Alpha Trading

Founded in 1807, John Wiley & Sons is the oldest independent publishing company in the United States. With offices in North America, Europe, Australia and Asia, Wiley is globally committed to developing and marketing print and electronic products and services for our customers' professional and personal knowledge and understanding.

The Wiley Trading series features books by traders who have survived the market's ever changing temperament and have prospered—some by reinventing systems, others by getting back to basics. Whether a novice trader, professional or somewhere in-between, these books will provide the advice and strategies needed to prosper today and well into the future.

For a list of available titles, visit our Web site at www.WileyFinance.com.

Alpha Trading

*Profitable Strategies That
Remove Directional Risk*

PERRY KAUFMAN

WILEY

John Wiley & Sons, Inc.

Published by John Wiley & Sons, Inc., Hoboken, New Jersey.
Published simultaneously in Canada.

For general information on our other products and services or for technical support, please contact our Customer Care Department within the United States at (800) 762-2974, outside the United States at (317) 572-3993 or fax (317) 572-4002.

Wiley also publishes its books in a variety of electronic formats. Some content that appears in print may not be available in electronic books. For more information about Wiley products, visit our web site at www.wiley.com.

Library of Congress Cataloging-in-Publication Data:

Kaufman, Perry J.
  Alpha trading : profitable strategies that remove directional risk / Perry Kaufman.
      p.   cm. – (Wiley trading series)
  Includes index.
  ISBN 978-0-470-52974-4 (cloth); ISBN 978-1-118-00120-2 (ebk);
  ISBN 978-1-118-00121-9 (ebk); ISBN 978-1-118-00122-6 (ebk)
  1. Pairs trading.   2. Futures.   I. Title.
  HG4661.K33 2011
  332.64'52–dc22   2010032753

Printed in the United States of America.

10 9 8 7 6 5 4 3 2 1

Contents

Preface

I wanted to write this book after the collapse of the tech bubble in 2000, but it wasn't until the subprime disaster of 2008 that I decided to do it. Investors should not be subject to the tremendous losses that the market serves up. And traders do not need to make a commitment to a long or short position all the time. There are other choices, and those choices do not necessitate compromising returns. They do require somewhat more complicated positions, but the reward is that, if the S&P collapses because of a terrorist attack, or program trading by one of the big investments houses runs amok and causes a 10 percent drop in the S&P, you are safe.

We've learned greater respect for risk in the past few years. It's a lesson that we all should have learned much sooner, but any time is a good time to improve your skills. Part of that advancement is to be aware of unconscious risks. When we trade more than one stock, each trade should have equal risk. That gives each trade an equal opportunity to contribute to the final results. If you don't do that, you are consciously or unconsciously saying that you think the trade with the largest risk is most likely to give you the best return. If that's the case, you should only make one trade in the best item and forget about diversification.

This book is as much about the process as it is about the results. Its target audience is active traders but not necessarily intraday traders. The intended reader is someone who spends time deciding which stocks or futures markets to buy or sell and doesn't hold a trade indefinitely when it goes the wrong way. Each step is explained, and there are examples of how the numbers should look. There is also a website that has the basic spreadsheets needed to do all the calculations.

The strategies in this book are well known to be profitable. They are called statistical arbitrage, or stat-arb, and they can be traded by holding positions for a few days, as suggested here, or for milliseconds, as implemented by the big investment houses. To trade, all you need is a spreadsheet to do a few calculations; then enter prices at the end of the day or anytime during the day when you think there is an opportunity. Trades have a high probability of success.

You cannot just believe that something works; you need to prove it to yourself. The black box approach is unacceptable and has proved a disaster to many investors. It's your money, and you owe it to yourself to understand and verify everything—even what is shown in this book.

It is one thing to be given a strategy and another to use it successfully. Once you have verified and paper-traded the strategies, you have a better chance of being successful because you have become part of the development process.

The development process is an exciting exploration. It begins with a sound premise and moves down various paths that may or may not turn out to be useful. But at the same time, it teaches valuable lessons. You understand why one idea works and another doesn't. You understand the robust and the fragile parts of the strategies. At some time in the future, you may be called upon to change the strategy because the market has changed—volatility has dropped to a level that limits opportunity or risen to a point of unacceptable risk. Markets that used to move together no longer do so, or as in the fourth quarter of 2008, markets moved together for no apparent reason.

Without having gone through the process, you do not have the knowledge to make these changes or the confidence that they will work. This book will present important strategies that should be part of any trader's portfolio. It will develop and explain the features that are incorporated, as well as choices that were not taken. But it is the sound premise of these ideas that is the underlying reason for its success. At the end, I hope you have learned a lot and that you trade successfully.

Perry Kaufman
January 2011

CHAPTER 1

Uncertainty

The investment world had a rude reminder in August and September of 2008 that forecasts and risk have more uncertainty than it would like to believe. From August 28 to the following March 9, the Standard & Poor's (S&P) 500 dropped 47%. Even more remarkable was that every investment was dragged down with it—hedge funds that were expected to offer diversification, commodity funds where you have the security of so-called hard currency, real estate, art, and of course, every possible stock in nearly every country.

Oddly, the U.S. dollar strengthened against the euro by about 15% during that time. It was odd because it was the United States that originated what we now call the *subprime disaster*. Yet in a crisis, investors still move money to the United States for safety.

What did we learn from this? Mainly, we learned that there is more uncertainty than we thought in the world of investments. Maybe that's not entirely correct. We just tend to ignore the risks when everything goes well for a long time. During the late 1990s, a similar move occurred in the tech stocks, with NASDAQ dropping from 5000 to below 1200. For those a bit older, or students of history, there was the crash of 1987 resulting in a drop of 39.8% in the S&P from October 6 to October 22. But the stock market had recovered by the end of the year, so investors who didn't react to the drop never suffered a sustained loss. By contrast, the recent drop in the S&P lasted from August 11, 2008, to March 3, 2009, far longer than 1987 but not comparable to the Black Monday of 1929.

At the time of this writing, the stock market is down only 15% from its highs. Again, investors who had closed their eyes are still suffering a loss in their pensions, but nothing devastating. Those who liquidated their portfolios and moved them to money market funds locked in their losses. The right decision is only known afterward.

IMPACT ON TRADING

But this book is about trading, not investing, and 2008 was a banner year for futures traders at the same time the equity markets were collapsing. The same could have been true for someone trading *exchange-traded funds* (ETFs) or any investment in which going short is a natural part of trading. The main beneficiaries were trend followers, who were able to get short (equity index markets), or long (interest rates), and stay with the trend for months, capturing what is known as the *fat tail*.

We can then say that many traders lost money and some profited, but the most important lesson is that the risk was enormous. Volatility rose from under 20% to 80%, a previously unthinkable level (see Figure 1.1). If you can't manage risk, then your interim losses may be too big to ever see the profits.

Money Moves the Markets

Normally, risk is reduced through diversification, but that wasn't true during this last crisis because the movement of money reversed the direction of all markets at the same time. In a crisis, most investors simply want to get their money out. If they are long equities, then equities fall; if they are long the Goldman Sachs Commodity Index (GSCI), then that falls; and

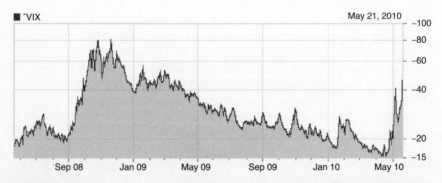

FIGURE 1.1 The volatility index (VIX) for S&P 500 from August 2008 through mid-May 2010.
© Yahoo!

if they are short the Japanese yen in the carry trade, the yen rises. Cash, or guaranteed government debt, is the only safe place, provided it's not Greece, Italy, Spain, Portugal, or a variety of emerging markets that may have even greater risk.

THE INEVITABLE PRICE SHOCKS

We all know that price shocks are extreme price moves that cannot be predicted. We also understand that they are worse when the investing public is holding the wrong position, that is, when we expect the Fed to lower interest rates to stimulate the economy, but instead they raise rates to prevent inflation. Of course, that's not supposed to happen in our new era of transparency. But what about a military coup in an oil-rich country that cuts off the needed flow of supply to the West? Or an assassination? Or a surprise election result? All of these have happened.

We might think of all price movement as a series of price shocks of different sizes—all reactions to today's news. Most often, these shocks are very small, but some are bigger, and occasionally one is gigantic. Do you ever wonder how these price shocks net against your market positions? Is it different if you are a long-term rather than a short-term trader? Is there something you can do to take advantage of a price shock, or at least not be hurt by it?

Biased against You

First of all, understand that you can't change the odds to have better than a 50% chance that you will profit from a price shock. Realistically, you would be lucky to have 50% of the price shocks in your favor. However, it does seem clear that when more people hold the same positions, any surprise that is contrary to that direction will have a greater impact while surprising news in a favorable direction will have little effect. But that information is not enough to make money because we still don't know when the next price shock will come.

Very few traders, professional or amateur, recognize the importance of price shocks and the effect that they have on profits. Given how ill-prepared and undercapitalized many traders are, one large price shock is all they need to be forced out permanently.

Price Shocks and Your Position   Do price shocks hurt the short-term or the long-term trader more? To find out, we ran a moving average test of a few different markets and totaled the value of the price shocks that caused profits or losses. Specifically,

- The moving average calculation periods ranged from 10 days to 200 days, in steps of 10 days.
- A *price shock* was defined as any day in which the ratio of today's price change to the standard deviation of the previous 10 day price changes was greater than 2.5. That means, if the standard deviation of the S&P daily price changes was 6 big points, then a gain or loss of 15 points would trigger a price shock. Specifically, if the threshold for a price shock $t = 2.5$ and $n = 10$, then if

$$|P_t - P_{t-1}| > \text{stdev}(P_i - P_{i-1}) \text{ where } i = t - 1, \dots, t - n$$

we can say that day t is a price shock.

By using the standard deviation of the daily changes, we can test using either the cash index or back-adjusted futures. Back-adjusting does not change the price differences or the standard deviation, although it will change any percentage calculation because the divisor is scaled to an artificial price. When working with futures, it's best to use price differences, and with stocks or stock indices, we should use returns.

S&P Price Shocks   The impact of price shocks on the S&P is unique. We believe that there is an upward bias in the index markets, caused by favorable tax treatment of capital gains as well as legal restrictions in some pension plans, which results in investors holding long positions. Short sales are limited to a far smaller group of professional traders, perhaps a few more now that inverse ETFs and bear funds (inverse mutual funds, such as ProFunds) allow easy access. Investors also seem to gravitate toward a clear bull market in any investment, whether the stock market or gold or oil. It should not be a surprise that downside shocks would hurt most investors. Our moving average system, however, is unbiased because it goes long or short according to the direction of the trend and not because of tax consequences.

Figure 1.2 shows the daily price changes of the S&P futures as a ratio of the standard deviation of the previous 10 days, as given in the previous formula. The data cover 13 years, ending in May 2010. Even though prices were well off the lows of the subprime crisis by February 2009, it is easy to see that there is still a bias toward downward price shocks. By looking at the ±4 lines on the left axis, we see that only seven events came close to that level, and not many moved above the 2 level, while there were many more both crossing –2 and penetrating –4. We might have expected that more computerized trading, and perhaps more investment sophistication,

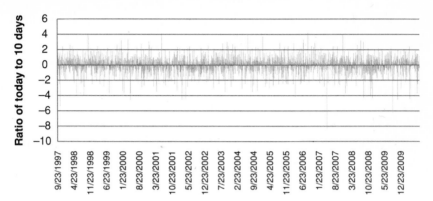

FIGURE 1.2 S&P 1-day volatility as a ratio to the standard deviation of the previous 10 days.

would cause shocks to be more symmetrical in recent years, but that doesn't seem to be the case.

Using this chart, we choose two price-shock thresholds, 3.0 and 4.0, to compare the impact of what we will call *more shocks* and *fewer shocks*. The *fewer* case is also larger shocks. We run a test of moving averages using calculation periods from 10 days to 200 days over the past 10 years. The rules are that a long position is entered when the moving average turns up, and a short is entered when the moving average turns down. The system is always in the market. A $25 round-turn commission is charged to cover all costs. Results are shown as Net PL in Figure 1.3, along with the net results of the 1-day price shocks. The performance pattern of the S&P begins with

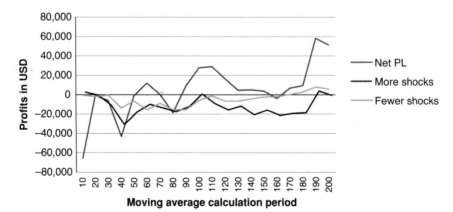

FIGURE 1.3 Comparison of the net returns for S&P moving average systems through May 2010 and the contribution from "more" and "fewer" 1-day price shocks.

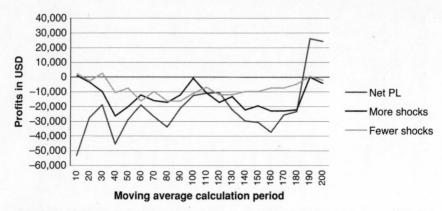

FIGURE 1.4 S&P price shocks for the period beginning January 1991 and ending on the last day of 2007, to avoid the effects of the subprime crisis.

large losses for faster trends and finally shows profits for trend periods approaching 200 days.

The lines representing the contributions from 1-day price shocks show that in nearly all cases, the net impact of price shocks are negative returns. This can be attributed to most investors holding the same long position when there is a sustained bull market. We would caution traders not to believe that price shocks will contribute to short-term profits, even though the chart shows some net gains for the 10-day average and again for the longest calculation periods. At best, you can assume a 50% chance of a price shock in your favor. Anything else is strictly luck.

We thought it would be interesting to compare the results of these tests without the impact of the subprime crisis; therefore, we retested the data beginning at the same point, 1997, when the e-mini S&P began trading, and ending on January 1, 2008. The results are shown in Figure 1.4. The results are actually very similar for the contribution of price shocks because only a few shocks would have been added. In addition, the measurement of a price shock is relative to the previous 10 days, so that the sustained high volatility during the months from August 2008 through February 2009 made it difficult to have any shock that would have been 3 times larger. Instead, we see that the S&P was a poor performer, using a simple moving average system, and that the large downward move and the following rally from August 2008 through the current mid-2010 boosted the profits from $25,000 for the longest trends to nearly $60,000. Simple systematic trend following can perform well when traders can't.

Interest Rates   Interest rates are a far less volatile and more orderly market than any equity index. Using the Eurobund as the representative,

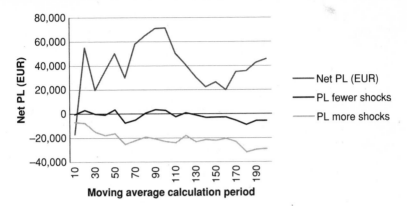

FIGURE 1.5 Impact of price shocks on Euro bund moving average returns.

we run the same tests as we did for the S&P, using €25 as the round-turn cost for each trade, and beginning in 1991. The results are shown in Figure 1.5. They differ considerably from the S&P results because more shocks total very negative returns, averaging about half of the net profits. The fewer, larger price shocks netted an impact closer to zero, but the more frequent shocks, the results of periodic economic reports, move consistently against the trend position.

The large losses due to price shocks can be attributed to the Eurobund trend over the test period, as seen in Figure 1.6. With prices moving higher over the past 18 years, we would expect most investors to be holding long positions. Then price shocks to the downside would most often generate losses. As the trend calculation period increases, the time holding a long position increases; therefore, price shocks to the upside become a larger profit component, and shocks to the downside a larger losing component.

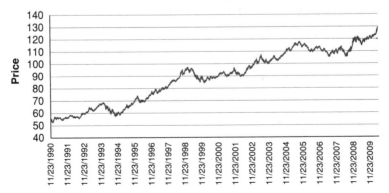

FIGURE 1.6 Eurobund futures prices, nearest contract, back-adjusted from 1990.

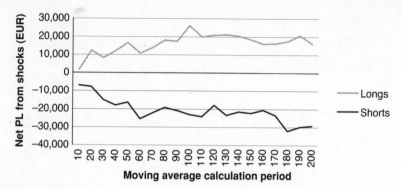

FIGURE 1.7 Net effect of price shocks on Eurobund long and short positions.

These can be seen in Figure 1.7, where the losses due to short-side shocks far outweigh the gains from upside shocks.

Crude Oil   Another market that has attracted a great deal of attention is crude oil, rallying from $40 per barrel to nearly $150 before falling back to $30 in just over three months, shown in Figure 1.8. A breakdown of the price shocks (Figure 1.9) shows that more shocks added to profits, while the largest shocks moved against the positions being held. This was a remarkable period for oil, and any news (more shocks) was taken as bullish. While there were big downside surprises, the market ignored them.

The profits from varying the calculation period of the moving average show that the slowest trends held the long position too far into the reversal that followed the peak of $150, giving back most of the gains. In hindsight, the perfect trend was about 110 days, but it's not likely we would have been trading it. Most macrotrend programs would have chosen something in the

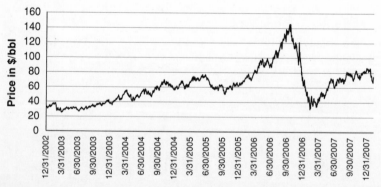

FIGURE 1.8 Crude oil, back-adjusted futures from 2003.

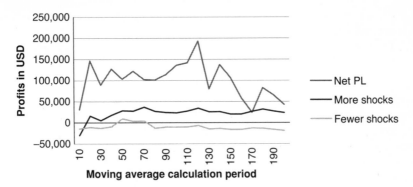

FIGURE 1.9 Crude oil effect of price shocks on the profits of a moving average strategy.

range of 60 to 80 days, all of which performed well and had small or some positive effect from price shocks.

WHY SO MUCH ABOUT PRICE SHOCKS?

Price shocks represent the worst-case scenario for traders. They are unexpected, violent, and most often generate losses. Even more important is that most traders don't plan for a price shock. You can plan to survive a price shock by holding large reserves so that a 4-standard deviation event will not produce a loss that you can't handle. But to do that, you need to give up leverage. More often than not, without the leverage, the result will be returns that are not justified by the risk.

Algorithmic traders are also guilty of ignoring price shocks. They test their programs on historic data that contain past shocks, and when they design their strategies and risk controls, the accumulated result of the way they traded during those past shocks can often produce net gains—a situation not likely to happen in real trading. The biggest offender was Long Term Capital Management, which, we are told, removed the price shocks from the data history because they believed them to be unrealistic (in the context of their trading) and not likely to be repeated. While it's true that the next shock is never a repeat of another past event, there are countless new market surprises.

What can you do to avoid price shocks, even if you can't predict them? The practical solutions are:

- Don't trade.
- Stay out of the market as much as possible.

- Choose a faster system so that you're not holding the same position as everyone else.
- Trade a hedged or market-neutral position.

Of course, no one reading this book would choose not to trade, so we'll ignore that point. On the other hand, staying out of the market as much as possible is very practical. That can be done easily with faster trading systems, where you target profits and have specific timing requirements to entering a new trade. If you end up holding positions for one-third of the number of trading days, then you have a 66% chance of missing a price shock.

Trading a faster system is also better. By not holding the same position as everyone else, and getting net long or short frequently, you have a good chance of a positive price shock 50% of the time.

Our choice is the last point, trading a spread or market-neutral position, which takes price shocks out of the picture completely. Of course, there is a chance that the two markets that are spread will not react as expected, but that is a very small chance. In addition, mean reverting strategies, which represent most of the market-neutral programs, are fast trading and require two or more markets to diverge; therefore, they are in the market for a relatively short period of time. As we will discuss later, long holding periods are not compatible with a mean reverting method because you then fight with the trend.

COMPLEXITY AND CONTAGION RISK

This generation of traders has recently experienced a series of contagion risks, where one seemingly modest financial event causes another seemingly controlled financial event, and in the end, we have a very large event. The first of these was the subprime meltdown. It first appeared to be limited to the U.S. housing market, then started to affect lending liquidity, and then moved to bank reserve requirements, until it had spread throughout the United States, Europe, and finally Asia. Equity markets all plunged, and investors ran to the safety of government treasuries.

We are now teetering on the problem of sovereign debt, first with Greece and probably some other countries in the European Union, but possibly spreading back to the United States. It's not yet a reality, but that's not because the financial news networks aren't trying to scare everyone into believing that it will happen.

The problem stems from a structural change in the way markets are used. Investors now diversify into a wide range of programs, placing money in hedge funds, bond funds, and real estate trusts. If one link in the chain fails, then investors must liquidate other holdings to cover losses. That leads to further liquidation. It is the complexity of the markets that we don't understand, the way money interacts with it all, causing the possibility of sequential failures.

THE UGLY SIDE

No discussion of uncertainty would be complete without recognizing that a different type of price shock occurs when we find out that we've been fooled. Of these, the greatest of all scams was Bernie Madoff, who fooled everyone into thinking that he had a lock on trading profits. Of course, he refused to discuss the specifics of his trading method because it was proprietary.

That brings up the issue of *black boxes*. A black box is usually a fully systematic, algorithmic trading model that is used for trading but not disclosed to anyone outside the company. Naturally, we can understand why a money manager would need to keep the specifics of a strategy secret. But then we don't really know what they're using or if they are using anything systematic at all. Fortunately, most investment managers, hedge fund operators, and commodity trading advisors (CTAs) are very credible. They give investors a general idea of what methods they use for trading and how they control risk. These can most often be verified by watching their performance under various market conditions. Unlike Madoff's results, which were up 15% each year regardless of market conditions, we expect to see periods of loss but more gains than losses over time.

Even in the best times, investing in someone else's trading program involves added risk—what we would normally call *counterparty risk*, the risk of one of the parties failing to perform their fiduciary responsibility. If you are the investor, that could be the stock or commodity exchange, but more likley the person or company managing your money.

If it is at all possible, you need to manage your own investment portfolio. Your common sense is enough to keep it on a safe track. If you're a trader, then all the better, because you can decide what strategy and how much leverage to use. And there is no penalty for stopping and withdrawing your money, and no waiting period. During the subprime crisis, many hedge funds refused to allow investors to withdraw their funds "for their own good" and because there was no market to liquidate their positions.

TAKING DEFENSIVE ACTION

We propose that the solution to all this risk and uncertainty is to trade in a way that removes exposure to directional risk. That include all forms of statistical arbitrage (stat-arb), from spreads to yield-curve trading to program trading, and from the simplest pairs trade to large-scale market-neutral strategies. These methods extract *alpha* from the market, profits over and above what might be gained, or lost, by a passive investment in the stock or bond market. Alpha is considered a measure of cleverness, although you will see that some of the methods do not require much more than common sense.

Not High-Frequency Trading

There has been a lot in the news about high-frequency trading, by which the major investment houses, such as Goldman Sachs and Morgan Stanley, trade hundreds or thousands of times each day to extract tiny but consistent profits. Much of this is conceptually simple but done on a massive scale only achievable by computerized trading. In fact, one of the main sources of success is pairs trading, which capitalizes on distortions between two related markets. Besides computerization, the edge in this method is that the cost of trading is near zero for these investment houses. We can't possibly compete with that, but we can compete in a different time frame.

In this book, we spend considerable time on pairs trading, but instead of holding a trade for microseconds, we will be looking at larger moves of one to three days. We will begin with the stock market but then look at futures markets and combinations of stocks and futures. Futures markets are more limited in selection but easy to trade, and they offer exceptional leverage.

The price movements of stock and futures markets are related for many reasons. Some of them are driven by common, long-term economic factors, and some are based on current geopolitical events. We often find ourselves commenting on how the S&P is moving with bond prices, or gold is moving with the EURUSD exchange rate, or that gold and crude oil are closely tracking one another. During extreme stress, markets move together, and we can take advantage of those opportunities, even if they last only three months or a year.

The methods discussed in this book are based on sound theory but are what we call *data driven*. Fundamentals play a role only in defining the strategy, such as *relative-value trading*, which is actually all relative and no value. But without a sound premise, we cannot expect to be profitable. On the other hand, we need to act often and precisely, which can be done only with a computerized trading program continually evaluating price changes. While it is possible to trade a few pairs using a simple spreadsheet, the true advantages come from a large-scale application which reduces risk due to diversification.

All of these methods fall into the category of *statistical arbitrage*, or *stat-arb*. Because they are computerized, they are also in the larger group of *algorithmic trading models*. Most important, these models are not exposed to price direction, so a shock to the market that moves all stocks in one direction will not itself cause an arbitrary profit or loss. Only the relative strength or weakness of one market compared with another will do that. Given the surprises of the past few years, that seems to be a much safer approach to trading.

ACCEPTING PERFORMANCE FOR WHAT IT IS

One final but important point: We cannot eliminate risk, no matter how clever we are or what powerful tools we use. Even when we express risk in terms of annualized volatility, we don't really believe that we will see that risk. A 12% *target volatility* means there is a 2.5% chance of losing 24% in one year. But if you lost 10% or 15%, then you would be looking to change trading systems or somehow alter your risk exposure, yet your returns are still within the range that you defined.

The only way to remove future risk is by reducing leverage. Unfortunately, lower leverage means lower returns. If you find a past situation that caused exceptionally large risk, and create rules to eliminate it from future trading, you'll be following in the steps of Long-Term Capital Management. These risks never repeat in the same way and may even get bigger.

Throughout this book, we will discuss ways to manage individual trading risk as well as portfolio risk. None of these approaches tries to eliminate risk. The methods are simple and should appeal to common sense. They are also very important for long-term success.

CHAPTER 2

The Importance of Price Noise

Market noise is an important but elusive component of price move-ment. It is the up-and-down, erratic price movement that goes nowhere and often causes you to be stopped out of a trade only to see prices reverse back in your direction. Traders have no trouble rec-ognizing noise. Most price shocks are an extreme case of noise, when the large move is followed by an equally sharp reversal the next day. A price shock is not noise if prices continue in the direction of the shock. That is most likely a structural change. The elusive part is:

- How do you tell the difference between a structural change and a price shock?
- When does a price move indicate a trend change, and when is it just noise?
- How do you take advantage of price noise?

These questions don't have simple answers, but what we learn from exploring them is still very valuable and will explain some of the important choices that are made in the following chapters.

NOISE EXPLAINED

The way we think about price noise is a day with very high volatility but a close nearly unchanged, or a day when prices closed sharply lower, then reversed nearly the entire move the next day. We also associate noise with the way prices react to our trading method. We get stopped out of a long position when prices break a key level, but that turns out to be the low of the move, and we're out at the worst price of the day.

In general, noise is a disorderly move. It doesn't need to be volatile, just erratic and unpredictable. Econometricians say that when you remove the trend, the seasonal pattern, and the cycle, the three main components of price movement, what you have left is noise. That's interesting but not very useful. We don't want to remove those three elements because the combination of everything causes price moves that can generate profits. Instead, we'll think of noise in the same way we approach the walk of a drunken sailor (no offense to sailors—it could be anyone).

If a sailor were to walk from point A to point B in a straight line, we can say that his route has no noise. If he meanders slightly off that straight path, we can see that as a small amount of noise; however, if he staggers first to the right, then sharply to the left, then backward and forward by different amounts, but ultimately heading slightly toward his goal, we would say there was a large amount of noise.

Once you understand the picture, seen in Figure 2.1, the concept should become clear: *the straighter the path, the less noise; the more erratic the path, the more noise.* This pattern can be expressed as a value we call the *efficiency ratio.* First, we measure the net distance gained from point A to point B, always taken as a positive number. Then we measure the actual path taken by the sailor in his journey from point A to point B.

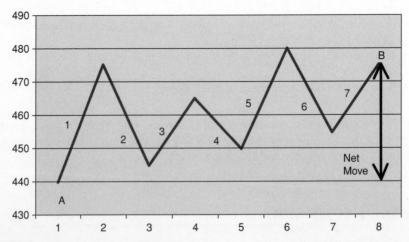

FIGURE 2.1 Noise is calculated as the net move (from A to B) divided by the sum of the individual moves (1 through 7). All values are taken as positive numbers.

Those values are also always positive, regardless of whether he is stumbling forward or staggering backward. The efficiency of his walk is given by the ratio

$$ER = \frac{\text{Net difference from A to B}}{\text{Length of the path actually walked}}$$

Referring now to the *efficiency ratio* (ER), if the sailor walked in a straight line, the ratio would be 1 because the numerator and denominator would be the same. As the sailor wobbles more, the denominator gets larger. If he wandered back and forth for a really, really long time, the denominator would get very big, and the ratio would move toward zero. Therefore, a walk with no noise will have the ratio of 1.0, and a completely directionless walk would be zero. This can be shown mathematically as

$$ER_t = \frac{|P_t - P_{t-n}|}{\sum\limits_{i=t-n+1}^{t} |P_i - P_{i-1}|}$$

where t represents today, P is the price, and n is the total number of days used in the calculation. As with many financial calculations, this is done over a fixed, relatively short period. By calculating the ratio each day based on rolling time periods, we get a history of the price noise. When we average those individual ratios over a long period of time, we get a profile of the amount of noise in a specific stock, index, or commodities market.

Note that the value ER_t can be zero (or near zero) if the denominator is extremely large or if the numerator is zero, which can happen if the starting and ending prices are the same. The ratio has no sign, so that we don't know if the prices have gone up or down over the calculation period.

Because the calculation is greatly dependent on the starting and ending values, some mathematicians consider it unstable. However, averaging the values over some period of price history minimizes that problem.

Volatility Neutral

The ratio also removes the volatility from the calculation. For example, if prices moved up an equal amount, say $0.50, every day for 10 days, then the total gain would be $5.00 and the ratio would be 1.0. On the other hand, if it moved up $0.10 each day, the gain would be $1.00, and the ratio would still be 1.0.

That is an important concept because it means that the efficiency ratio may not be sufficient for trading. An arbitrage or relative value strategy that profits from trading against the current move usually needs sufficient volatility to clear a profit. This ratio doesn't have that information, although a separate calculation could easily solve that problem.

Fractal Efficiency

The efficiency ratio was developed and used by this author in the late 1970s. It wasn't until Benoit Mandelbrot wrote *The Fractal Geometry of Nature* (W. H. Freeman, 1982) that the concept of fractals became clear.* Up to then, fractals were not thought of as having common properties, but Mandelbrot used them to measure the roughness of the coastline, distinguishing this from classic, orderly, Euclidian geometry. Realists, such as Mandelbrot, believe that straight lines exist only in theory.

It's not clear where the formula or naming of *fractal efficiency* first appeared, but it's a good description of the efficiency ratio. The concept of a fractal applies to all dimensions, and it appears that the ratio is equally descriptive when used for daily, weekly, and monthly price data as well as 5-minute and hourly data. Noise is noise.

In this book, we'll use the term efficiency ratio because it best describes the way prices move from one point to another.

Calculation Example   Using Excel, the efficiency ratio is calculated in a few easy steps, shown in Table 2.1. Beginning with the S&P cash index, SPX, in August 1998, the date and closing prices are placed into columns B and C. The calculation period will be 10 days, appearing in cell D1. This technique will be used with the Excel feature *offset*, which will allow us to change the calculation period, and the results will automatically be recalculated.

- In column D, beginning in row 12, calculate the absolute value of the 10-day price difference. The Excel formula is `abs(C13-OFFSET(C13, -$D$2,0))`. This value will be the numerator of the ratio.
- In column E, beginning in row 3, calculate the 1-day absolute differences, `abs(C4-C3)`.
- Column F, beginning in row 13, will be the 10-day sum of the values in column E, `sum(E13:OFFSET(E13,-$D$2+1,0))`. This will be the denominator.
- Column G is the efficiency ratio, `D13/F13`.

---

*Prior to this, Mandelbrot published *Fractals, Chance and Dimension* (W. H. Freeman, 1977).

TABLE 2.1 Example of calculating the efficiency ratio using SPX.

A	B	C	D	E	F	G
1	Date	Close	10	← Days in Calculation		
			Abs n-day differences	Abs 1-day differences	Sum of 1-day diff	Efficiency ratio
2	8/3/1998	1112.44				
3	8/4/1998	1072.12		40.32		
4	8/5/1998	1081.43		9.31		
5	8/6/1998	1089.63		8.20		
6	8/7/1998	1089.45		0.18		
7	8/10/1998	1083.14		6.31		
8	8/11/1998	1068.98		14.16		
9	8/12/1998	1084.22		15.24		First full
10	8/13/1998	1074.91		9.31		calculation
11	8/14/1998	1062.75		12.16		needs
12	8/17/1998	1083.67	28.77	20.92	136.11	0.21 ← 10 days
13	8/18/1998	1101.20	29.08	17.53	113.32	0.26
14	8/19/1998	1098.06	16.63	3.14	107.15	0.16
15	8/20/1998	1091.60	1.97	6.46	105.41	0.02
16	8/21/1998	1081.24	8.21	10.36	115.59	0.07
17	8/24/1998	1088.14	5.00	6.90	116.18	0.04
18	8/25/1998	1092.85	23.87	4.71	106.73	0.22
19	8/26/1998	1084.19	0.03	8.66	100.15	0.00
20	8/27/1998	1042.59	32.32	41.60	132.44	0.24
21	8/28/1998	1027.14	35.61	15.45	135.73	0.26
22	8/31/1998	957.28	126.39	69.86	184.67	0.68
23	9/1/1998	994.26	106.94	36.98	204.12	0.52
24	9/2/1998	990.48	107.58	3.78	204.76	0.53
25	9/3/1998	982.26	109.34	8.22	206.52	0.53
26	9/4/1998	973.89	107.35	8.37	204.53	0.52
27	9/8/1998	1023.46	64.68	49.57	247.20	0.26

DIFFERENT MARKETS

Before trying to figure out how to use the ratio, we can discover interesting information from calculating the ratio over a wide range of markets. An 8-day calculation period was chosen because it will show the greatest differences between the data. The efficiency ratio over only 8 days should bounce around quite a bit, offering the opportunity for each market to show its patterns. If the efficient ratio is robust, then using a longer calculation period should simply scale the results. Remember that a ratio value of 1.0 can happen only if prices move in the same direction for every day of the

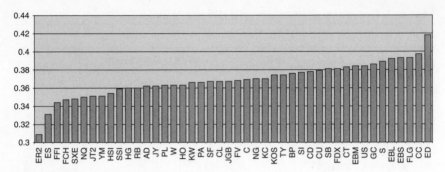

FIGURE 2.2 Average noise level from 2005 through 2009 for selected markets.

calculation period, so using a value of 40, or even 20, is unnecessarily large and simply compresses the ratio values.

Figure 2.2 shows 44 of the most liquid futures markets, including equity index, fixed income, currency, energy, metals, and agricultural commodities. The ratios span a range of only about 0.11 ratio points, but for a test of nearly five years, the differences are significant. For convenience, the actual ratios are shown from lowest to highest, in four columns, in Table 2.2.

Both Figure 2.2 and Table 2.2 paint an interesting picture. The lowest 10 ratios, in the first set of columns in Table 2.2, are all equity index markets. The only missing indices are the Deutscher Aktienindex (DAX), which

TABLE 2.2 Efficiency ratios for 44 markets.

1 to 11		12 to 22		23 to 33		34 to 44	
Market	**Ratio**	**Market**	**Ratio**	**Market**	**Ratio**	**Market**	**Ratio**
Russell	0.309	Unleaded	0.360	5-year notes	0.368	DAX	0.381
SP	0.331	AUDUSD	0.362	Corn	0.369	Cotton	0.383
FTSE	0.344	USDJPY	0.362	Natural gas	0.370	Eurobobl	0.384
CAC	0.347	Platinum	0.363	Coffee	0.370	US 30-year bond	0.384
EuroStx	0.348	Wheat	0.363	Kospi	0.374	Gold	0.386
Nasdaq	0.350	Heating oil	0.363	US 10-year notes	0.374	Soybeans	0.389
Topix	0.351	KC Wheat	0.366	USDGBP	0.376	Eurobund	0.392
DJIA	0.351	Palladium	0.366	Silver	0.377	Euroschatz	0.393
Hang Seng	0.354	USDCHF	0.367	CADUSD	0.378	Long gilt	0.393
Nikkei	0.359	Crude	0.367	EURUSD	0.379	Cocoa	0.397
Copper	0.360	JGB	0.367	Sugar	0.381	Eurodollars	0.418

appears at the top of the last set, and the Korea Composite Stock Price Index (Kospi), in the middle of the third set. That means the index markets, as a whole, are the noisiest of all markets traded. Is that a surprise? Even during the remarkable period from mid-2008 through the first quarter of 2009, when index markets seemed to go straight down, the ratio says that it was noisy—or at least relatively noisier than other markets.

Of the nine equity index markets leading the pack, the Russell and the Standard & Poor's (S&P) are the noisiest. Other studies have shown that volume and noise are related. That is not to say that they are at all the same, but the observation is that newly trading markets and emerging markets with lower volume and often dominated by a few large companies tend to have lower noise. Trading in new markets with low volume tends to be dominated by commercials. These are businesses and institutions using the markets to hedge or those with an arrangement with the exchange to provide liquidity. Commercial positions tend to be single large orders, and many commercials have the same view of the market. The result is that prices move in the same direction more often than is normal, the result of fewer and larger trades. We'll discuss why this is important a little later. Meanwhile, note that the closest we come to an emerging market is the Kospi, which is in the middle of the sorted sequence of ratios. The DAX is not emerging but has much lower volume and much higher volatility than the other index markets, which provides a reason for it to have a high ratio.

On the other side of the scale, the market with the highest ratio and the least noise is the Eurodollar interest rate, and it's much higher than all the other markets. We could say, in general, that interest rates are the group with the lowest noise, with five of them in the last set of columns and almost all of them in the second half. Had we included other 3-month rates, such as the short sterling, Euribor, Euroswiss, or Euroyen, they would have all fallen at the end. The other groups of markets—currencies, metals, agriculturals, and energy—are mostly scattered in the middle two columns. Of the foreign exchange (FX) markets, the EURUSD has the most trend, and the AUDUSD the most noise.

A CLOSER LOOK AT EQUITY INDEX MARKETS

Because the concept of noise is important, we will look at a larger set of equity index markets, using a 40-day calculation period. We noted in the previous section that increasing the calculation period would scale down the ratio values but do little to change the order of ranking. Figure 2.3 shows the results of calculating the efficiency ratio for 24 world equity index

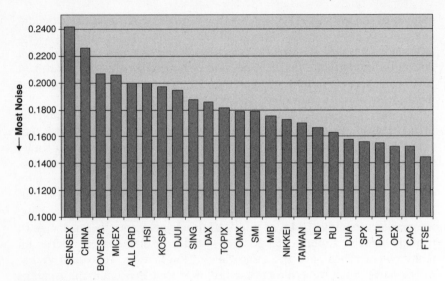

FIGURE 2.3 The efficiency ratio calculated for 24 world equity index markets, using a 40-day period.

markets. The ratio on the left ranges from 0.14 to 0.24 instead of 0.30 to 0.41. The markets with the highest noise are on the right, beginning with London's FTSE and the Paris CAC, then the U.S. markets: the S&P 100 (OEX), Dow Transports, S&P, Dow Industrials, Russell, and NASDAQ. These are a combination of actively traded markets, as in the case of the U.S., or moderately traded markets not dominated by commercial use. On the far left are the emerging markets: India's Sensex, China, Brazil's Bovespa, and Russia's Micex indices. These markets tend to make large, sustained moves in one direction.

IMPORTANCE OF NOISE

The two pieces of information we should come away with from the noise study are that index markets are very noisy and that interest rates have a low level of noise. What can we do with that?

When we look at various trading strategies that hold outright long and short positions, the primary choices are *trend following*, taking a position in the direction of the current price move, and *mean reversion*, trading against the current move in expectation of prices correcting back the mean (average price). If prices move very smoothly, going from one price level to another with only small retracements, then a trend approach should work well. On the other hand, if prices keep changing direction and rarely sustain a continuous move in one direction, then mean reversion should be the preferred approach. This is exactly what the level of noise tells us.

According to the ratios in Table 2.2, we should be using a trend strategy to trade the Eurodollars and all other interest rates but a mean reverting method to trade the equity index markets, with the exception of the DAX. We don't know exactly what threshold value of noise tells us to change from mean reversion to trending.

This premise can be easily proved by calculating the profitability of a typical trend strategy for equity index and interest rate markets. At the same time, we can find the noise level that distinguishes a trend candidate from a mean reversion one. We'll use a 10-day calculation period, which is close to the 8-day period used for the noise calculation. The rules for entering and exiting are:

- *Buy* (close out shorts and enter a long) when the 10-day moving average turns up.
- *Sell* (close out longs and enter a short) when the 10-day moving average turns down.

No commissions or slippage was used, so the lower volatility or frequency of trades did not influence the results. For this test, we are interested only in the pure trend results compared with the corresponding noise. For technical traders, we point out that using the direction of the moving average, rather than a price penetration, for determining the change of trend works best for longer-term trends. It reduces the number of false penetrations and greatly reduces the costs. For very short-term trends, when you want the first sign of a change, using the price penetration is more responsive even though there are more false signals.

The markets used were heavily weighted with equity indices, but there was a broad sample of others.

- Index markets: Russell, S&P, Dow Jones Industrial Average (DJIA), DAX, Kospi, and Tokyo Stock Price Index (Topix).
- Interest rates: U.S. 30-year bonds, Eurobund, Eurodollars.
- Currencies: Euro, Japanese yen, Swiss franc.
- Energy: Crude oil.
- Metals: Gold.
- Agricultural: Wheat, soybeans.

The test was run using TradeStation, and the same test interval, 2005 to May 2009, was used for all markets. The results available were the net profit or loss and the *profit factor*, the gross profits divided by the gross losses.

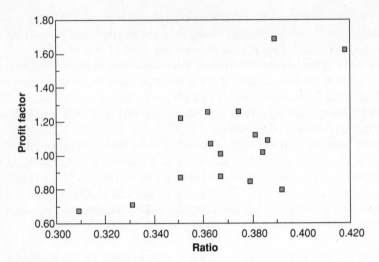

FIGURE 2.4   Dispersion of profit factors for 10-day moving average test.

When the profit factor is above 1.0, the market is net profitable. The profit factor is not as useful as the Sharpe ratio or information ratio (the more commonly used ratio, without the risk-free rate of return), but it does give some measurement of risk and reward, and is better than using only net profits for comparing results.

The pattern to see in Figure 2.4, which plots the profit factor against the efficiency ratio, is that there is a general tendency for the profit factor to move in the same way as the ratio, shown along the bottom axis. Granted, there is a large blob in the middle of the chart, reflecting the variance of results when the ratio is in the middle of the range. Remember that moving average profits can vary based on other price patterns, so that noise will not be a perfect description of expected results. However, the extremes conform to our expectations. The lower left part of the chart shows that the worst performance is associated with the lowest ratio, and the upper right shows that the best trend performance has the highest ratios. The lower left markets are the Russell and S&P, and the upper right are soybeans and Eurodollar interest rates.

Isolating the equity index markets gives a clearer example of this relationship. If we plot the ratio against the profit factor, we see fewer points but a clear pattern from the lower left to the upper right (see Figure 2.5). The three lower points are the Russell, S&P, and DJIA, showing losses, while the upper points are the DAX, Kospi, and Topix, all profitable. As mentioned earlier, the Kospi and Topix might benefit from a combination of lower liquidity and/or larger commercial trading.

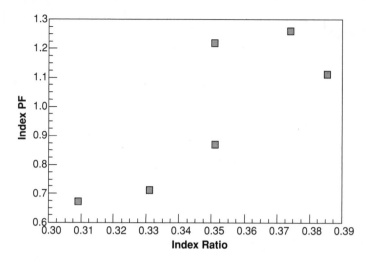

FIGURE 2.5 Dispersion of profit factors for 10-day moving average, index markets only.

DETERMINING THE STRATEGY

What was the purpose of all this analysis? We can see from the index markets that high ratios are profitable with a trend-following approach. We can infer that the low ratios will be profitable using a mean-reverting strategy. At least we can say that a trend-following strategy should not be used with those markets showing the greatest amount of noise, the lowest ratios.

Naturally, there are times when even the noisiest market, the Russell, will produce a profit with a moving average of some calculation period. But a few profits do not make a successful trading program, and the underlying premise is very important. Our premise is that the Russell should not be traded with a trend system but most likely will be successful with a mean-reverting one.

The Time Frame Helps

The calculation period for the trend or mean-reverting method can greatly help the performance of the strategy. This is based on the observation that longer moving averages, or lower-frequency data (weekly instead of daily, daily instead of hourly), implicitly smooths the data. Chartists can recognize the trend in prices more easily when they see a weekly chart rather than an hourly one.

Based on this premise, a trend system is more likely to be successful if the calculation period is longer, for example, 40, 60, or 80 days, and a mean-reverting system is best when using calculation periods from 3 to 8 days. This could be why macrotrend strategies use calculation periods from 40 to 200 days, with most of them closer to 80 days. Mean reverting is often applied to intraday moves.

We conclude that noise appears to be a greater part of price movement when seen up close, and the trend is more visible when viewed from afar. When choosing a strategy, the nature of the market (the underlying noise) and the calculation time frame are both critical.

Volatility Is Still Important

It was mentioned earlier that volatility is removed from the noise calculation. But volatility is a critical ingredient for mean-reverting or any short-term trading. Without volatility, the individual trades may not exceed the cost of doing business, commissions, and slippage. This will be an important issue in the chapters that follow.

Robustness of the Noise Measurement

The concept of fractal efficiency is particularly important because it claims to be robust. That is, whether we look at very high frequency data (such as intraday, hourly prices) or low frequency (weekly), the relative price noise in all markets should remain about the same. To show this, the average noise for the past 10 years was calculated using 8-, 20-, 40-, and 80-day periods for a wide range of futures markets, shown in Table 2.3. The four columns have been sorted with the highest noise at the top for each of the calculation periods. From our previous work, we expect the equity index markets to have the most noise and the interest rates the least noise.

In fact, the results in Table 2.3 confirm our expectations, although we also find other information. Viewing it in the most general sense, the short-term maturities, the short sterling, the European *Interbank Offered Rate* (Euribor), and Eurodollars are all consistently at the bottom, showing the least noise and the most trend. As the maturities get longer, the prices show increasing noise, although with only a few exceptions the interest rate markets all remain in the lower half of the table.

We see a similar case for equity index markets, clustering near the top of the table. The DAX is the bottom market in each column, indicating the least noise of that group.

As we look from the fastest calculation period, 8 days, to the slowest, we see a shift upward of the longer-term U.S. interest rates. This seems to

	Futures markets sorted by their average noise over 10 years based
TABLE 2.3	on four calculation periods. Those markets with the highest noise are on top.

Ratio and Average Calculation Period			
8	**20**	**40**	**80**
CAC	CAC	Russell	30-year bond
Russell	S&P 500	S&P 500	Gold
S&P 500	Russell	CAC	Russell
Nasdaq	CADUSD	Gold	S&P 500
Copper	Heating oil	30-year bond	Crude oil
Unleaded	Nasdaq	Crude oil	10-year note
Platinum	DAX	Heating oil	CAC
DAX	Platinum	Nasdaq	Unleaded
Heating oil	Crude oil	CADUSD	USDJPY
Natural gas	Unleaded	Unleaded	Heating oil
Crude oil	Copper	USDJPY	CADUSD
Eurobobl	Gold	DAX	Nasdaq
Eurobund	30-year bond	Platinum	Jap govt bond
10-year note	USDJPY	Jap govt bond	DAX
CADUSD	Jap govt bond	10-year note	5-year note
30-year note	10-year note	Eurobund	Eurobund
USDJPY	EURUSD	Copper	EURUSD
5-year note	Natural gas	EURUSD	Eurobobl
EURUSD	Eurobobl	Eurobobl	Natural gas
Gold	5-year note	Natural gas	Platinum
Jap govt bond	Eurobund	5-year note	Copper
Palladium	Palladium	Palladium	Palladium
Short sterling	Short sterling	Short sterling	Short sterling
Euribor	Euribor	Euribor	Euribor
Eurodollars	Eurodollars	Eurodollars	Eurodollars

reflect the trendiness of the past 10 years. The U.S. 30-year bonds spent a number of years moving sideways with relatively low volatility, even when the short-term rates continued lower.

Most other markets scatter throughout the center of the table with the exception of palladium, which is consistently classified as very low noise.

We take one last look at the trend performance using both noise and a moving average taken over the same calculation periods, 20, 40, and 80 days. We find that doubling the calculation period gives a better test sample. As before, we scatter the results using the average noise as the bottom scale and the information ratio as the left scale, shown in Figures 2.6a, b,

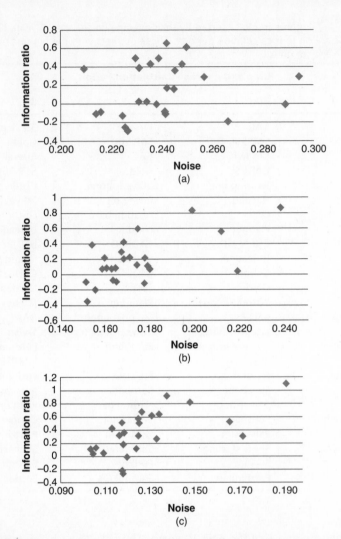

FIGURE 2.6 (a) Results of a 20-day trend applied to 25 markets and scattered by average noise and information ratio. (b) Results of a 40-day trend. (c) Results of an 80-day trend.

and c. Figure 2.6a seems to have no particular pattern, but that can easily be caused by a mixture of poor performance because 20 days is not long enough to capture macrotrends in most of these futures markets.

The 40- and 80-day calculation periods show an increasingly clear pattern where higher values of noise (less noise) produce better returns, indicated by a higher information ratio. Any information ratio below zero indicates a loss. The three diamonds at the far right are the results of the three short-maturity futures markets, Euribor, short sterling, and Eurodollars. The negative ratios are generally the equity index markets, but the 80-day trend shows that 30-year bonds and gold also generated net losses from 2000.

CAPITALIZING ON THE TREND OF NOISE

We've looked at the long-term average of noise for each of the markets. These averages create an orderly ranking that shows which strategy is most likely to succeed. But over the short, 8-day calculation period, the noise of any market can vary considerably. Figure 2.7 shows the SPX, along with the 8-day efficiency ratio for the first quarter of 2009. During this interval, the SPX drops to its lowest point in March 2009, and the efficiency ratio is seen to peak twice and touch bottom four times. The average of the ratio for the period in the chart is 0.37, although it ranges from near zero, 0.01, to 0.87 in February.

Observing the patterns on a chart always gives rise to hopeful ideas. In this case, we see that the S&P dropped twice, from about 930 to 800 in January and again from near 850 to under 700 in February and March. At the same time, the ratio shows two insightful patterns. After the ratio peaks in mid-January, it drops quickly and stays low during an interval

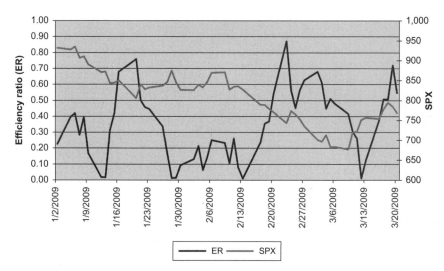

FIGURE 2.7 SPX with an 8-day efficiency ratio, first quarter, 2009.

where the S&P goes sideways. Then, just after February 13, 2009, it starts up sharply, indicating an improved trend, and stays high through the entire period when the S&P drops 150 points. Can the trend of the ratio be used to switch from a trending strategy to a mean-reverting one? Or can it be used to tell us when to stand aside using either strategy?

It's an interesting idea that will be left to the reader to pursue. Once such a pattern is observed, we each approach a solution differently, and this is an exercise worth some investment of time.

CHAPTER 3

Pairs Trading: Understanding the Process

airs trading is not an industry secret. It is a basic market arbitrage and can be done by any conscientious trader. It may be that greater competition in recent years means that you will need to be more selective about the choice of trades, but the opportunities are still there.

The basic stock market pairs trade begins by choosing two companies that are fundamentally related. We can use a simple correlation tool, which we will discuss later, but that's not necessary. By observing the chart of one company against another we can see that the two companies move in much the same way, reacting to news in a similar manner.

The best pairs trades will be between direct competitors, such as Dell and Hewlett-Packard. There may be periods of time when prices move significantly apart, but even during those intervals, there will be a lot of similarity. We don't want the two stocks to track each other too closely, because that also means there is limited opportunity. We also need to be vigilant about structural changes in one of the companies and how that might affect their relationship to other companies in the same industry. A price jump following an earnings release is not a structural change. Most often the first chip manufacturer to report indicates that other manufacturers in that industry should follow with similar performance.

The trade itself will sell the stronger stock and buy the weaker, looking for their prices to correct, or come back very close to each other. When they do correct, the trade is exited. The number of shares traded for each stock will be calculated to equalize the risk of the long and short. This approach is the basic statistical arbitrage (stat-arb) trade. What differs from trader to trader is the selection of pairs, the size of the distortion being targeted, the size of the positions, and the exit criteria, but not the concept.

THE PROCESS

This section steps through the process of developing a pairs trading strategy. A similar procedure is used for the other strategies in the chapters that follow, but it is important to understand how it comes about. There are clear rules to be followed; otherwise, you cannot have confidence that the final system will work. Both our computers and development tools are extremely powerful, perhaps too powerful. It is easy to beat the problem into submission. Our challenge is to keep it simple and robust. We must think of the problems that can be encountered in advance and use our data and tools wisely. At the end, we will review the process and comment on critical steps.

An important advantage of a rule-based system is that, once implemented for one pair using a spreadsheet or computer program, it can be easily extended to others. That will allow us to test for robustness. If we are doing it correctly and it worked on Dell and Hewlett-Packard, then it should work on similarly related pairs. Once we have a number of pairs checked out successfully, hopefully in different sectors, you have gained confidence in the method as well as diversification.

All trades will be entered and exited on the daily closing prices, although that won't be necessary for actually trading. You could enter prices into the spreadsheet at any time during the day, perhaps 15 minutes after an economic report when volatility is high, and enter a trade any time there is a distortion that satisfies our minimum threshold.

We will try to approach each problem as we would without any foresight as to what is the correct solution or the best markets. When exploring a new method, there are always false starts. Each time we uncover a problem, we learn more about the process and the solution.

THE BASICS

We'll start by choosing four U.S. airline stocks, which we intuitively believe react to the same economic fundamentals. If the economy is strong and there is more disposable income, then more people fly for both business and pleasure, and if the economy is weak, they stay put. The candidates are American, Continental, Southwest, and U.S. Airways, all large companies, with Southwest the only domestic carrier. We will use American and Continental as the primary example in the following sections. They were chosen

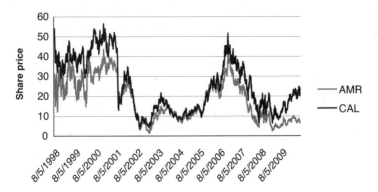

FIGURE 3.1 The price history of American Airlines (AMR) and Continental Airlines (CAL), 10 years ending July 2010.

because both had the maximum amount of data and both were major domestic and international carriers. They turn out to be neither a very good example nor a very bad example. By the time you read this, one or the other of the airlines may have a different name, but that won't affect our results.

If we show American (AMR) and Continental (CAL) on the same chart (Figure 3.1), we can see the similarity in their price movement. Most of the time Continental trades above American, but there are obvious differences that could be turned into either profit opportunities or large trading losses. Most important, we see that on September 11, 2001, both companies took a plunge of more than 50%, based on the public perception that no one was ever going to get onto an airplane again. For those readers who are good with spreadsheets, the correlation of the daily changes over the 10 years is .94, quite high. Remember that correlations always use the price differences and not the actual prices and that the differences are actually *returns* and are best calculated as a percentage change,

$$\frac{P_{today}}{P_{previous}} - 1$$

It may also seem from the chart that the volatility of Continental is higher than that of American. That would be a good guess because the average price of Continental was higher than that of American during this period. But that's not the case. Over the full 10 years, Continental had an annualized volatility of 69% while American was 81%. Because the volatility is calculated in the standard way used by financial institutions,

$$\text{Annualized volatility} = \text{Standard deviation of daily returns} \times \sqrt{252}$$

where the daily returns are percent changes, these values are somewhat self-adjusting to the differences in price.

Time Perspective

We need to decide if our trading should target a few big profits or many small ones. My own preference is for many faster trades, even though a series of small losses could total the same as one large loss generated by a longer-term strategic trade. With faster trading, it is possible to have more consistent performance because the individual trade risk is smaller. If you hold a trade for a long time, then the risk increases proportionally (but not linearly) with the holding period, so it's not possible to have a long-term trade with low risk. More trades also give greater statistical confidence.

If we think of the conclusions given in Chapter 2, "The Importance of Price Noise," we should remember that operating in a shorter time period emphasizes price noise, and taking a longer view emphasizes the trend. Pairs trading assumes that differences between the two stocks will be corrected; therefore, we are dealing with noise. Using a shorter time horizon will benefit us.

A more intuitive, convincing argument may come from looking at the chart of the two stocks in Figure 3.1. It appears that, about September 2000, Continental moves higher while American moves lower. This is certainly a big opportunity. Within two weeks, prices converge again, and by 9/11 they are virtually the same. Buying American and selling Continental short would have been highly successful. In August 2006, we get another separation, where Continental gains over American, and Continental appears to remain higher until August 2008. In this case, if you consider that the size of the risk increases with time (as do the profits), we have another argument in favor of shorter trades.

The principal argument against frequent trading is the increase in cost. More trades mean accumulated execution slippage and commissions, and a shorter time frame also means less volatility and smaller profits per trade. Volatility is the main enemy of many of these strategies, which are mean reverting. Prices must move apart by some minimum amount to offer enough profit opportunity.

Note on Data and Costs   Be sure to check that all the data are in the same format. Even within the same data service, the stocks series that are automatically created may be without any decimal points, so a share price of $22.15 could be shown as 2215. Data downloaded specifically by the user, for example, a stock that is not in the S&P 500, may be shown in decimal form, such as 14.50. For most programs to work correctly, all of the data should be in the same format.

TABLE 3.1	Cross-correlations of American (AMR), Continental (CAL), U.S. Airways (LCC), and Southwest Airlines (LUV) from September 2005 to February 2009. Southwest is clearly different.

	Correlations			
Airlines	AMR	CAL	LCC	LUV
AMR	1			
CAL	0.766	1		
LCC	0.758	0.773	1	
LUV	0.392	0.390	0.392	1

The examples that follow using stocks do not reflect any costs. Instead, the results will always show the returns per share. Costs vary considerably from trader to trader, with professionals paying less than $0.001 per share. You will need to decide whether the potential returns are sufficient given your own costs.

Correlations and Common Sense

In expectation of adding U.S. Airways (LCC) and Southwest Airlines (LUV) to the mix of pairs when we are done with American and Continental, we will look at data beginning on September 29, 2005, when U.S. Airways began trading on the NYSE. We'll call that the beginning of our test period. When we compare the correlations of the price changes for the four companies (see Table 3.1), we get a wide range, with American, Continental, and U.S. Airways closely tracking one another, but Southwest very different. We can explain this because Southwest is exclusively a domestic carrier, but we don't know if that will make a difference to our trading. It will give us the opportunity to see if the greatest profits come from markets that are more or less correlated while still in the same transportation group. Although we're sure from the 0.766 correlation that American and Continental will correct any differences, we don't yet know if those divergences may turn out to be too small for practical trading, or if the correlations are good but the volatility needs to be watched.

If we were fundamental traders, we could explain that Southwest has a different, discount business model. We could remember the news articles that credited Southwest with extensive jet fuel hedging success. But we can't confirm these statements, and we don't know when an average jet-fuel price that's 40% under the market will turn around to become 10% over the market. We do know that Figure 3.2 shows a very different price pattern for Southwest than for the other airlines. Again, we'll let the trading results

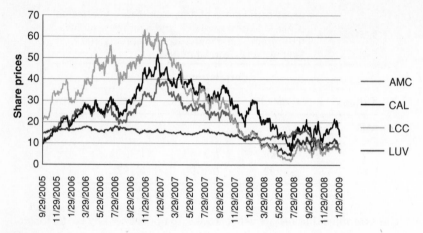

FIGURE 3.2 Comparison of four airlines, September 29, 2005, to January 30, 2009.

confirm whether it should be included in the pairs trading mix. For now, we can feel comfortable that three of the four airlines have similar price moves; therefore, they are candidates for pairs trading.

Percentage Deviation

The basic approach to pairs trading is to look at the percentage differences in the daily moves of the two stocks, in this case AMR minus CAL. When the difference is too high, we sell short the stronger (AMR) and buy the weaker (CAL); if too low, we buy AMR and sell short CAL. Based on our observation and the correlations, we can expect this divergence to correct within a few days.

Before you express concern about short selling, it is very common today for actively traded stocks; however, at the end of the airline example, we will show how to use sector ETFs as a simple alternative for the short side.

As an example of using percentage differences, suppose that American gained 1.5% today and Continental gained 0.9%. Then the difference (AMR − CAL) would be +0.6%. We now need to know if +0.6% is unusually high. To gain a better understanding of the range of these values, we calculated them for our test period and got the results shown in Figure 3.3.

We can see from this chart that the volatility of the AMR-CAL differences changes drastically over the four years. First, from the beginning in September 2005 until September 2006 volatility was uniform, with daily percentage differences ranging from about +5% to –5%, with a maximum of

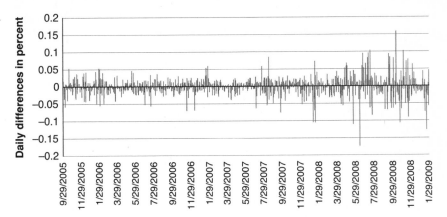

FIGURE 3.3 Daily percentage difference in American Airlines (AMR) and Continental (CAL).

about 8%. For the next 9 months, volatility dropped. Had we been trading before July 2007, we might have created the following trading rules:

- Sell short AMR and buy CAL on the close when the daily change in AMR exceeds the change in CAL by 2.5%.
- Sell short CAL and buy AMR on the close when the daily change in CAL exceeds the change in AMR by 2.0%.

Selling AMR with a 2.5% threshold and selling CAL with a 2.0% threshold accounts for the upward bias we can see on the chart, where the maximum was 8% and the minimum about 5%.

After May 2007, volatility begins to increase until by mid-2008 when the maximum difference has become 17.5%, far greater than the previous 8%. Had we sold AMR at a 2.5% difference over CAL using our previous rules we would have, theoretically, been holding the same trade when the difference reached 15%. But that would never have happened. When the trade reached 10%, we would have all rushed for the exit, forgetting the opportunities. Without going through the tedious exercise of figuring out all the trades, we can see that the basic method has too much risk and too much variability. This method may have worked during the 1960s, but it is not the one we want now.

It is also good to see that we used the chart to decide buy and sell levels that were not symmetric. These levels, 2.5% and 2.0%, clearly fit the pattern but are not a good way to find a solution. Generally, we see this skew in the prices because the stocks have been moving in one direction, in this case up, or the volatility of one stock is greater than the other. When prices change direction so does the skew. A solution that is going to last will need to be more robust, and the safest approach will always be a symmetric solution.

Changing volatility is also a good lesson in why using more data is better than fewer data for testing. If you were to choose only the last year of data, then you get a narrow, unrealistic idea of market patterns. Whatever program you develop will have a short life span. When you see a structural change in the volatility, you need to consider a more dynamic way to adjust to the market. In Figure 3.3, there are three distinct volatility regimes: moderate, low, and high. By finding one method that adjusts to these situations, you can create a more robust approach.

What is needed is a way to adapt the entry levels to changes in market volatility. We not only are concerned with increased volatility and the associated increased risk but also realize that if volatility falls, as it did in 2006, and we're waiting for a 2.5% difference for an entry trigger, then we could wait months before seeing a new trade. The problem needs to be solved for both increasing and decreasing volatility.

Relative Differences

The solution to adapting to changing volatility is to recognize *relative differences*. One method of showing relative differences is to use a momentum indicator, such as *relative strength* (RSI), stochastic, or *moving average convergence-divergence* (MACD). They all accomplish the same thing in slightly different ways. In our examples, we'll use the stochastic indicator because it is easier to calculate and, interpreted correctly, will give you the same results. In addition, it has less lag than the other indicators. The basic calculation for the stochastic is

$$\text{Stochastic indicator} = \frac{C_t - \min(L_{n-\text{days}})}{\text{Max}(H_{n-\text{days}}) - \min(L_{n-\text{days}})}$$

where C_t is today's close, $\min(L_{n-\text{days}})$ is the minimum price (the lows of the day) over the past n days, and $\max(H_{n-\text{days}})$ is the maximum price (the highs of the day) over the past n days. The denominator is then the maximum to minimum price range of the past n days. The stochastic indicator actually shows the positioning of today's close within that range, essentially expressed as a percent measured from the low of the n-day range to the high of that range.

The value of the stochastic can vary from 0 to 100. If the past range for AMR was from $22.00 to $18.00 and the close is now at $19.00, then the stochastic will be 25. If today's close was a new high, the stochastic would be 100.

For those familiar with this momentum indicator, our definition is for the *raw stochastic*. Most trading software show a much slower version, created by taking the 3-day average of the raw stochastic, then again taking the 3-day average of that result, giving essentially a 4.5-day lag (half of 9 days). For our purposes, that creates an indicator that is too slow.

Table 3.2 gives an example of the raw stochastic calculation from the beginning of the data. The calculation period is 10 days; therefore, the first 9 data rows are blank. Beginning in row 11 on February 3, 2000 (row 1 has the headings), column H shows the high of the past 10 days = `max(B2:B11)` and column I shows the 10-day low = `min(C2:C11)`. Using the highs and lows of the past 10 days, we can calculate the AMR stochastic in column J as = `(D11-I11)/(H11-I11)`. Once both AMR and CAL stochastics are calculated in columns J and M, the differences = `J11-M11` are entered into column N.

If we calculate the traditional 14-day stochastic (usually the nominal calculation period found on charting services) for AMR and CAL during the second half of 2007, we get the picture shown in Figure 3.4. Both markets move in a similar way between 0 and 100; however, they do not reach highs at the same time, and some of the lows are also out of phase. Without those differences, there would be no opportunity. Based on this view of the divergence in the two stocks, we can devise trading rules that profit from it. Although we think that we can see where the momentum values are farthest apart, the first step is to show those differences more clearly. That can easily be done by plotting the differences between the AMR and CAL stochastics, as shown in Figure 3.5. We'll refer to that as the *stochastic difference* (SD), in column N on the spreadsheet.

Stochastic Difference

Figure 3.5 shows both the annualized volatility and the stochastic differences for AMR and CAL. The second half of 2008 was chosen because of its historically high volatility, when everyone thought that the end of the world was coming. It is interesting to see that the stochastic difference did not peak at the same place as the volatility spike. Instead, the bottom line in Figure 3.5, *M1-M2*, shows that the stochastic differences peaked in May 2008 at a value of about 50 and had numerous lows of about –50 throughout the year. The low levels are more consistent than the peaks, but this is only six months, or 5% of the test period.

Experience teaches us that we should not attempt to fine-tune these levels or bias our trading to expect the extension on the upside to be smaller than the downside. At some point, whatever causes these charts to be asymmetrical will change. Those readers familiar with trend-following systems may have noticed that during the 1990s, when there was a clear

TABLE 3.2 Stochastic indicators created from AMR and CAL daily prices.

A	B	C	D	E	F	G	H	I	J	K	L	M	N
	American			Continental			American 10-Day Stochastic			Continental 10-Day Stochastic			
Date	High	Low	Close	High	Low	Close	High(10)	Low(10)	Stochastic	High(10)	Low(10)	Stochastic	AMR-CAL
1/21/2000	25.53	24.74	24.74	35.75	34.44	34.63							
1/24/2000	24.74	24.21	24.48	35.00	33.63	33.88							
1/25/2000	24.56	23.63	23.68	34.25	32.94	33.13							
1/26/2000	24.50	23.71	24.03	33.81	33.06	33.50							
1/27/2000	24.34	23.21	23.31	33.88	33.19	33.25							
1/28/2000	23.74	22.81	22.81	33.88	32.81	33.19							
1/31/2000	23.21	22.65	22.78	33.75	31.06	31.63							
2/1/2000	23.42	22.76	23.39	32.50	31.69	32.44							
2/2/2000	24.19	22.92	23.89	33.75	32.13	33.50							
2/3/2000	24.40	23.60	24.26	33.44	32.06	33.00	25.53	22.65	0.559	35.75	31.06	0.414	0.145
2/4/2000	24.77	24.05	24.21	32.94	32.13	32.19	24.77	22.65	0.736	35.00	31.06	0.287	0.449
2/7/2000	24.40	23.74	23.76	32.63	32.13	32.31	24.77	22.65	0.524	34.25	31.06	0.392	0.132
2/8/2000	24.48	23.76	24.24	33.13	32.44	32.69	24.77	22.65	0.750	33.88	31.06	0.578	0.172
2/9/2000	24.56	23.87	23.87	32.81	30.88	30.94	24.77	22.65	0.575	33.88	30.88	0.020	0.555
2/10/2000	23.87	22.78	22.97	31.00	29.00	29.19	24.77	22.65	0.151	33.88	29.00	0.039	0.112
2/11/2000	23.23	22.33	22.62	31.06	29.38	30.88	24.77	22.33	0.119	33.75	29.00	0.396	−0.277
2/14/2000	23.02	22.54	22.86	31.50	30.38	31.06	24.77	22.33	0.217	33.75	29.00	0.434	−0.216
2/15/2000	22.99	22.23	22.41	32.25	31.06	31.88	24.77	22.23	0.071	33.75	29.00	0.606	−0.535
2/16/2000	22.78	22.12	22.70	33.44	31.75	33.00	24.77	22.12	0.219	33.44	29.00	0.901	−0.682
2/17/2000	23.13	22.54	22.99	34.63	33.25	33.25	24.77	22.12	0.328	34.63	29.00	0.755	−0.427
2/18/2000	22.99	21.57	22.25	33.81	32.94	33.00	24.56	21.57	0.227	34.63	29.00	0.710	−0.483

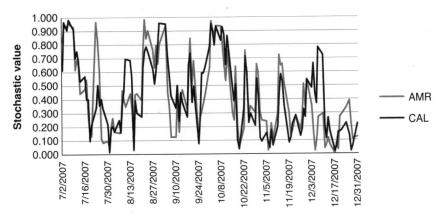

FIGURE 3.4 14-day stochastic momentum of AMR and CAL, second half of 2007.

bull market in stocks, long positions would have been held longer and shown larger profits than short sales, making the performance noticeably asymmetrical. If we had decided to optimize only the long positions or bias our trading to the long side, the result would have been to hold the longs even longer and possibly not trade any shorts. That would have been a financial disaster after 2000, when prices headed down for more than three years. If we don't know when the next major economic cycle will start, using symmetrical trading rules is the safest approach.

Exits   When planning a trading strategy around these numbers, our nominal exit should always be at a stochastic difference of zero, indicating that

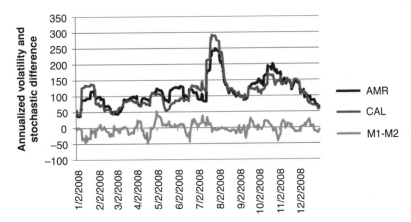

FIGURE 3.5 The stochastic difference (SD) of the AMR stochastic minus the CAL stochastic, shown with the AMR and CAL prices during the second half of 2008.

the relationship between the two stocks has gone back to equilibrium. For some traders, that might be unnecessarily strict. We should also consider exiting shorts above zero and exiting longs below zero. This would cut profits short but assure us that we would safely exit more often.

There is always a temptation to hold a short position until the stochastic difference moves from the high entry to the low point, where we would reverse and enter a long position, for example, from a stochastic value of 80 down to 20. Profits would be much bigger and transaction costs less important. But that's not the way the market works. A relative distortion, as we recognize with the momentum indicator, is likely to return to near normal but has no reason to reverse. In our 6-month example, CAL tends to lead AMR, then fall back to normal, and then lead again. We would be exposing ourselves to very high risk unnecessarily if we waited for AMR to lead CAL in order to exit a long position.

Implicit Bias   As we look at Figure 3.5 and consider the rules, we see that if we sell above 45 and buy below –45, there is only one short trade and four longs. If we choose ±25, there would be a lot more trades on both sides, but that would force us to hold those trades with larger unrealized losses. Those are classic trade-offs that we will consider later in the development process.

None of the strategy rules will consider asymmetrical parameters. There has always been a bias in the stock market because history has shown a steady increase in the average price of a stock or an index. One example of this bias is the traditional definition of a bull and bear market. A bear market begins when the DJIA turns down by 20%, and a bull market begins after the DJIA turns up by 20%. However, after a decline of 50%, a rally of 20% is actually a recovery of only 10% of the value lost in the downturn. Then the threshold can be twice as large to enter a bear market as a bull market, a definite bias toward the upside.

The 2008–2009 stock market decline of 50% points out that those upward biases may have provided small improvements during good times and large losses when they go wrong.

The rules in this strategy, and others given later in this book, will all use symmetrical thresholds. A short sale signal will occur when the stochastic difference moves above 40, and a buy on the first day that the stochastic falls below –40. Exits will initially be at retracements to zero.

Results for Stochastic Difference

In tracking the performance, there are five trades during this period with a total return of $350.39, or $0.468 per share (as shown in Table 3.3). At that level of return, the method would still be very profitable after costs and

TABLE 3.3 AMR-CAL trades based on the difference in stochastics, 2008.

Date	AMR Position			CAL Position			AMR Stoch	CAL Stoch	Stoch Diff	PL	PL/Share
	Pos	Size	Price	Pos	Size	Price					
1/14/2008	Buy	100	13.04	Sell	58	23.35	41.8	82.2	−40.4		
2/4/2008	Exit	100	14.41	Exit	58	27.94	71.9	69.1	2.7	−129.22	−0.82
4/17/2008	Buy	100	8.54	Sell	49	21.11	7.5	56.3	−48.9		
4/22/2008	Exit	100	7.02	Exit	49	17.20	0.6	0.3	0.3	39.59	0.27
5/1/2008	Sell	100	9.90	Buy	46	19.25	97.2	45.1	52.0		
6/13/2008	Exit	100	5.46	Exit	46	13.50	20.6	37.0	−16.4	179.50	1.23
6/19/2008	Buy	100	6.31	Sell	54	15.59	46.6	90.3	−43.7		
6/23/2008	Exit	100	5.73	Exit	54	11.96	28.8	4.1	24.8	138.02	0.90
10/30/2008	Buy	100	9.20	Sell	62	16.94	26.6	68.1	−41.5		
11/4/2008	Exit	100	11.05	Exit	62	17.94	69.1	65.3	3.8	123.00	0.76

slippage. However, this is a single example and not typical of a wide range of performance.

The list of trades also confirms the rules. In the first trade, on January 14, 2008, the stochastic values were both very positive, but CAL was much stronger than AMR, 82.2 compared with 41.8. The difference, AMR – CAL, was –40.5, below the –40 threshold to trigger a buy of AMR and short sale of CAL. On February 4, 2008, the stochastic difference moved above zero, and the trade was exited for a loss. Four of the five trades during 2008 were triggered on CAL being stronger than AMR.

It shouldn't be surprising that there are profits because we picked our buy and sell thresholds off the charts and then just verified that those values generated profits. The advantage of this method is that the stochastic should adapt to many different price patterns, including changes in volatility. Remember that the intention is to find a method that would adapt to the more volatile period beginning June 2007. In this first test, the threshold values of ±40 generated only five trades in a year. We would prefer to trade more often.

Different Position Sizes

Notice that the sizes of the CAL positions are different from the nominal AMR position of 100 shares. That is because a volatility adjustment was used. As we go through this process, the size of the two positions will be an important way to control the risk and improve the chance for a profit. In this case, a rolling volatility measurement was used.

To find the volatility-adjusted position size, we begin by assigning a fixed size to one leg. In the previous example, AMR always traded 100 shares. Next, we calculate the *average true range* (ATR) of each leg, measured over the same n days. For any day, the true range, TR, is the largest of the high minus the low, the high minus the previous low, and the previous close minus the low:

$$TR_i = \text{Max}(H_t - L_t,\ H_t - C_{t-1},\ C_{t-1} - L_t)$$

The ATR is the average of the past n values of TR. Then, if the ATR of AMR was \$0.50 and over the same period the ATR of CAL was \$1.00, we would trade twice as many shares of AMR as we would CAL. It is important to remember that this is a critical step in trading two markets simultaneously. They must each have the same risk exposure. If you miss this step, there is no way to correct for it later. This will be discussed in more detail in the section "Alternative Methods for Measuring Volatility," later in this chapter.

Had we not adjusted the position size of each leg, the only alternative would have been to trade 100 shares each, with the results shown in Table 3.4. This method returns a total profit of $178.00 with $0.18 per share compared with the volatility-adjustment method of $350.89 and $0.47 per share. Of course, this is a very small test period, and the results could have greatly favored taking equal positions, especially if it was the CAL leg that was most often profitable. But the performance would have depended on the chance that the leg with higher volatility was the one generating profits, which is not good risk management. There is no substitute for volatility-adjusting each leg of the trade.

Alternate Approach to Position Size

The idea behind volatility-adjusted position sizes is that every trade should have an equal risk. That way you maximize diversification and are not making the unconscious decision that one trade is better than another.

In the previous process, we started by fixing the position size of one leg at 100 shares and then finding the number of shares in the other leg that caused risk to be equal. An alternative approach is to assign some arbitrary investment size to each stock, say, $10,000, and then:

- Calculate the average true range of the stock price over the past 20 days.
- Divide the nominal investment size by the average true range.

The result is the number of shares needed to equalize the risk of the two stocks. These can be done for any number of stocks, and all will have been adjusted to the same risk. When you're done testing using these position sizes, the results can be scaled up or down by multiplying all stock positions by the same factor to reach a target volatility or an investment amount.

Testing a Range of Stochastic Values

At this point, it is impossible to avoid some amount of optimization. We are hopeful that the underlying premise of the method is good, and we would like to vary the calculation period as well as the entry and exit parameters to see if we can increase the number of trades, as well as the returns. The pattern of these relationships is predictable, so we might be on safe ground. For example, as we make the entry thresholds farther apart, we will get fewer trades, the profits should be bigger (if we keep the exit at the same level), and the risk should get larger because we're holding the trade longer.

TABLE 3.4 AMR and CAL with equal position size.

Date	AMR Position			CAL Position			AMR Stoch	CAL Stoch	Stoch Diff	PL	PL/Share
	Pos	Size	Price	Pos	Size	Price					
1/14/2008	Buy	100	13.04	Sell	100	23.35	41.8	82.2	−40.4		
2/4/2008	Exit	100	14.41	Exit	100	27.94	71.9	69.1	2.7	−322.00	−1.61
4/17/2008	Buy	100	8.54	Sell	100	21.11	7.5	56.3	−48.9		
4/22/2008	Exit	100	7.02	Exit	100	17.20	0.6	0.3	0.3	239.00	1.20
5/1/2008	Sell	100	9.90	Buy	100	19.25	97.2	45.1	52.0		
6/13/2008	Exit	100	5.46	Exit	100	13.50	20.6	37.0	−16.4	−131.00	−0.66
6/19/2008	Buy	100	6.31	Sell	100	15.59	46.6	90.3	−43.7		
6/23/2008	Exit	100	5.73	Exit	100	11.96	28.8	4.1	24.8	305.00	1.53
10/30/2008	Buy	100	9.20	Sell	100	16.94	26.6	68.1	−41.5		
11/4/2008	Exit	100	11.05	Exit	100	17.94	69.1	65.3	3.8	85.00	0.43

If we hold the entry levels constant and make the exit points closer, then we should increase the number of trades, reduce the size of the profit, and decrease the overall risk because the trades will be held for a shorter time.

We will also vary the calculation period for the stochastic indicator. As that value gets larger, the indicator will reach its extremes less often, generating fewer trading signals. A shorter calculation period will produce more signals. We would like to have as many signals as possible but recognize that a faster frequency of signals will also have smaller price moves and consequently smaller potential profits. There are always trade-offs that must be balanced. In addition, we know from Chapter 2 that when we look at shorter time intervals, we see more price noise. We expect that for this mean-reverting method, shorter calculation periods should favor our trading strategy.

Because we are testing different combinations and must be concerned about overfitting, we will watch carefully to see that the pattern of results has the shape that we expect and that the numbers do not jump around.

Using In-Sample and Out-of-Sample Data

If we were working in completely uncharted waters, that is, developing a strategy from a new concept, we would want to divide the data into *in-sample* and *out-of-sample* partitions. We would then test all of the new concepts on the in-sample data until we were satisfied with the rules and the test results. Finally, we would run our best rules and parameters through the unseen, out-of-sample data. We expect the results to be worse than the in-sample performance because there are many more patterns that we could not have anticipated. Still, if the ratio of return to risk of the in-sample test was 2.0 and the out-of-sample test was 1.2, we would consider that a success. It would be ideal if the out-of-sample data performed the same as the in-sample data, but that rarely happens because there is always some degree of overfitting, even if it is unconscious and unintended.

However, if the out-of-sample test is a complete failure, yielding a ratio near zero, then the method is also a failure. You cannot review the new results, find the problem area, and fix it, because that is feedback. You no longer have true out-of-sample data, and there is good reason to believe that your improvements are simply overfitting the data more and will result in trading losses.

Specifying the Tests

Our primary measurement statistic is the *information ratio* (annualized return divided by annualized volatility), and the results are shown in

Table 3.5. The overbought entry levels are varied from stochastic values of 50 to 30 and the corresponding exit levels from 10 points under the entry to zero. Rather than test only the pair AMR-CAL, we will show the average of all tests for the combinations of four airlines:

LCC—CAL
LCC—AMR
LCC—LUV
AMR—CAL
AMR—LUV
CAL—LUV

We take this approach because the choice of parameters should work for all the pairs, not just for AMR-CAL. When we look at average results of all tests, we won't be able to see how the individual pairs performed, but we will know if one set of thresholds is better than others when applied to all markets. This will prevent us from looking too closely at the detail. We also expect to get smoother results by averaging the ratios for each pair.

Which Parameter First?

There are three parameters to test: the stochastic calculation period, the entry threshold, and the exit threshold. The general rule is that we test the parameter that has the most effect on performance. That seems to be the stochastic calculation period. We should expect that longer periods (larger values) will generate fewer trades. The entry threshold will also be a major factor in determining the number of trades: The greater the threshold, the fewer the trades. The exit threshold will have only a small effect on the frequency of trading. If we exit sooner, then there is a chance that prices will reverse and allow us to enter again, but that should happen much less often. Then the order of testing will be

- Stochastic calculation period
- Entry threshold (with exit set to zero)
- Exit threshold

To begin, we need to pick some reasonable values, which will be a calculation period of 20, an entry of ±60, and an exit of zero. We expect that the best calculation period will be less than 20 and the entry may be less than 60. Exiting at zero is normal, but exiting a short at 10 might be safer. Table 3.5 shows the results of these tests beginning in January 2000; however, some of these stocks start later due to mergers.

TABLE 3.5   Initial tests of four airline stocks, six pairs.

Parameters			Performance Statistics				
Mom	**Entry**	**Exit**	**Trades**	**AROR**	**Per Share**	**Ratio**	**Prof Pairs**
20	60	0	17	−4.70	−0.379	−0.389	0 of 6
14	60	0	23	−1.83	−0.040	−0.152	1 of 6
10	60	0	30	4.20	0.225	0.335	3 of 6
8	60	0	34	2.47	0.103	0.207	4 of 6
7	60	0	36	4.52	0.159	0.375	5 of 6
6	60	0	42	3.48	0.095	0.292	5 of 6
Average			30	1.36	0.027	0.111	

The ratio will be the key statistic for determining success or failure. In Table 3.5, the ratio increases in a reasonably orderly way as the momentum calculation period declines from 20 to 6, as shown in Figure 3.6. The calculation periods are shown along the bottom and the ratios along the left scale. Periods of 10 and lower are clearly better, with 7 the best. The period 7 also had the highest profits per share, which is critical to success. We could have tested all calculation periods, but the difference between 20 and 19 days (a change of 5%) would not be as significant as the difference between 7 and 8 (a change of 14%), so we've skipped some values at the high end and included all of them at the lower end.

We expect that everyone would choose the period 7, not just because it has the highest ratio but because it falls in the middle of the profitable set of tests. It is best to avoid the value 6 because faster trades are likely to have smaller profits per trade. The 10-day test may be better because of the profits per trade, but readers will need to perform these tests themselves to verify the results, and they can make other choices at that time. You

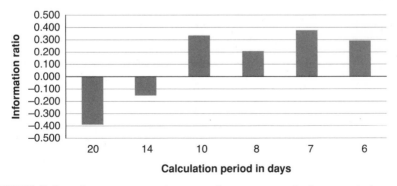

FIGURE 3.6   Information ratios for tests of momentum calculation periods.

TABLE 3.6 Airline pairs with entry threshold of ±50.

Parameters			Performance Statistics				
Mom	**Entry**	**Exit**	**Trades**	**AROR**	**Per Share**	**Ratio**	**Prof Pairs**
20	50	0	28	−2.88	−0.098	−0.240	1 of 6
14	50	0	37	0.40	0.082	0.034	3 of 6
10	50	0	48	3.60	0.154	0.300	3 of 6
8	50	0	57	3.02	0.103	0.251	4 of 6
7	50	0	61	5.67	0.149	0.472	6 of 6
6	50	0	67	5.00	0.104	0.415	5 of 6
Average			50	2.47	0.082	0.205	

can use these results to convince yourself that this is a viable approach to trading, but you can never simply accept someone else's work without verifying it yourself.

The greatest concern is the average number of trades. Because U.S. Airways (LCC) started trading in October 2005, all combinations using LCC will be more than 5 years shorter than the other pairs. If we consider all pairs trading for the full 10 years, an average of 36 trades is only 3.6 trades per year. That may not be enough to hold our attention. One way to increase the number of trades is to lower the entry threshold below ±60; however, by lowering the threshold, we will also expose ourselves to greater risk because we will enter more trades before they reach their extremes. Tables 3.6 and 3.7 show the results of lowering the threshold to ±50 and ±40. The averages show that the number of trades increases along with all of the other statistics—the annualized rate of return, per share return, and information ratio—but the entry threshold of ±50 is noticeably better than the threshold of ±40. For the threshold of ±50, more of the

TABLE 3.7 Airline pairs with entry threshold of ±40.

Parameters			Performance Statistics				
Mom	**Entry**	**Exit**	**Trades**	**AROR**	**Per Share**	**Ratio**	**Prof Pairs**
20	40	0	40	−3.30	−0.104	−0.274	0 of 6
14	40	0	53	−1.37	0.005	−0.113	1 of 6
10	40	0	67	0.97	0.052	0.082	3 of 6
8	40	0	82	3.43	0.091	0.285	4 of 6
7	40	0	93	4.02	0.087	0.335	4 of 6
6	40	0	101	4.85	0.093	0.406	4 of 6
Average			73	1.43	0.037	0.120	

individual pairs were profitable (see the far right column) than with the entry threshold of ±40. Calculation periods of 10 and lower are still best, and 7 is again the peak performer.

The number of trades has increased by making the threshold lower, but the profits per share are, on average, at only $0.082, which is below what we believe is a safe margin of error, given execution costs. We would consider testing the exit level of 10, compared to zero, to assure us that we exit the trade more often. But because the profits per share are marginally small, exiting sooner would reduce those profits, and it would be unlikely that these stocks would generate a net profit. One answer is to look at the volatility of the market for each individual stock and trade only when the volatility is relatively high. That will reduce the number of trades but should increase the profits per trade. It will probably add risk because there are fewer trades and less diversification, and risk is always associated with higher volatility. But low volatility isn't an option if it doesn't produce sufficient profits.

Before looking at volatility, let's inspect the returns of the individual pairs. Up to now, we have looked at the average of the tests, which is a good way to avoid overfitting. But we need to understand the profits per trade. Table 3.8 shows that results are significantly skewed, with the first two pairs, U.S. Airways (LCC)–Continental (CAL) and U.S. Airways–American (AMR), posting very large per share returns, and all other pairs posting returns that are below what we would consider sufficient for netting a profit. Still, all pairs are profitable, which can be seen as a good start.

If we go back to the original test that used a ±60 entry threshold, we expect the profits per trade to increase, although there would be fewer trades. Table 3.9 shows that results are as expected. The per share results go up on average, and the LCC-LUV pair increases from 4.1 cents to 12.5 cents, enough to produce a real profit. There are some differences in the results of the first two pairs, LCC-CAL and LCC-AMR, due to better

TABLE 3.8 Results of individual pairs for airlines, momentum period 7, entry threshold ±50, exit threshold 0.

Pair	#Tr	TotPL	AROR	Std	Corr	PL/Share	Ratio
LCC-CAL	23	1993	15.9	12	0.765	0.424	1.325
LCC-AMR	24	1718	10.7	12	0.754	0.299	0.889
LCC-LUV	47	978	2.6	12	0.591	0.041	0.216
AMR-CAL	52	693	1.8	12	0.753	0.073	0.150
AMR-LUV	113	801	1.2	12	0.577	0.022	0.096
CAL-LUV	107	1442	1.8	12	0.572	0.037	0.154
Average	61		5.67			0.149	0.472

TABLE 3.9   Results of individual pairs for airlines, momentum period 7, entry threshold ±60, exit threshold 0.

Pair	#Tr	TotPL	AROR	Std	Corr	PL/Share	Ratio
LCC-CAL	13	940	9.1	12	0.765	0.354	0.759
LCC-AMR	10	935	9.4	12	0.754	0.423	0.784
LCC-LUV	34	2255	8.6	12	0.591	0.125	0.717
AMR-CAL	23	140	0.1	12	0.753	0.033	0.005
AMR-LUV	67	466	0.7	12	0.577	0.021	0.055
CAL-LUV	70	−52	−0.8	12	0.572	−0.002	−0.069
Average	36		4.52			0.159	0.375

entries or few trades, but the gains of those two pairs hold up nicely. The number of trades drops predictably, as do the net profits. Three of the six pairs are tradable.

One last approach is to visually inspect the individual *net asset value* (NAV) streams. In Figure 3.7a, these results are messy. If we look closer at the more recent U.S. Airways pairs in Figure 3.7b, the returns are much more orderly.

Are These Results Robust?

Now we come to the difficult part, deciding whether these results are robust. If they are, then we can comfortably trade these pairs. The answer, if any, comes partly from a more philosophic view of this process.

On the positive side, the idea of trading distortions between two fundamentally related stocks is a basic and believable concept. We used a stochastic indicator to measure the relative momentum of the two stocks and then found those points where they diverged. This was simply the difference between the two stochastic indicator values. The larger the difference that determined the entry threshold, the fewer the trades and the larger the profits per trade. That is all according to expectations. We exit when the stochastic values come back together.

When we run a set of tests, varying the calculation period of the stochastic, we get more trades for shorter holding periods. Again, this is very normal and conceptually correct if we are trying to emphasize the price noise. The results are continuous in terms of the number of trades, profits per trade, and information ratio.

On the negative side, we have clearly tested combinations of parameters. If we test enough, then some are very likely to be profitable, but statistics tell us that a small number of profitable results within a larger set of tests do not have predictive qualities. There are also not as many trades

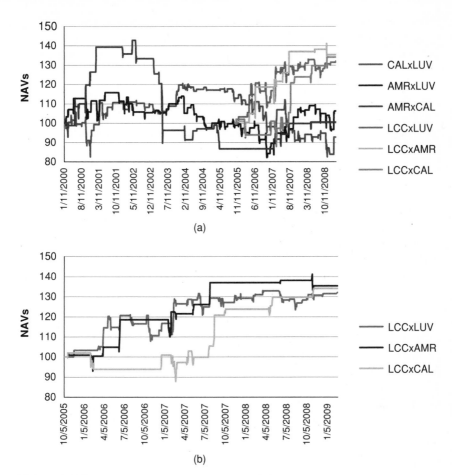

FIGURE 3.7 NAVs for (a) all airline pairs and (b) airline pairs using U.S. Airways (LCC) as one leg.

over the test period as we would like, but that may be the normal outcome of highly correlated stocks that don't diverge often, rather than just spurious price moves. And some of the results show very small net profits and even some losses.

One way to determine robustness is to consider the percentage of profitable results over all tests. In other words, if we used a reasonable range of calculation periods for the momentum indicator and reasonable entry and exit thresholds, and we found the percentage of profitable tests, then a large percentage would tell us that this method is sound, even though some returns were small and others large. It would remove the possibility that this method worked for only a narrow set of conditions. We find this a strong measurement of robustness.

Another confirmation of robustness is to apply this exact method on other sectors with similar fundamental relationships. If the results were similar, then we would be more confident and, at the same time, have additional pairs to trade that would provide valuable diversification.

For now, we can say that there is nothing wrong with the current results, but they are not sufficient to draw a conclusion. We would also prefer pairs that had more trades.

TARGET VOLATILITY

Before moving on, notice that the standard deviation of returns in Table 3.7 is 12% for all pairs. That is called the *target volatility*. To compare the returns of different pairs, we need to make the risk equal for each of the pairs' NAV streams. We use 12% annualized volatility as the industry standard.

There are a number of steps needed to equalize the risk of all the pairs that will be traded. This has the consequence of maximizing diversification by avoiding the arbitrary allocation of more or less of the investment risk to any one pair. The first step was to volatility-adjust the two legs so that each stock in the pair had the same risk exposure. The exact way of doing that was given in the section "Different Position Sizes." The next step is to equalize the risk of each pair relative to each other. To do that, scale the number of shares traded in each pair to a level that represents a target volatility, in this case, 12%.

A 12% target volatility is where the annualized standard deviation of the daily returns is equal to 0.12. To get to that number after the fact, based on all data, follow these steps:

- Record the daily net profits and losses of both legs of the pairs trade.
- Find the standard deviation of the entire series of profits and losses.
- Multiply that standard deviation by the square root of 252 in order to annualize.
- The investment size necessary to trade pair i with 12% volatility is

$$\text{Investment}_i = \frac{\text{Annualized standard deviation}_i}{\text{Target volatility}}$$

Therefore, if the standard deviation of daily returns is $100, the annualized volatility is $1,587. For a target volatility of 12%, we would need an investment of $1,587/0.12 = $13,229 for that pair.

- Create a NAV series by applying the normal formula for the compounded rate of return, but divide each daily profit or loss (expressed in dollars) by the investment size calculated in the last step.

$$\text{NAV}_t = \text{NAV}_{t-1} \times \left(1 + \frac{r_t}{\text{Investment}}\right)$$

As seen in Table 3.9, the risk for all of the pairs is shown as 12% (the column headed Std) so that the annualized returns and other statistics can be compared on an equal footing. The investment in each pair will be different, depending on its volatility.

Combining Pairs into a Portfolio

This method of adjusting to a common volatility works well for comparing the performance of individual pairs, but does not work for combining the pairs into a portfolio. For that we need to have the same performance volatility for each pair relative to the same investment size. The steps are nearly the same.

- Choose an arbitrary investment or an actual one. If the amount is $100,000 and there are six pairs, then each pair gets 1/6, or $16,666.
- Divide the dollar value of the daily returns by the investment size to get the percentage returns each day.
- Find the annualized volatility of the returns: the standard deviation times the square root of 252.
- Divide the target volatility, for example, 12%, by the annualized volatility of this pair, giving us the *adjustment factor*, AF_i.
- Multiply all position sizes for the ith pair by AF_i.

This process adjusts all position sizes for all pairs to create the same risk for each trade. We also know that the volatility of the portfolio of pairs will be less than the target volatility due to diversification. Again, we would want to increase our position sizes to bring the volatility back up to the target level, but there may not be excess money to allow that. This will be discussed later in this chapter under "Benefiting from Pseudo-Leverage," but it will be most important in the chapters concerned with futures markets.

Note that a target volatility of 12% means that there is a 16% chance that we will lose more than 12% and a 2.5% chance that we will lose more than 24% over a one-year period. The target volatility is simply one standard deviation of the returns; therefore, it has the same properties as a normal distribution. The comfort range for most traders can be as high as 17% volatility; for fund managers, it may be as low as 6%.

One of the major limitations in trading stocks is that just because we want a target volatility of 12% doesn't mean that the system performance will permit that much leverage. In the stock market, we are limited by having to pay the full share price, which is not the case with futures or options. Near the end of this chapter, we will look again at what happens when the total cost of buying and selling shares exceeds the maximum investment that we determined in advance was needed to achieve a target volatility of 12%.

Filtering Volatility

Volatility has been discussed in different ways up to now. Rather than try to pick buy and sell thresholds based on absolute price differences between two stocks, we decided to use the difference between two stochastic values to normalize volatility and make the buy and sell levels adaptive. We also used volatility to determine the size of the positions traded in the two legs. By adjusting the position size, we prevented the returns of one stock from overwhelming the other when one of the stocks had much greater volatility. We now need to address the relationship between profits and volatility. It seems reasonable that there is a point where price volatility is too low to produce a profit. On the other side of that question, we might want to know if there is a point where volatility is so high that the risk does not compensate for the returns.

Alternative Methods for Measuring Volatility

The original reason for finding the volatility was for adjusting the position sizes of the two legs. In the extreme, what if CAL was much more volatile than AMR, or if CAL was trading at $150 and AMR at $10? Then the success of every trade would depend entirely on the success of CAL because both its profits and its losses would overwhelm AMR, if trading an equal number of shares of each. During this test period, that situation is not a problem because the prices of both stocks were similar, although CAL was twice the price of AMR during short periods in the fourth quarter of 2008. We know that, under normal circumstances, there is a direct relationship between price and volatility; therefore, CAL should be significantly more volatile than AMR most of the time. We should expect to trade more shares of AMR than CAL to adjust for that volatility. Our solution needs to be general because other pairs may not trade near the same price. In an early section, "Different Position Sizes," we introduced the use of the average true range.

The traditional way of measuring annualized volatility, V, uses the standard deviation of the returns, multiplied by the square root of the number of data points in a year:

$$V = \text{Stdev}(r)_n \times \sqrt{252}$$

where r are the 1-period returns, $\frac{p_t}{p_{t-1}} - 1$ over n days. For monthly returns, we would multiply by $\sqrt{12}$. However, using only the closing price differences when the high and low are also available has been shown to give inferior results. Instead, we'll use the *average true range*, ATR, measured over the same n days. For any day, the true range, TR, is the largest of the high minus the low, the high minus the previous low, and the previous close minus the low,

$$\text{TR}_t = \text{Max}(H_t - L_t,\ H_t - C_{t-1},\ C_{t-1} - L_t)$$

The ATR is the average of the past n values of TR.

When we calculate the volatility based on the standard deviation during the last three quarters of 2008, we find that AMR has a higher volatility than CAL, even though it is trading at a much lower price. Of course, it is possible that prices jump around more if one stock is in the news more than the other. It is also likely that stocks at very low price levels, and in the news, make moves that are proportionately greater than stocks trading at higher prices. Regardless, the volatility numbers generated by the traditional standard deviation method do not seem intuitively correct. Results are shown in Table 3.10. For the first trade, we set the AMR position to 100; then the CAL position is $100 \times (.903/.748) = 121$. The position size of CAL is larger because its volatility is lower.

In recalculating volatility using the average true range, we find the opposite relationship: CAL had significantly higher volatility than AMR. Where the ATR of AMR was \$0.768 in the first trade, the ATR of CAL was \$1.558, twice the amount. This is a remarkable difference, considering both measurements were based on the same time period. The only reasonable explanation is that the intraday volatility of CAL was very high, but it tended to close nearer to its previous close. That is, the closing price volatility did not reflect the wide price swings that occurred during the trading day. When we think of volatility, we must consider the intraday price swings. It is an interesting lesson in volatility, but it may be more pronounced for shorter calculation periods. But it seems likely that if the average true range is twice the value of the close-to-close price changes, the annualized volatility would also be quite different. This brings to mind that there are many risk calculations based on this traditional volatility measurement, and they may yield results that are far too low. Underestimating risk can have serious repercussions. Options traders will also know that *implied volatility* is calculated using the same standard deviation method. Is that value also too low and does that present a trading opportunity?

Returning to our position size calculation, to normalize the volatility using the ATR, we calculated the CAL position as $100 \times (.768/1.558) = 49$. The smaller position reflects the higher volatility. These results are shown in Table 3.11. Based on using the annualized standard deviation method,

TABLE 3.10 AMR-CAL continuous results during 2008 using annualized standard deviation to determine position size.

Date	AMR Position			CAL Position			AMR PL	CAL PL	Net PL	PL per Share	Annual Std AMR	Annual Std CAL
	Pos	Size	Price	Pos	Size	Price						
4/17/2008	Buy	100	8.54	Sell	121	21.11						
4/22/2008	Exit	100	7.02	Exit	121	17.20	−152	473	321	$1.45	0.903	0.748
5/1/2008	Sell	100	9.90	Buy	112	19.25						
6/13/2008	Exit	100	5.46	Exit	112	13.50	444	−644	−200	$(0.94)	1.216	1.082
6/19/2008	Buy	100	6.31	Sell	109	15.59						
6/23/2008	Exit	100	5.73	Exit	109	11.96	−58	396	338	$1.62	1.199	1.103
10/30/2008	Buy	100	9.20	Sell	115	16.94						
11/4/2008	Exit	100	11.05	Exit	115	17.94	185	−115	70	$0.33	1.689	1.470

TABLE 3.11 AMR-CAL continuous results during 2008 using average true range to determine position size.

Date	AMR Position			CAL Position			AMR PL	CAL PL	Net PL	PL/Share	ATR AMR	ATR CAL
	Pos	Size	Price	Pos	Size	Price						
4/17/2008	Buy	100	8.54	Sell	49	21.11						
4/22/2008	Exit	100	7.02	Exit	49	17.20	−152	192	40	$0.27	0.768	1.558
5/1/2008	Sell	100	9.90	Buy	47	19.25						
6/13/2008	Exit	100	5.46	Exit	47	13.50	444	−270	174	$1.18	0.796	1.705
6/19/2008	Buy	100	6.31	Sell	55	15.59						
6/23/2008	Exit	100	5.73	Exit	55	11.96	−58	200	142	$0.91	0.691	1.266
10/30/2008	Buy	100	9.20	Sell	62	16.94						
11/4/2008	Exit	100	11.05	Exit	62	17.94	185	−62	123	$0.76	1.401	2.251

the sum of the four trades was $529 and $0.61 per share. Using the ATR, the sum was $478 with $0.78 per share. It's difficult to tell from four trades which method will produce better results, but we'll stay with the average true range as a more intuitively robust measurement.

Volatility Threshold Filter

Having settled on a way to measure volatility, we now need to decide if performance is dependent on the volatility level, that is, are we more likely to be successful during periods of high or low volatility? Again, we'll use the ATR as our measure of volatility because we believe it is more robust and it is intuitively easier to explain. We'll revert to our original example, AMR and CAL, using a 7 period momentum indicator, but this time we will reduce the entry threshold to ±40 to increase the number of trades. This pair was a modest performer because the ratio was not high, but if a volatility filter works, the results should be improved.

Low Volatility Filter   The first step is to show how the profits for any trade are dependent, if at all, on the volatility of either stock at the time the trade is entered. We recorded the entry ATR values, the final trade PL, and the profits per share and created the three-dimensional surface chart shown in Figure 3.8. This chart may look a bit bumpy at first, but closer inspection will show a hump near the middle and lower points around the

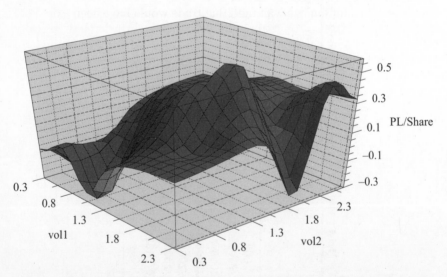

FIGURE 3.8 Surface chart showing the relationship between trade PL and the volatility of the two stocks, measured using ATR, at the time of trade entry.

outside. It's the outside that is of particular interest. In the left corner, where the volatility of both legs (vol1 and vol2) are at low values, the chart makes its steepest dip. There may be other areas, but for now we are interested in only this one. We can also see that, as volatility increases, there is a sharp drop along the right front of the chart. We may also be able to remove trades with very high volatility, which translates into risk, but we'll save that for the next section.

The vol1 and vol2 values used in Figure 3.8 are in dollars per share. It turns out that both AMR and CAL had volatility ranges that were nearly the same. If we were to use those values to define our threshold and we wanted to isolate the lower left corner, then we would need to say:

> *Do not enter any trade if the AMR volatility is less than $1.50 and the CAL volatility is less than $0.80, based on a 7-day average true range.*

It doesn't take much analysis to realize that we are seriously overfitting the data by looking at this much detail. We can try to make this more general by reverting to the traditional annualized standard deviation measurement. Although we prefer the average true range, that measurement is very specific to each stock, while we can express the annualized standard deviation as a single percentage value that makes sense for every stock price.

For this filter to be triggered, we require that *both* legs be less than the volatility threshold. If that occurs at the time of entry, then we do not enter that trade. In addition, we wait until that trade would have been exited before we enter another. The reasoning for the entry rule is that low volatility is expected to produce low per share returns. We did not look at the case where only one leg was under the low volatility threshold.

Table 3.12 and Figure 3.9 show a sequence of tests from low to high annualized volatility, beginning at 10%, which did not have any effect, and ending at 50%, which reduced trades from 98 to 60. The reason that the annualized volatility reaches such high levels so often is that the annualizing process uses only seven days of data. During a very volatile few days, the annualization of those price moves will look unusually high and cannot be sustained for long.

The low volatility filter was able to increase the profits per share only from 9.4 cents to 12.8 cents. That may be enough to net a profit after costs, but it also removed 27 trades to achieve that gain.

High Distortion Filter   A more interesting filter is one that recognizes that large differences in the volatility of the two legs of a pair cannot easily be resolved by volatility adjusting, even if it makes sense in theory. For example, if we were to trade a pair where leg 1 traded at $100 and leg 2 at

TABLE 3.12	Results of low volatility entry filter on AMR x CAL show some improvement but only when 27 trades are removed, 28% of all trades.

Ann Vol	Trades	AROR	Per Share	Ratio
10%	98	3.9	0.094	0.321
15%	98	3.9	0.094	0.321
20%	97	3.7	0.092	0.309
25%	95	3.5	0.089	0.290
30%	93	3.6	0.094	0.304
35%	86	3.6	0.098	0.298
40%	80	3.7	0.109	0.311
45%	71	4.0	0.128	0.337
50%	60	1.4	0.063	0.116

$2, we would expect to trade a very large amount of leg 2 for each share of leg 1. Then, if the $2 share were to jump, it might gain 25% or 50% in one day, while that size move would be nearly impossible for a $100 per share stock. Perhaps this can be recognized using annualized volatility; however, we have decided that the ATR is a better measure. Even using annualized volatility, there is still a large risk of imbalance.

An easy way to recognize that two legs are not compatible is to take the ratio of the shares needed to be traded after applying volatility adjusting. We'll call this the *distortion ratio*. If leg 2 needs to trade 100 shares to offset the volatility of 10 shares in leg 1, we get a distortion ratio of 0.10, calculated as

Distortion ratio = Min(leg 1 shares/leg 2 shares, leg 2 shares/leg 1 shares)

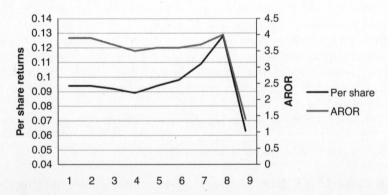

FIGURE 3.9 Results of low volatility filter applied to AMR x CAL shows that removing trades at low volatility increases both returns and per share profits through 40% annualized volatility.

TABLE 3.13 AMR x CAL filtered with the high distortion ratio.

Distortion	Trades	AROR	Per Share	Ratio
None	98	3.9	0.094	0.321
0.4	96	4.4	0.107	0.370
0.5	93	4.9	0.119	0.409
0.6	85	6.9	0.155	0.577
0.7	69	6.2	0.158	0.520
0.8	45	3.8	0.138	0.315
0.9	25	5.9	0.258	0.495
1.0	0	0	0	0

By using the min function, we get the minimum value of the two-share ratios, regardless of whether leg 1 or leg 2 is bigger. Table 3.13 shows the results of a small set of tests using the distortion ratio. When the ratio is 0.4, then all trades with share ratios more extreme than 40 to 100 are filtered. At a ratio of 0.5, all trades with share ratios more extreme than 50 to 100 are filtered. The best results come from a ratio of 0.60, which means the shares must be no more extreme than 60 to 100, which essentially puts the restriction on the two legs that they have reasonably similar volatility—that the volatility of one leg is less than twice the volatility of the other leg.

The results of these two filters—the low volatility filter and the distortion filter—can be seen in Figure 3.10. The NAVs of the original case (No Filters) are very similar to the low volatility returns. The high-distortion filter does much better, avoiding a sharp drawdown but generally selecting better trades. This results in a final NAV above 180 and much higher than the previous peak at 160, while the other two NAV streams are only able

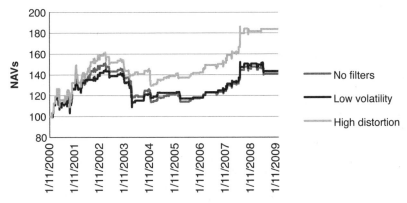

FIGURE 3.10 Comparison of filters applied to AMR x CAL shows that the high-distortion filter was best.

to return to their previous highs. One concern is that the distortion filter is removing trades that are only modestly unbalanced, rather than extremes. That may be another sign of overfitting. Because this method improved results at every level that was more extreme (where 0.1 is most extreme), the general solution that works on all pairs may not be as good as this example.

What We Have Learned from Airline Pairs

We would like to conclude that our premise was correct: low volatility is not good for this strategy, and two stocks that are out of balance with regard to volatility present unwanted risk and unstable expectations.

We could fiddle around further with the parameters and volatility filters and perhaps find a combination that produces enough profit and enough trades to be worth trading, but that is clearly going in the direction of overfitting. Some might question whether we have already overfit the problem, but the concept has been kept fairly clean. So far, we have

- Identified a pairs trading opportunity based on a fundamental market relationship.
- Used a relative value measurement, the stochastic, to identify when two fundamentally related stocks have diverged.
- Isolated the entry point based on normal trade-offs, that is, greater potential but fewer trades if we entered at larger extremes.
- Exited the trade when the relative differences approach or are equal to zero. We did not consider holding the trade looking for a reverse distortion.
- Adjusted the position sizes to the same volatility using the average true range, which we considered a more robust measurement than the annualized standard deviation of the daily changes.
- Applied the same rules and parameters to each pair in our test sector.
- Filtered trades with low volatility to increase profits per share but also reduced the number of trades.
- Removed trades in which the volatility of the two legs were significantly different, arguing that such a trade presented unexpected and unreasonable risks.

We believe that low volatility is a problem, but filtering the volatility removes too many trades. These setbacks are part of the reality of system development. At each step, there is another problem to solve, but continuing with specific solutions to each problem will eventually result in overfitting the data.

The market doesn't hand profits to you. There are some alternative ways of identifying entry and exit points, but none of them will create larger profits from low volatility. Unless we choose to believe that the two pairs,

LCC-CAL and LCC-AMR, will perform in the future as they have in the past, and better than the other airline pairs, we need to refocus on sectors with greater volatility. At the moment, banking is very active, but share prices range from exceptionally low for those banks that were hurt in the sub-prime crisis (Bank of America) to unusually high (Goldman Sachs and J. P. Morgan & Company) if they were perceived as safe. That might produce good profits, but the shares needed to equalize the volatility of these companies will be highly skewed and could lead to unexpected, unpleasant consequences. Volatility adjusting might not be enough to control risk.

Instead, we can turn to the housing construction sector. Although it has been at the center of the financial crisis, companies have not been bailed out or nationalized, and stock prices continue to respond to market forces, but with greater volatility.

HOME BUILDERS

Five of the biggest home builders are Lennar (LEN), Pulte Homes (PHM), KB Homes (KBH), Toll Brothers (TOL), and Hovnanian (HOV). The first three are part of the S&P 500. Their stock performance is an excellent view into the recent mortgage crisis and economic recession. Five companies give us 10 pairs, with the cross-correlations shown in Table 3.14. The average correlation is .58, which is nearly the same as the airlines, but there were fewer airline stocks and the correlations were as low as .39. Figure 3.11 shows the five home builders' stocks together. The run-up in prices parallels the real estate market, peaking in 2006. From the chart, these five stocks seem to be performing the same way, so there is no reason that we shouldn't use all combinations of them as pairs.

Testing the Home Builders

We follow exactly the same process to test the home builders as we did for the airlines. From five related stocks, we get 10 pairs. Each of these pairs

TABLE 3.14 Cross-correlations for home builders, 10 years ending March 2009.

	LEN	PHM	KBH	TOL	HOV
LEN	1				
PHM	0.767	1			
KBH	0.787	0.804	1		
TOL	0.472	0.503	0.495	1	
HOV	0.449	0.460	0.495	0.708	1

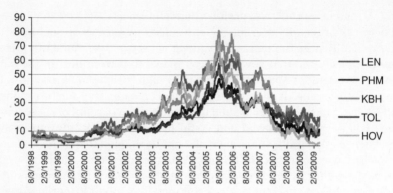

FIGURE 3.11 Prices of five home builder stocks. All five react in a similar manner to the economic changes.

is tested by calculating the individual stochastic values, then taking the difference in the two stochastic values (SD, the stochastic difference). A new trade is entered when the difference exceeds our entry threshold, which, from our previous experience with airlines, should be between 60 and 40 for shorting the pair, and –40 to –60 for buying the pair. *Shorting* the pair means entering a short sale in the first leg of the pair and buying the second leg, while *buying* the pair means buying the first leg and selling short the second leg. The stochastic difference is the stochastic of the first minus the stochastic of the second. No costs were considered in the process, but results show the profits per share, net of both legs, so that it should be simple to reduce those results by your expected costs. Table 3.15 shows the results of tests covering a range of calculation periods and a range of entry criteria.

As with the airlines, tests cover the most recent 10 years. In this case, all the stocks traded for the full period. Our first concern is the information ratio (annualized return divided by annualized volatility) resulting from trading each pair. We want an average ratio greater than 0.25; otherwise, we know that the final performance will be very erratic, with large drawdowns.

Table 3.15 shows the most important statistics for the 10 pairs:

LEN—PHM
LEN—KBH
LEN—TOL
LEN—HOV
PHM—KBH
PHM—TOL
PHM—HOV
KBH—TOL
KBH—HOV
TOL—HOV

TABLE 3.15 Average results of 10 home builders varying the momentum calculation periods from 3 to 14 days and the entry criteria from stochastic values of 40 to 60.

(a) The results of 10 home builder pairs varying the momentum calculation periods and using a ±60 entry threshold and zero exit threshold.

Period	Entry	Trades	AROR	Per Share (in $)	Ratio
14	60	16.8	−0.62	0.0051	−0.050
10	60	22.0	0.73	0.0322	0.062
8	60	26.2	2.18	0.0413	0.181
7	60	28.5	3.14	0.0624	0.262
6	60	30.1	4.05	0.0713	0.337
5	60	33.6	5.12	0.0759	0.426
4	60	42.5	4.98	0.0595	0.414
3	60	51.0	4.13	0.0444	0.344
Average	60	31.3	2.96	0.0490	0.247

(b) Average results of home builder pairs using an entry threshold of ±50.

Period	Entry	Trades	AROR	Per Share (in $)	Ratio
14	50	35.9	−1.05	−0.0083	−0.088
10	50	45.1	0.24	0.0163	0.019
8	50	52.0	2.23	0.0383	0.186
7	50	56.5	3.07	0.0443	0.256
6	50	64.0	3.88	0.0430	0.323
5	50	70.5	4.66	0.0547	0.388
4	50	79.4	5.86	0.0601	0.489
3	50	94.2	6.04	0.0528	0.502
Average	50	62.2	3.12	0.0377	0.259

(c) Average results of home builder pairs using an entry threshold of ±40.

Period	Entry	Trades	AROR	Per Share (in $)	Ratio
14	40	61.6	−0.45	0.0068	−0.037
10	40	78.1	1.07	0.0245	0.088
8	40	90.3	2.27	0.0333	0.190
7	40	99.3	1.74	0.0232	0.145
6	40	109.4	3.13	0.0328	0.260
5	40	125.5	3.88	0.0370	0.324
4	40	137.5	5.07	0.0450	0.423
3	40	163.9	6.37	0.0478	0.531
Average	40	108.2	2.89	0.0313	0.240

Columns 1 and 2 show the parameters. Column 1 is the momentum calculation period, ranging from 14 down to 3. The value 3 was included to show at what point the pattern fails. We must recognize that a stochastic calculation based on three days will jump from zero to 100 nearly every other day, making the results erratic. Column 2 shows the entry threshold of 60. Part a of Table 3.15 shows the results for an entry threshold of 60, and Tables 3.15b and 3.15c show the results of entry thresholds of 50 and 40, respectively.

The statistics shown in Table 3.15 are the number of trades, the *annualized rate of return* (AROR), the profits per trade in dollars, and the information ratio. We expected the relationship between the parameters to change in the following ways:

- As the calculation period decreases from 14 to 3, there would be more trades but the profits per share would get smaller. The less time you hold a trade, the less opportunity there is for gain. Similarly, we would expect the AROR to decline, but we cannot forecast the information ratio because both returns and risk will drop, but we don't know which will drop faster.
- As the entry threshold decreases from 60 to 40, we will also get more trades, but we should see a smaller return per share and more risk. When a mean-reverting trade is entered sooner, we can expect prices to move against us both in magnitude and time. Both of these will affect the ratio. If there are many more opportunities at the entry thresholds of ±40, those good results might offset the fewer trades in which the prices continued to diverge, but we will also not be able to tell the extent of that in advance.
- If we also change the exit threshold, then, as it moves closer to the entry level (for example, entering a short at 60 and exiting at 0, 10, or 20), the size of the profits will decrease, the number of profitable trades should increase, and the total number of trades will increase. If we exit a short sale at 20, not having to wait for zero, and prices reverse to the upside, we would get another short sale that we would have missed had we needed to wait for zero to exit.

Our goal is to have very continuous results; that is, our statistics should move smoothly in one direction as the test parameter values change. We also need profits per trade that are large enough to net a profit after costs. Finally, we want enough trades to make it worthwhile to use this strategy, although that should be reflected in the rate of return. Our confidence in the results also deteriorates if there are too few trades.

It is easier to see the results as a chart. Starting with Figure 3.12, we can see that the number of trades increases as the momentum calculation

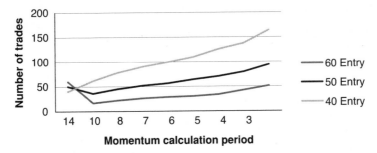

FIGURE 3.12 Home builders, comparison of the number of trades.

period decreases. It does this uniformly for the three entry thresholds, but the number of trades also increases as the entry threshold gets smaller. The fastest trading combination, an entry threshold of ±40 with calculation periods of 5 or less, generated an average of more than 100 trades in 10 years. Although that's only 10 per year for each of the 10 pairs, it is enough to give us confidence in the method.

The profits per share may be the most important statistic because, above all, it tells us whether we can net a profit after costs. In these tests, shown in Figure 3.13, we see that the pattern is good, but the highest average profit per share falls below 8 cents. That may be enough for a professional trader, but we would like it to be higher. When we consider that the entry threshold of ±40 generated the most trades, we see that it cleared only 4 cents per share using the faster calculation periods. Because there were more trades, we can try to be selective by using a volatility filter.

The last statistic, the information ratio, is also important because it gives you an idea of how much risk you will take to get these returns. Figure 3.14 shows that, for the most part, the ratio continues to increase as the calculation period declines. We can explain this in hindsight by

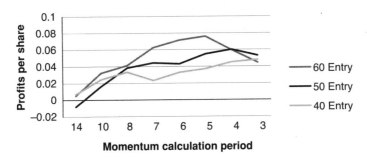

FIGURE 3.13 Home builders, average profits per share.

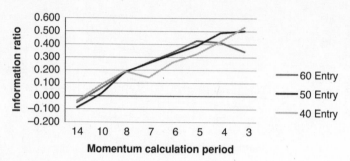

FIGURE 3.14 Home builders, average information ratio.

recognizing that pairs trading, like other mean-reversion strategies, flourishes in environments of market noise. Chapter 2 pointed out that a closer look at prices—that is, looking at hourly instead of daily data—accentuated the noise. Also, using shorter calculation periods focuses on more noise and less trend. The trend is emphasized by using longer calculation periods and less frequent data (weekly instead of daily). Figure 3.14 shows that ratios were above 0.25, our objective, for all calculation periods from 6 and lower.

The good news is that the three figures show consistency. As the calculation period declined, results changed in a very orderly fashion. Even better, they were nearly all profitable. If you remember, an important criterion of robustness is that a large number of combinations of parameters should produce profitable returns, given a reasonable test range. Our only problem, which could be insurmountable, is that we want larger profits per share.

Selecting the Threshold Levels

The best choice will be some combination of the number of trades, profits per trade, and information ratio. We will use the average values of all pairs, even though looking at the detail of each pair would give us more information. We think that using the averages is an attempt to avoid unnecessary overfitting. However, the shape and consistency of the statistics have convinced us that this is a sound approach, so choosing any set of parameters, or more than one set, should be safe.

If we think back to the airline tests, we also saw that the performance ranges were very similar. For airlines, there were fewer pairs, so the results might be less consistent.

Because we plan to test a low-volatility filter that may remove up to 25% of the trades, we will choose the calculation period of 4 with an entry

TABLE 3.16 Results of home builder pairs for momentum 4 and entry threshold ±40.

Pair	#Tr	AROR	Std	Corr	PL/Share	Ratio
LEN-PHM	128	4.3	12	.769	0.043	0.357
LEN-KBH	108	9.3	12	.790	0.107	0.776
LEN-TOL	121	2.7	12	.746	0.031	0.221
LEN-HOV	160	7.6	12	.656	0.055	0.636
PHM-KBH	104	−0.2	12	.820	0.005	−0.015
PHM-TOL	110	2.2	12	.778	0.025	0.185
PHM-HOV	186	9.0	12	.654	0.056	0.754
KBH-TOL	119	3.8	12	.776	0.040	0.320
KBH-HOV	168	6.9	12	.674	0.048	0.572
TOL-HOV	171	5.1	12	.658	0.040	0.421
Average	138	5.1			0.045	0.423

threshold of ±40, one of the fastest trading combinations. We can now look at the detail of each pair, shown in Table 3.16. All but one pair, Pulte-KB Homes, was profitable, and all were reasonably consistent. Only one pair, Lennar-KB Homes, showed a return of greater than 10 cents per share, and all had at least 100 trades. The consistency, which is good, removes the temptation of discarding one or two pairs that performed badly or selecting a few that had large profits per share. An average ratio of 0.423 is very good if only we can increase the profits per share.

Low-Volatility Filter for Home Builders

As with the airlines, we can test the low-volatility filter. If results improve, it will confirm the method that we were unable confirm with fewer airline pairs. Using the same pairs and parameters shown in Table 3.17, we applied the low-volatility filter with values ranging from 0% to 120% and got the results in Table 3.17. Of course, 120% would be impossible except that we're using only four days to project an entire year of volatility, so an unusually volatile interval will produce a very large annualized volatility.

It is easier to see the results of Table 3.17 in Figures 3.15 and 3.16. The first shows how the number of trades drops and the profits per trade increase as we filter out more low-volatility trades. However, the highest per share returns average only about 11 cents, while the number of trades drops to about 20 for each pair over 10 years, two per year. If we can accept 7 cents per trade, then we could double the number of trades. That's still not much.

Figure 3.16 shows a parallel decline in both the annualized rate of return and the information ratio as trades are removed using the

	TABLE 3.17	Home builder pairs using momentum 4, entry ±40, and a low-volatility filter.		
Ann Vol	**#Tr**	**AROR**	**PL/Share**	**Ratio**
0%	137.5	5.07	0.0450	0.423
10%	137.3	5.06	0.0446	0.421
15%	135.5	5.17	0.0459	0.431
20%	131.2	5.04	0.0450	0.421
25%	124.3	4.63	0.0423	0.387
30%	115.5	5.72	0.0513	0.477
35%	106.5	5.98	0.0553	0.498
40%	94.5	5.98	0.0594	0.498
45%	82.5	5.85	0.0622	0.487
50%	72.8	5.68	0.0628	0.473
55%	62.7	5.17	0.0611	0.431
60%	55.5	4.33	0.0554	0.361
65%	48.6	4.17	0.0545	0.346
70%	43.2	4.91	0.0699	0.410
80%	33.2	4.90	0.0793	0.409
90%	26.6	3.77	0.0764	0.315
100%	20.3	3.77	0.1131	0.314
120%	13.4	2.52	0.1110	0.210

low-volatility filter. We can explain that because fewer trades spread over a longer time period will always reduce the rate of return. Similarly, if the risk of the individual trades remained the same but the annualized return was lower, then the information ratio would decline. Those results show that there is less to earn, but the most important statistics are the profits

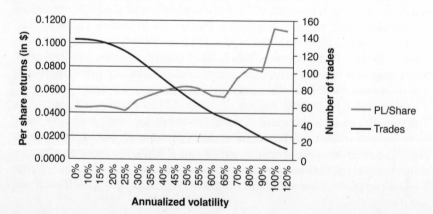

FIGURE 3.15 The low-volatility filter for home builders shows a steady drop in trades and a corresponding increase in per share returns as more trades are filtered out.

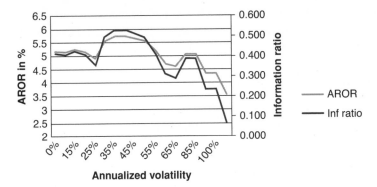

FIGURE 3.16 The low-volatility filter for home builders shows a parallel decline in both returns and the information ratio as more trades are removed.

per share and the number of trades, both of which are too low to be very interesting.

At this point, we've gained confidence in the method but still need to find pairs with more volatility or those that allow some form of leveraging.

A Sure Way to Avoid Overfitting

Before moving forward, we must consider whether our selection and filtering process, no matter how well considered, has resulted in overfitting. We must continually return to this question if we are to create a successful trading method. If we have overfitted the data, then our expectations of profits will never become a reality. One way to avoid this problem is to reject the idea of selecting one or more parameter sets.

Throughout the development and testing of this pairs model, we showed the ratios resulting from tests of reasonable entry combinations and the entire range of possibilities for filtering trades. In almost all cases, the results were profitable, although those profits varied in a predictable pattern according to the parameter and filter values. The biggest danger still lies in selecting one set of parameters to trade. How do we know that it will be the best set, or even a good set, in the future?

To avoid that question, which probably does not have an answer, why not trade a number of different parameters, or even all of them? We don't need to decide on a 4-day stochastic when we can use 4, 5, 6, and 7 days. If you have a large enough investment, then trading all combinations with equal allocations could not be considered overfitting. Some combinations will be better than others, but we know that, over a long period of time, they all performed well. Your result should be the average performance of all pairs. Because this performance will vary, the average results should have less volatility and greater predictability than any one pair that we might choose. You will also increase your diversification and reduce your slippage because, for the same pair, trades will occur on different days and each trade will be smaller.

Benefiting from Pseudo-Leverage

Supposing we are prepared to go forward with small per share returns, we now have what appears to be a viable pairs trading program. Returns are high enough to support costs, and the information ratio indicates that risk is reasonable. We now need to look deeper into one of our original assumptions: that we wanted to target a portfolio of 12% volatility. That's important because our returns and our profits per share—actually all the statistics—scale up and down based on our choice of target volatility.

In the section "Target Volatility," we calculated the necessary investment size for each pair by taking the daily net profits and losses (expressed in dollars or the currency of the stocks), finding the standard deviation, annualizing it, and then getting the investment size necessary to make that annualized standard deviation equal to 12% (our choice of target volatility). We will have to look at some actual numbers to find out whether this is really possible. In the next chapter, in which we use futures, leveraging the returns will be much easier, but for stocks it is not always possible to increase leverage.

Evaluating Leverage for the Pulte–Toll Brothers Pair   If we create a series of daily dollar returns for the Pulte–Toll Brothers pair (PMH-TOL), then take the standard deviation of those returns, we get $26.89. Annualizing that value by multiplying by $\sqrt{252}$ gives $426.90, then dividing by 0.12 to find the investment size that yields a 12% volatility gives an investment of $3,557.50. The question now is, Are there any trades in which the amount of purchase plus the amount of short-sale exceeds the investment of $3,557?

Unfortunately, the answer is *yes*. In Figure 3.17, the daily cost of shares, also called *market exposure*, is shown to exceed the investment size during the period from the first quarter 2004 until about August 2007, or about 3.5 years out of a little more than 9 years. The maximum cost was $6,098, 71% higher than our investment. What can be done to save our strategy?

> **Raise the Investment Amount.** The easiest solution is to increase the investment size by 71% to $6,098. But we would still have the same profits and losses, so we would need to multiply all of our statistics by 0.58 to get the new result. That would reduce our 10-pair average profits per share from, for example, $0.11 to

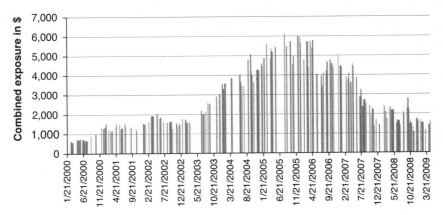

FIGURE 3.17 PMH-TOL total cost of shares ("market exposure").

$0.0638 for the filtered case, and put it at a marginally profitable level.

Borrow the Excess Investment. Stocks can be leveraged by as much as 50% by borrowing capital. Because the share cost exceeds the original investment by amounts varying from very small to 71%, that money can be borrowed at the current interest rate, say 5%. Because trades are not held long, funds would not be needed continuously. Estimating the cost, we have an average excess of $1,270 (the average of $3,557 and $6,098, less $3,557) for 3.5 years at 5%, or $222. That added cost represents an adjustment in total returns of 222/3557, or 6.2%. Then a per share return of $0.11 would drop to $0.103, a more manageable option.

Cap the Amount Traded. The cost of shares does not always exceed the original investment size; therefore, an alternative is to limit each trade to the amount of the investment. For example, if our investment is $3,000 and the total share value for this trade is $4,000, then the position size is reduced to 75% of the original amount. Instead of 100 shares, we trade 75 shares. The amount of this reduction will vary for each trade, depending on the ratio of actual cost to investment size. Once the trade is entered, the cost remains the same until the trade is closed out.

Figure 3.18 shows the results of capping the exposure at the investment size for the pairs LEN-TOL (Figure 3.18a) and TOL-HOV (Figure 3.18b). In both cases, capping resulted in much better returns. The capping ratio, shown as bars across the top of the chart, and read on the right scale, shows the reduction in the size of the daily position needed to bring the

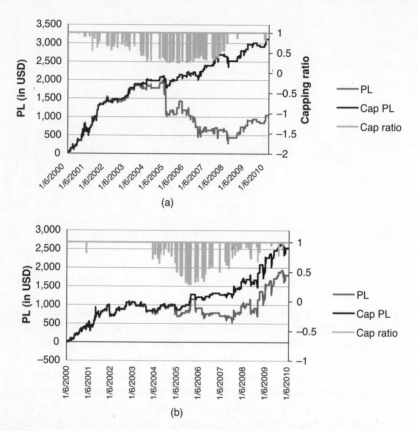

FIGURE 3.18 Comparison of capped and original PL for (a) LEN-TOL and (b) TOL-HOV.

exposure down to the investment size. Note that the largest losing period in the original profit/loss stream occurs at the same time that the capping ratio is most active in reducing the position size. This can be explained in terms of market volatility.

In the pairs trading strategy, we not only equalize the risk of both legs but also enter a larger position when the volatility is lower. This is intended to give each trade an equal chance to contribute to the returns. However, when the volatility is low and more positions are entered, the total exposure has a greater chance of exceeding the investment size.

Because cutting the position size during periods of low volatility makes such a drastic improvement in performance, we can conclude that those periods were not good for the strategy. We thought that trades set during periods of low volatility could be removed using the low-volatility filter, but that does not seem to have been as effective as letting the exposure control the process. Table 3.18 shows the results of all 10 home builder

TABLE 3.18 Comparison of capped and original results for 10 home builder pairs.

		Not Capped					Capped			
Pair	#Tr	TotPL	AROR	Std	PL/ Share	Ratio	TotPL	AROR	Std	Ratio
LEN x PHM	128	1524	4.3	12	0.043	0.357	2740	8.8	9.4	0.932
LEN x KBH	108	2355	9.3	12	0.107	0.776	3263	13.7	9.9	1.383
LEN x TOL	121	1047	2.7	12	0.031	0.221	3114	10.0	9.2	1.090
LEN x HOV	160	3147	7.6	12	0.055	0.636	4574	11.8	11.0	1.071
PHM x KBH	104	88	−0.2	12	0.005	−0.015	1134	6.8	9.0	0.764
PHM x TOL	110	546	2.2	12	0.025	0.185	1696	9.0	9.0	1.008
PHM x HOV	186	2592	9.0	12	0.056	0.754	3370	12.3	10.8	1.140
KBH x TOL	119	1287	3.8	12	0.040	0.320	2392	8.3	9.1	0.912
KBH x HOV	168	2917	6.9	12	0.048	0.572	4177	10.5	10.8	0.965
TOL x HOV	171	1803	5.1	12	0.040	0.421	2531	7.6	10.9	0.697
Average		1731	5.1	12	0.045	0.423	2899	9.88	9.91	0.996

pairs. While the number of total trades remains the same, the cumulative profits (TotPL) increased by 67%, and the information ratio jumped from 0.424 to 0.996. We could estimate the improvement in the profits per share by taking the accumulated capping ratio divided by the number of days. If the capping ratio was effective 30% of the time, and the average ratio was 0.85 (a 15% reduction), then the net impact would have been $0.30 \times 0.15 =$ .045. We actually estimated the reduction in position size for LEN-TOL at about 6.5%. By itself, that would not be enough to be a major change, but combined with a 67% increase in profits, it should net a 75% increase in the profit per share.

Summarizing the Capping Results

Was that just an anomaly, or does capping actually improve performance? For home builders, the improvement is very good, but we must remember that all home builders moved in the same way at the same time. For this to be a robust solution, it would need to work on other markets. But even then, there is a similarity in the price movement of all stocks on the same exchange.

Table 3.19 shows the results of applying the same capping method to the airline pairs, based on the momentum period of 7 and entry threshold of ±40. As with the home builders, all the results were improved, although not quite as dramatically. Cumulative profits rose from an average of $1,356 to $1,927, and the information ratio increased from an average of 0.335 to 0.572. Overall, the results confirm our previous tests, but it is not a comprehensive study.

TABLE 3.19 Comparison of capping for airline pairs with momentum 7, entry ±40.

Pair	#Tr	TotPL	AROR	Std	PL/Share	Ratio	TotPL	AROR	Std	Ratio
LCC × CAL	44	2051	11.4	12	0.213	0.95	2556	14.8	10.2	1.456
LCC × AMR	42	1784	7.4	12	0.173	0.618	2096	9.1	10.8	0.838
LCC × LUV	61	−114	−1.1	12	−0.004	−0.088	447	0.8	10.6	0.074
AMR × CAL	98	1687	3.9	12	0.094	0.321	2127	5.3	9.7	0.549
AMR × LUV	152	−306	−1.3	12	−0.006	−0.108	676	0.7	11.0	0.063
CAL × LUV	158	3032	3.8	12	0.052	0.317	3662	4.9	10.8	0.454
Average		1356	4.0	12	0.087	0.335	1927	5.9	10.5	0.572

The Problem with Zero-Value Returns For those who are interested in the mathematics, one of the reasons that the actual cost of buying and selling the pair exceeds our investment is that the annualized standard deviation of the returns is too low. How can that be? After all, it's just a simple statistical calculation. Of course, the number is technically correct, but it includes all of the zero returns on those days when we had no position. Therefore, the less often the pair trades, the smaller the standard deviation. The actual risk on the days that a position was held would be much higher, and we could see that if we had only used the days on which returns were nonzero, that is, when we were holding a position. But then, we would still have had the same returns, but the volatility measure would give us a bigger number. Then our target volatility would have required a larger investment. A larger investment with the same returns would have resulted in a lower rate of return!

The idea of using only nonzero returns when annualizing the volatility is important for infrequent trading. If we are using only 10 days to calculate the annualized volatility and only one of those days has activity, then the volatility is going to look unreasonably small. And if you followed 10 days of being out of the market with 10 days of trading, then the volatility will be increasing every day as the zero returns drop off. That creates an unstable volatility measure. Instead, we really want to know, When we are in the market, what is our risk? To know that, we should only calculate the volatility on days with nonzero returns.

USING ETFs

Exchange-traded funds (ETFs) can be used in pairs trading as either one of the legs or as a substitute for short sales; however, they are an index, not an individual stock. As one of the legs, they offer additional diversification, and as a substitute for short sales, they may make trading easier. Short sales can be executed as easily as entering longs, and it will not be affected if the government reinstates the uptick rule or even limits short sales during periods of financial stress. The ETFs can always be traded long or short in the same way as futures, without bias and without additional expense.

Cross-Margining and Counterparty Risk

One very important advantage of using ETFs is *cross-margining*, a facility also available for trading futures and options. Cross-margining is the recognition that a pairs trade, or any spread between two related markets, has less risk than being long or short both markets. Then the amount of margin (good-faith deposit, not share value) required by the broker or dealer is much lower than the face value of the ETFs because the risk is offset. It is not clear whether there is cross-margining between a stock and an ETF; however, these can be negotiable items if both trades are placed at the same electronic communication network (ECN).

One note of caution: An ETF is guaranteed by the creditworthiness of the issuer. During a time when banks have been bailed out or, in the case of Lehman Brothers, collapsed, this level of counterparty risk may be unacceptable to some investors. They should carefully assess this aspect of risk before using ETFs. They are not guaranteed by the exchange clearing house as are futures markets. Although the New York Stock Exchange has a fiduciary responsibility to handle the transactions correctly, they do not guarantee the firms listed on the exchange. And with American depositary receipts (ADRs) listed, there is very little oversight as to whether any of their financial disclosure is correct.

Composition of an ETF

A sector ETF is an average of a selection of stocks within that sector. An ETF is usually *capitalization weighted* (the number of outstanding shares times the price of a share), similar to the S&P or DJIA, or less often, *equally weighted* (the same number of shares). Because it is an average, the price of the ETF compared with a single stock will not be as volatile, nor will it reach the stochastic extremes that are used for single stock thresholds. Based on that, we would expect fewer trades with the same profit per share as individual stocks, or the same number of trades with smaller profits per share. But before we eliminate it because of purely theoretical reasons, we need to see how the numbers look.

There are two viable ETF candidates for the home builders, and both have reasonable liquidity:

1. XHB, SPDF S&P Homebuilders ETF, with data from February 6, 2006.
2. ITB, ISHARES DJ US Home Construction with data from May 5, 2006.

Figure 3.19 shows that these two ETFs track very closely.

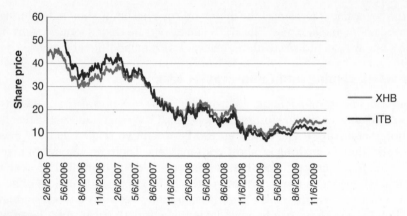

FIGURE 3.19 The home builders ETFs, XHB and ITB, both track one another closely.

Using an ETF as One Leg of a Pair

Considering the ETF as one leg of a pair, we can choose either XHB or ITB, creating five additional pairs. The data for these ETFs begin in February 2006 for XHB and May 2006 for ITB; therefore, we will create the statistics for the full 10 pairs from February 2006 using the same parameters, a momentum of 4, and an entry threshold of ±40. The results are shown in Table 3.20 and are not as good as for the longer interval, beginning January 2000, but they will give us a benchmark to compare the use of an ETF.

The first case is to treat the ETF as another home builder stock, leg 2 in our test. Table 3.21 shows the results. In both cases, there are only two

TABLE 3.20 Home builder pairs from February 6, 2006.

Pair	#Tr	TotPL	AROR	Std	PL/Share	Ratio
LEN-PHM	37	449	4.0	12	0.053	0.334
LEN-KBH	36	159	1.2	12	0.024	0.100
LEN-TOL	38	4	−0.7	12	0.001	−0.056
LEN-HOV	46	778	4.5	12	0.051	0.379
PHM-KBH	37	−98	−2.2	12	−0.016	−0.183
PHM-TOL	31	68	0.1	12	0.012	0.012
PHM-HOV	60	851	7.0	12	0.051	0.579
KBH-TOL	34	−779	−7.1	12	−0.095	−0.589
KBH-HOV	57	750	3.7	12	0.036	0.310
TOL-HOV	55	889	5.1	12	0.050	0.425
Average	43	307	1.6	12	0.017	0.131

TABLE 3.21 Home builders.

(a) Using the ITB ETF as leg 2

Pair	#Tr	TotPL	AROR	Std	PL/Share	Ratio
KBH-ITB	80	−2653	−7.0	12	−0.071	−0.584
TOL-ITB	74	−2609	−7.9	12	−0.088	−0.660
LEN-ITB	76	−2503	−6.5	12	−0.085	−0.540
HOV-ITB	88	1723	7.2	12	0.073	0.599
PHM-ITB	77	691	1.7	12	0.028	0.141
Average	69	−426	−0.3	12	−0.005	−0.022

(b) Using the XHB ETF as leg 2

Pair	#Tr	TotPL	AROR	Std	PL/Share	Ratio
KBH-XHB	91	1731	3.2	12	0.039	0.267
TOL-XHB	79	−2388	−7.3	12	−0.075	−0.606
LEN-XHB	93	−2648	−6.5	12	−0.069	−0.545
HOV-XHB	96	1171	4.0	12	0.042	0.333
PHM-XHB	89	−1158	−4.3	12	−0.038	−0.360
Average	85	−163	−0.3	12	−0.001	−0.024

winning pairs and three losing ones. Surprisingly, they are not the same pairs, even though the chart of the ETFs seemed nearly identical. There are also many more trades than the pairs without ETFs, which was unexpected, and needs to be explained.

The stochastic indicator will take on values from 0 to 100 regardless of volatility. It simply adjusts to the current volatility level and identifies the extremes within its current framework. We expected the ETF to have less volatility than a single stock because it is an average, and averages benefit from diversification (an upward move offsetting a downward move). To prove that, we applied the low-volatility filter at the arbitrary level of 100% and show the results for ITB in Table 3.22a and XHB in Table 3.22b. When we applied the low-volatility filter to the test beginning in January 2000, the filter level of 100% annualized volatility reduced trades from 137 to 20, showing a somewhat normal distribution. With the interval beginning in 2006, trades were reduced less, indicating a flatter distribution.

Capping the Pairs Using ETFs

As further confirmation that capping benefits the performance, we applied the same capping principle to the five pairs after the 100% low-volatility filter was applied. Results are shown in Table 3.23. As with the earlier test,

TABLE 3.22 Using an ETF as leg 2 with a low-volatility filter of 100% annualized.

(a) Pairs using ITB as leg 2 with a low-volatility filter of 100% annualized.

Pair	#Tr	TotPL	AROR	Std	PL/Share	Ratio
KBH-XHB	11	619	5.5	12	0.149	0.462
TOL-XHB	6	639	11.1	12	0.274	0.926
LEN-XHB	19	262	1.4	12	0.043	0.114
HOV-XHB	28	−642	−6.4	12	−0.103	−0.532
PHM-XHB	10	−172	−2.8	12	−0.057	−0.236
Average	15	141	1.8	12	0.061	0.147

(b) Pairs using XHB as leg 2 with a low-volatility filter of 100% annualized.

Pair	#Tr	TotPL	AROR	Std	PL/Share	Ratio
KBH-ITB	9	548	6.6	12	0.153	0.552
TOL-ITB	7	443	9.7	12	0.168	0.805
LEN-ITB	16	693	6.3	12	0.137	0.526
HOV-ITB	29	−747	−6.5	12	−0.112	−0.544
PHM-ITB	10	271	4.0	12	0.090	0.333
Average	14	242	4.0	12	0.087	0.334

TABLE 3.23 Using an ETF as leg 2 with a volatility filter and capping.

(a) Pairs using ITB as leg 2, 100% volatility filter, and capping.

Pair	#Tr	Capped		
		TotPL	AROR	Std	Ratio
------	-----	-------	------	-----	-------
KBH-ITB	9	767	9.8	11.1	0.883
TOL-ITB	7	385	8.7	7.6	1.152
LEN-ITB	16	894	8.6	11.0	0.776
HOV-ITB	29	−319	−3.1	10.5	−0.293
PHM-ITB	10	546	9.2	10.1	0.919
Average	14	455	6.6	10.1	0.687

(b) Pairs using XHB as leg 2, 100% volatility filter, and capping.

Pair	#Tr	TotPL	AROR	Std	Ratio
KBH-XHB	11	736	7.2	8.0	0.893
TOL-XHB	6	623	11.1	10.0	1.104
LEN-XHB	19	616	4.5	10.0	0.452
HOV-XHB	28	−204	−2.3	10.0	−0.234
PHM-XHB	10	373	4.3	9.4	0.460
Average	15	429	5.0	9.5	0.535

performance improved drastically, with the ratio jumping from 0.147 to 0.687 for ITB (Table 3.23a) and from 0.334 to 0.535 for XHB (Table 3.23b). Overall, ITB seems to be a better performer, but it is still necessary to filter trades in to create a profile that would be profitable after transaction costs.

Using ETFs as a Substitute for Short Sales

A practical use for the ETFs is as a substitute for short sales, because there are no restrictions on trading ETFs on the short side, and new regulations are not likely to affect them. The ETF comes into play at the time of execution; the signal to buy or sell the pair is still based on the two stock legs.

In addition to executing the ETF instead of the short leg of the pair, we need to consider whether the position size of the short leg should change. The position size was intended to equalize the risk of both legs and was calculated based on the average true range of each stock price over the recent past. If we substitute an ETF with significantly different volatility, then the long and short positions will not have offsetting risk. Then it seems logical that we would recalculate the position size using the volatility of the ETF.

In many cases, only the closing prices are available for the ETFs. If the high, low, and close are available, then the volatility calculation would be performed in exactly the same way as the underlying stocks, using the average true range. However, if only the closing price is available, as it was for our data, then the average true range becomes the average of the close-to-close differences, which would be a much lower volatility value. With only the closing prices, we went ahead and tested the use of both ETFs as a substitute for short sales. The results, using the standard values of a four-day momentum and ±40 entry threshold, are shown in Table 3.24.

Although the chart shows that ITB and XHB are very similar, and the correlation of their returns is .957, the effect of substituting them for the short sales yields very different results. The ITB ETF performs better than the benchmark case, and the XHB results are much worse. Profits per share increase from 1.7 cents to 4.0 cents, and the ratio gains from 0.131 to 0.149. At the same time, using XHB turns those profits into net losses. When we look at the individual pairs, we see that the ratio for KBH-TOL jumped from −0.589 to +0.919 using ITB but was little changed with XHB, and both ETFs performed very badly when used for LEN-HOV. In fact, ITB has a very different performance overall.

We can conclude that using an ETF as a substitute for short sales can work, but each ETF needs to be tested because just looking at the chart doesn't tell us enough.

TABLE 3.24	Comparison of ETF shorts using ETF volatility to determine position size.					
	PL/Share			**Ratio**		
Pair	**None**	**ITB**	**XHB**	**None**	**ITB**	**XHB**
LEN-PHM	0.053	0.016	0.054	0.334	0.006	0.374
LEN-KBH	0.024	0.259	0.109	0.100	0.903	0.527
LEN-TOL	0.001	0.086	0.023	−0.056	0.328	0.087
LEN-HOV	0.051	−0.149	−0.112	0.379	−1.060	−0.902
PHM-KBH	−0.016	−0.052	0.047	−0.183	−0.229	0.235
PHM-TOL	0.012	0.073	0.114	0.012	0.397	0.708
PHM-HOV	0.051	0.043	0.007	0.579	0.412	0.000
KBH-TOL	−0.095	0.140	−0.049	−0.589	0.919	−0.443
KBH-HOV	0.036	0.007	−0.05	0.310	0.008	−0.523
TOL-HOV	0.050	−0.019	−0.058	0.425	−0.197	−0.616
Average	0.017	0.040	0.009	0.131	0.149	−0.055

PORTFOLIO OF HOME BUILDER PAIRS

The final step in creating performance expectations is to build a portfolio from the results of the 10 pairs. This will show our anticipated returns and the risk associated with those returns. We expect that the risk will be reduced due to diversification, but we also know that these stocks are highly correlated, and the reduction might be small.

Because the construction of a portfolio is important, we will go through the process in six steps. The values for the pair LEN-TOL will be used as an example. The first steps can also be followed in Table 3.25.

1. *Create a series of daily profits or losses for each pair of stocks.* The net profit for the pairs is the sum of the gain or loss in one stock (the number of shares held on day t times the change in price from day t through day $t + 1$) plus the gain or loss in the other stock. If you are using capped results, then the daily profits and losses reflect the net return after capping the position size. The capped results are shown in the second column (B) of Table 3.25.

2. *Find the annualized volatility of the daily profits and losses in (1).* For this pair, first create a column with the daily differences in the PL (column 3). Then find the standard deviation of those differences, 18.03. To annualize, multiply that value by $\sqrt{252}$ to get 286.21. Note that this annualized change seems lower than expected because there were many days with no trading, giving zero returns on those days.

3. *Find the investment size needed to trade this series at your target volatility.* If the target is 12%, divide the annualized standard deviation

TABLE 3.25 Construction of NAVs from daily profits and losses for LEN-TOL.

Date	Capped PL	PL Diff	Return	NAV
1/6/2000	0			100
1/7/2000	0	0	0	100
1/10/2000	0	0	0	100
1/11/2000	0	0	0	100
1/12/2000	0	0	0	100
1/13/2000	11	11	0.00461	100.4612
1/14/2000	25	14	0.00587	101.0509
1/18/2000	25	0	0	101.0509
1/19/2000	25	0	0	101.0509
1/20/2000	53	28	0.01174	102.2371
1/21/2000	53	0	0	102.2371

in (2) by 0.12. The capped series yields an investment of $2,385. The capped series actually has lower volatility and a lower investment than the noncapped returns. This lower investment will translate into an increase in portfolio returns. When using futures in the next chapter, we will be able to adjust the leverage freely while keeping a close eye on risk.

4. *Create the volatility-adjusted returns in column 4.* Divide each PL difference (column 3) by the investment size calculated in step 3.

5. At this point, we have volatility-adjusted each pair to the target volatility of 12% using the capped returns, so that each PL series has an equal risk. We now create a NAV series (column 5) from the capped PL for each of the pairs. Starting with the value 100, we multiply the previous day's NAV by the value 1 + Returns for the current day. For example, on January 13, the strategy had a positive return of 0.00461, or about 46 basis points. Up to this point, there were no trades. We get the new NAV value as follows:

$$NAV_{today} = NAV_{previous} \times (1 + Returns_{today}), \text{ or}$$
$$NAV_{today} = 100 \times (1 + 0.00461)$$
$$= 100.461$$

On the next day there was another gain of 0.00587. The new NAV would be:

$$NAV_{today} = 100.461 \times (1 + 0.00587)$$
$$= 101.0509$$

6. Repeat steps 1 through 5 for each pair of stocks.

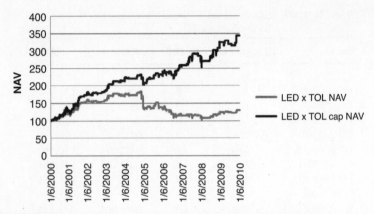

FIGURE 3.20   LEN-TOL comparison of capped PL and capped NAV.

When all the changes are processed, the final NAV for the pair LEN-TOL is 343.56. Because this is a compounded rate of return, results will sometimes increase faster or slower than the simple profit and loss returns, as seen in Figure 3.20, which shows the NAVs of both the noncapped and capped results.

Putting the Portfolio Together

When the individual pairs results have been converted from PL to NAVs, we get the NAV streams shown in Figure 3.21. All show good returns at the same target volatility of 12%. The final step in creating a portfolio is to begin with the daily returns for each pair, shown in column 4 of Table 3.25.

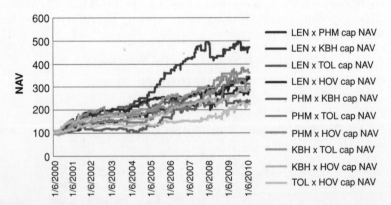

FIGURE 3.21   All 10 capped NAV streams from home builder pairs.

Our portfolio will equally weight the returns for each pair because we believe that all have the same chance of being profitable in the future. You may know that modern portfolio theory states that a portfolio should be maximized using the information ratio, the annualized returns divided by the annualized risk. Then those pairs that have a better payoff (higher return for the same risk) should be given more of the investment, which is the same as giving them a larger weight or larger allocation.

Although modern portfolio theory was religiously accepted when it was first proposed by Markowitz, the years have tempered enthusiasm for it. No one has actually proved that it has predictive ability, only that the optimized returns are better than any other combination. We shouldn't be surprised that optimized returns are better.

We prefer to assume that we don't know which of the 10 pairs will give the best returns next year. They all seem good, and the economy, as well as individual corporate management, always seems to surprise us. The best company this year can be out of business next year. Had we heavily favored Enron in an energy portfolio, we would have been both disappointed and broke.

This portfolio will equally weight all pairs. This approach is called *removing returns from the picture*. It's simpler than portfolio optimization, we can do it on a spreadsheet, and it assumes less. Because of that, we also believe that the results, or expectations, are more realistic. The steps are simple:

- If you don't already have the daily returns for each series, you can start with the NAVs and calculate the daily returns, r, as

$$r_{\text{today}} = \frac{\text{NAV}_{\text{today}}}{\text{NAV}_{\text{previous}}} - 1$$

- For each day, average the returns of all 10 pairs. This is the same as equally weighting the results. We'll call the average daily return of the portfolio of 10 pairs R. Note that you will not equally weight the pairs if the liquidity of one or more stocks is restrictive.
- Create the portfolio NAVs from the average returns using the same formula that was given in step 5 when creating the individual NAVs. The final portfolio NAV using capped returns is 327.77 and using noncapped is 173.36, both shown in Figure 3.22.
- Find the annualized rate of return

$$\text{AROR} = \left(\frac{\text{NAV}_{\text{ending}}}{100} \right)^{\frac{1}{\text{years}}} - 1$$

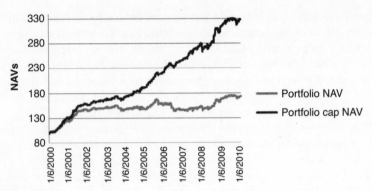

FIGURE 3.22 Final portfolio NAVs for home builders using noncapped and capped returns.

- The ending capped NAV was 327.77, and the total number of days was 2,530, then

$$AROR = \left(\frac{327.77}{100}\right)^{\frac{1}{(2530/252)}} - 1 = 01255$$

- The number of years is a decimal number, the result of dividing the total number of trading days by the number of trading days in a year (typically 252). The annualized return for this portfolio is 12.55%, without commission costs or other fees.
- The information ratio, the final measurement of return for risk, is

$$\text{Information ratio} = \frac{\text{Annualized return}}{\text{Annualized risk}}$$

$$\text{Information ratio} = \frac{12.55}{5.359} = 2.34$$

- A ratio of 2.34 is comfortably high and likely to remain above 1.5 even after costs are deducted. Any value over 1.0 means that you are getting more return for each unit of risk. The information ratio for a passive investment in the S&P index may be as low as 0.4 over a long period of time, and even lower in recent years that include the 2008 decline.

The final NAV stream for the portfolio of capped pairs is smoother than the individual streams because of the unexpected diversification gained from the different pairs and the final annualized volatility of only 5.35%, down from 12%. Unless you choose one of the available leverage options, such as financing part of the position with borrowed funds, you can't boost the returns because the capped result is already using all of the investment.

EXECUTION AND THE PART-TIME TRADER

Success of a short-term trading program depends on the timely execution of orders. Even though this program uses only the closing prices to generate signals, it's not likely to be successful if calculations were done after the market closed, then entered the next morning on the open. An extreme price on the close is very likely to have corrected by the next opening. It might work if executions were done in the aftermarket on the same day, provided trading was done in small numbers. However, we could be pleasantly surprised.

The most likely way of executing this program is to enter prices shortly before the close, calculate the new positions, and enter those orders for execution on the close or as soon as possible. As long as the pair satisfied the entry threshold, you should have a good trade. If there are differences between the price entered and the final closing price that would have affected the position size, adjustments can be made after the close; however, that may be unnecessary.

You may also want to choose a different time of day to trade, preferably a few minutes after a key economic report, such as a Federal Reserve Open Market Committee (FOMC) meeting. Statements of interest rate changes and policy are released at 2:15 P.M. on the second day of the meeting, usually a Tuesday. Capturing prices and trading somewhere between 2:20 and 2:30 P.M. is likely to take advantage of price distortions during a short but volatile reaction. Similarly, you might want to trade after the official close on a day when the first chip manufacturer announces quarterly earnings. There is a 15 minute window where you might find greater price distortions between similar companies.

Pairs trading does not require that you enter a trade on the close. The method holds up, or might even be better, if you can take advantage of obvious shifts in prices. Exiting from a trade, however, is still best on the close.

STOP-LOSSES

Many traders are concerned about unexpected price moves causing large losses, and they often try to solve this problem using a stop-loss. Normally, you would use a stop-loss for a trend trade or fundamental position, one where you are net long or short. For a pairs trade, you have equal, balanced positions, long and short, in related stocks. Any price shock will affect both stocks and should cause offsetting profits and losses unless that shock was related specifically to only one of the stocks in the pair. Whether one stock of the pair moves more or less than the other is arbitrary.

But what if the pair continues to post a loss and that loss gets larger? How do you deal with controlling the maximum loss? It's not possible to handle this with a stop-loss because both stock prices are moving, and the loss is relative to the difference between the two. You could monitor the profits or losses and close out the trade if the losses persisted. But the nature of the method is that the stochastic indicator adjusts to higher or lower prices and establishes a new norm. Then a smaller relative price change will trigger an exit.

Using stops changes the performance profile of a system. Pairs trading has a high probability of a profit, and there are many smaller profits and a few larger losses. If you use a stop, then there will be more losing trades, and in some cases you will have captured a loss when the trade would have eventually produced a profit. The balance of the system will be altered, and there is no assurance that the final result will be profitable.

TRADING INTRADAY

Our application has used closing price data; however, intraday price changes can generate many more trades, and taken to an extreme, it is similar to the high-frequency trading done by the big investment banks. Those trades are entered and exited in milliseconds and costs are negligible, but the principles are the same. In the previous section, "Execution and the Part-Time Trader," we discussed that trading after economic or corporate announcements could be an advantage.

A compromise between daily and milliseconds is hourly data. The strategy posts prices each hour and looks for the stochastic difference to generate a trade. Of course, profits per trade would be smaller because the holding period would also be shorter, so your costs would be the limiting factor rather than the opportunities.

KEY POINTS TO REMEMBER

- This chapter was as much about the *process* as about the strategy. It was intended to be a step-by-step explanation of the process needed to take an idea and create a trading strategy.

- We began with what we believe to be a *sound premise*, that pairs trading is based on the fundamental concept that two stocks in the same sector, affected by the same macrofundamentals, will perform similarly. Because of that, we skipped the process of using in-sample and out-of-sample data, which would be a requirement if we were *exploring* for a new solution. Instead, we tested our method on one market and one sector, then applied it to other markets and other sectors. It is a weaker out-of-sample approach but we felt that it was sufficient.
- We selected our set of markets by what seemed reasonable. We picked those that were most liquid. We did not reject any because their charts looked bad. We calculated the cross-correlations but did not find those values useful. Had one of the stocks been negatively correlated, we would have rejected it.
- We created the trading rules based on simple calculations that showed the relative, not absolute, differences between the pairs.
- We volatility-adjusted the position sizes to equalize the risk of both legs. In doing that, we avoided a price move in one leg overwhelming the results.
- We ran tests on multiple pairs but looked at the average results of all pairs, not at the individual profits and losses. When we selected a parameter value, it was because it improved the net performance of all pairs.
- We confirmed our belief in the robustness of this strategy because nearly all combinations of parameters were profitable for the average results. We observed that the pattern in performance was continuous when parameter values were increased or decreased.
- You don't need perfect performance to have a profitable trading program. When we selected our final parameters, some of the pairs showed losses. We did not remove those from the set because we don't know what will happen in the future. If we could justify removing the losing pairs, we could have justified removing all but the most profitable pair.
- We volatility-adjusted each of the pairs to the same target volatility.
- We tested a low-volatility filter, under the premise that small price movement is the worst-case scenario for this strategy.
- By creating a profit and loss series, we found the investment size that was needed to trade each pair at our target volatility. We then checked to see if the cost of trading the volatility-adjusted positions on any day exceeded our investment size. It did, in about a third of the days.
- We needed to cap the size of the positions on days when they would have exceeded our investment size. We scaled down the position size to satisfy the cap and adjusted the daily returns by that ratio. The result

was that the capped performance exceeded the original returns before capping.

- Using the capped profits and losses, we found the new investment size and created return series for each pair, each with its own investment size. We averaged the daily returns and found that the risk had dropped by about 40%. We created the new portfolio NAVs from the aggregate investment size and the average daily returns. Because of the nature of stock investments, we were unable to leverage our returns to the target volatility and needed to settle for about half of that, or 6%.

CHAPTER 4

Pairs Trading Using Futures

A lthough pairs trading clearly works, the returns for many stocks are small, and the demands on good execution are high. In the previous chapter, we looked at airlines and home builders and found that airline stocks did not have enough volatility, and home builders are more active but give only marginally good results. Using volatility and distortion filters will improve results but at the cost of fewer trades. Capping provided an unexpected gain while reducing the risk. The concept of trading pairs, however, is fundamentally sound and can be considered robust because it shows profits across a wide range of parameter values. What is needed is more volatility or leverage.

It is possible to leverage returns in stocks by borrowing part of the capital needed to trade. If interest rates were very low and trading returns were high, then borrowing would be a profitable alternative. It is also possible to use stock options rather than stocks. The companies that we are trading are mostly large and liquid, so that options could be a viable choice. In addition, options have no restrictions on going long or short. In fact, by selling (writing) one leg, you receive the premium, offsetting the cost of buying the other leg. Given the bullish or bearish bias in the market, costs may be kept very small. It would be necessary to evaluate the slippage, or bid-asked spread, combined with the net premium of the two legs, to know the viability of using options. That is not our focus here.

FUTURES

Futures contracts offer a completely different approach, satisfying all liquidity and leverage problems but providing far fewer choices in the markets that can be traded. While there may be 30 to 50 different companies within the energy complex, there are only six viable energy futures markets: crude oil, natural gas, heating oil, and unleaded gasoline trading at the New York Mercantile Exchange (NYMEX) in New York and Brent and gas oil traded on the International Petroleum Exchange (IPE) in London.

Another complication is that the trading hours are different in New York and London. Even though crude oil has become a 24-hour market, the bulk of liquidity occurs during the normal business hours in the country where the commodity is being traded. Crude oil in New York is officially open from 10:30 A.M. to 2:30 P.M.; in London, the pit session (open outcry if there are still humans on the floor) is open from 10:02 A.M. to 7:30 P.M. On the ICE (the all-electronic Intercontinental Exchange), trading is from 1:00 A.M. to 10:00 P.M. Given the five-hour time difference between New York and London during all but one week in the spring, we see that both the New York and London markets are open during the entire time that New York trades its pit session, from 3:30 P.M. to 7:30 P.M., and they both close at the same time.

Our approach has been to trade on the close, which also assumes that prices posted on the close are realistic approximations of the price of two markets at the same time. Even then, no one ever gets a fill at the settlement price. If you're a buyer on the close, expect to get a price above the settlement, and if you're a seller, below the settlement. A bid-asked spread exists no matter what time of day you're trading and no matter how liquid the market.

In futures, the settlement price is a volume-weighted average price of all trading during the last 30 seconds of the session. This is similar to the close of the stock markets. Because of that, getting the closing price for your execution is not realistic, and on volatile days, the range of the last 30 seconds can be wide. It may be safer to trade a few minutes before the close to have better control of your fill price. Unfortunately, because this trade may have one leg in New York and one leg in London, it's not possible to enter the order as a spread, which guarantees a minimum differential between the two prices. For pairs on the same exchange, spread orders are the best way to go.

Technically, the popularity of 24-hour markets and extended pit sessions makes it possible to trade both legs of a spread at the same time, at almost any time, albeit with different amounts of liquidity. But it is more important to know that the prices used to decide the trade actually occurred at the same time. If the two markets that make up the pair are not actively trading, the screen price will not be the price you would get when you execute the trade. For example, you think there is an opportunity to arbitrage gold because a COMEX (Commodity Exchange) deferred contract is trading at $1,150 and London forward of a comparable delivery is showing a print of $1,154. The cost of delivery is $2. But London gold hasn't traded for two minutes. If you were to look at the bid-asked, you might see $1,149.5 and $1,150.5, showing that the next trade would bring prices back together, eliminating any arbitrage possibility.

Even with these complications, the closing price is the most realistic assumption that both markets have traded at the same time. The close tends to have very high liquidity. Still, when you buy one leg, you often get a price in the upper half of the closing range, and as a seller, you get the lower half. It's necessary to be sure you wait for a spread difference large enough to absorb a poor fill and still net a profit.

For the equity index markets, which we will apply in these examples, only the U.S. and European markets will be used. In April 2005, EUREX changed its trading hours to remain open until the close of the U.S. sessions. The German DAX, EuroStoxx, French CAC, and other European index markets (although not the London FTSE) all close at 10 P.M. in Germany, or 4 P.M. in New York, except for one week in the spring when the United States adjusts to daylight savings time earlier than Europe or Great Britain. This allows us to assume that the closing prices are close enough and base our trading signals on the close.

Different Holidays

There are many days in which either the U.S. or European markets are not open due to holidays. Over the years, many countries have aligned their holidays so that the markets are open and closed at the same time; however, London does not close when the U.S. celebrates Independence Day, July 4, even if there is little trading. It's the principle.

To account for these differences, and the errors it would cause if the strategy didn't recognize that one market was closed and the other open, we have adopted the rule:

If either market posts no price change, we cannot enter or exit a trade.

There will be days when the market actually closes unchanged, and the system will not change its position. These differences seem small compared with entering or exiting with a large profit (or loss) because one market traded and the other did not. Those traders who are more ambitious can keep an accurate calendar of market holidays, which are available on each of the exchange web sites.

Trading Habits in Different Countries

Although markets now stay open at all hours to accommodate traders, most activity is still concentrated during local business hours. That is to our advantage. The results will show that the best performance is when we trade a U.S. against a European market. There are two primary reasons.

While the fundamentals of the economy are different, globalization causes traders to push similar markets in the same direction. When the release of a U.S. economic report causes the U.S. stock market to jump higher, European index markets tend to follow before deciding to what extent that report actually affects them.

The second reason is that traders in Germany just don't want to stay up until 10 P.M. to trade the U.S. close. Naturally, professional hedge funds hire traders to do just that—to keep the same hours as U.S. markets. But that's not enough to make the volume high.

Check the Data Carefully

Many futures markets have day sessions (once called the pit session, before most of the pits became extinct), night sessions, and overnight sessions. For convenience, these will be called *open outcry* and *electronic sessions*.

For a pit session, or open outcry session, the trading day starts at the beginning of business hours for the country in which the futures market is trading. In the United States, stocks and stock index markets open their pit sessions at 9:30 A.M. New York time. The stock market closes at 4 P.M., but futures close at 4:15. The extra 15 minutes allows reaction to some earnings reports released just after the close of the NYSE. The close of the pit session is also the price used for marked-to-market accounting, the settling of all profits and losses for the day.

After a pause of from 15 minutes to one hour, the electronic session starts. For some markets, there is side-by-side trading. For example, there is an S&P pit session trading a big contract worth $250 per big point change, and an electronic e-mini contract with a $50 per big point change. The e-mini contract trades 24 hours and has most of the volume.

"Big point" or "handle" is the insiders' way of saying that the price to the left of the decimal point has changed. In the days when the pit session was active, traders used hand signals to indicate the price at which they wanted to buy or sell. Those signals showed only the decimal place, not the handle. Even today in crude oil, trading is so active that prices could stay between, for example, $71.00 and $72.00 for hours, so that only the cents are needed to show your bid or asked price.

When you look at combined session data, which are very common now, you are seeing the trading from both the pit and electronic sessions. For the

U.S. markets, the new trading day starts *after* the close of the pit session when the electronic session opens (for the S&P) at 6 P.M. the same evening. Both the pit and electronic sessions close at 4:15 P.M. the next day.

For Europe, the electronic session becomes an extension of the current day. But even in Europe, the official settlement price occurs between 2:30 P.M. and 4:15 P.M. local time, essentially tied to when the banks traditionally closed for the day and posted all debits and credits.

It is important to know that, in Europe, the DAX day session closes at 5 P.M., electronic at 10 P.M., and some data series have the high and low until 10 P.M. but the official settlement at 5 P.M. Whoops! That doesn't work for your trading system because the high or low could have occurred after the 5 P.M. close, and you would be using data that did not exist at 5 P.M. You'll need to be sure that you have a data series that has the last price instead of the settlement.

Markets Close at Different Times

For some of the examples in this chapter, the futures markets used in a pair may not close at exactly the same time. These are mainly in the section that looks at inflation-related markets, gold, crude oil, and the EURUSD. The biggest impact on the results is that there may be some additional trades due to price moves that occur after one market is closed. However, when we compared the periods when the S&P and EuroStoxx did not close at exactly the same time with the later period when they did, we could not see a significant difference in the number of trades. Of course, when actually trading these pairs, entries and exits to both legs must be done simultaneously, when both markets are trading.

MECHANICS OF A PAIRS TRADE IN FUTURES

The mechanics of a futures trade are slightly different from the trades using stocks that we covered in the previous chapter. The two exceptional advantages are:

1. There is no distinction between entering a long trade and a short sale (simply called a "short" in futures). When you place an order to buy, you don't tell the broker that you're setting a new position or covering a previous short. If you are previously long 10 contracts and you place an order to sell 10, you end up flat. If you are long 5 contracts and sell 10, you end up short 5. There are no uptick rules and no likelihood

that shorts would be restricted in any way. You don't need to borrow stock to sell short; it's a normal process when you trade futures. Selling short in futures simply means that you believe prices will go down. The person who takes the other side of that trade expects prices to go up. You can both be right if your time frames are different; prices could go down in the short term, then up in the long term.

2. You can leverage the trades without borrowing funds. In fact, you earn interest on most of the money on deposit in your account. That can offset the commission costs. In trading futures, you only need to put up *margin*, but this is not the same as margin for stocks. It is simply a good faith deposit. For most futures trades, that deposit amounts to about 10% of the contract value. If you are a commercial trader—that is, if you are trading gold and your business is jewelry—then your margin might be as low as 5%. For example, if gold is trading at $1,100/ounce and the contract is 100 ounces, then one contract is worth $110,000. The typical margin would be about $10,000, but the exact number can be found by going to the COMEX or Chicago Mercantile Exchange (CME) web site or checking with your broker.

Putting up $10,000 to trade a gold contract, with gold at $1,100 an ounce, is the same as buying assets of $110,000 at a leverage of 11:1. In reality, the leverage is lower because the brokerage firm will require more in the event your trade goes the wrong way. In futures, you are required to restore margin to the full amount ($10,000 in our example) once your balance falls below 75% of the initial margin. To avoid continuous problems, a broker may want you to deposit $20,000 or $30,000 just to trade one contract. That means they won't have to chase clients who lose all their investment and more. In futures, you are responsible for your losses, even if they exceed the amount on deposit in your account. A typical investment manager will keep leverage to 4:1. Then, for one gold contract, they will have $40,000 on deposit, earning either money market interest or 3-month T-bill rates on up to 90% of the balance.

Example of Trading Signals for Futures

As an example of a pairs trade in futures, we use a heating oil–natural gas pair. Table 4.1 shows two trades, both profitable, but with large equity swings. In this example we use a 14-day calculation period and enter a new trade when the momentum difference exceeds ±50 and an exit when the momentum falls to 10 for shorts and rises to –10 for longs.

In the first trade, lasting only two days, the momentum difference on 6/9/2009 is –58.37, below the –50 entry threshold. This is the difference

TABLE 4.1 Two sample trades for the pair natural gas and heating oil.

Date	Natural Gas (NG)			Heating Oil (HO)			Momentum (Stochastic)			Volatility		NG Position		HO Position		Trade PL			Total PL
	High	Low	Close	High	Low	Close	NG	HO	NG-HO	NG	HO	Ctrs	Entry	Ctrs	Entry	NG	HO	Net PL	PL
6/9/2006	16.010	15.770	15.782	2.7510	2.7085	2.7444	29.55	87.93	-58.37	2837	2424	10	15.782	-12	2.7444	0	0	0	0
6/12/2006	15.880	15.720	15.834	2.7575	2.6845	2.6898	36.18	36.71	-0.53	2664	2523	0	15.782	0	2.7444	5200	26840	32040	32040
6/13/2006	15.920	15.750	15.773	2.6610	2.6285	2.6301	28.41	1.21	27.20	2585	2433	0	0	0	0	0	0	0	32040
6/14/2006	16.278	15.978	16.200	2.6399	2.6129	2.6344	82.80	14.52	68.29	2694	2323	-10	16.200	12	2.6344	0	0	0	32040
6/15/2006	16.948	16.198	16.823	2.6544	2.6309	2.6337	91.06	14.04	77.01	3109	2219	-10	16.200	12	2.6344	-62300	-341	-62641	-30601
6/16/2006	16.868	16.648	16.803	2.6379	2.6109	2.6283	89.63	11.59	78.04	3137	2135	-10	16.200	12	2.6344	2000	-2631	-631	-31232
6/19/2006	16.548	16.408	16.501	2.6219	2.5879	2.5948	68.03	3.99	64.04	3255	2092	-10	16.200	12	2.6344	30200	-16319	13881	-17351
6/20/2006	16.398	16.038	16.085	2.6299	2.5979	2.6087	38.27	12.02	26.25	3311	2010	-10	16.200	12	2.6344	41600	6771	48371	31020
6/21/2006	16.238	16.048	16.146	2.6529	2.5899	2.6409	42.63	30.62	12.01	3179	1989	-10	16.200	12	2.6344	-6100	15686	9586	40606
6/22/2006	16.098	15.918	15.962	2.6809	2.6379	2.6757	29.47	50.72	-21.25	3127	1948	0	16.200	0	2.6344	18400	16953	35353	75959

between the natural gas momentum of 29.55 and the heating oil momentum of 87.93, indicating that natural gas was moderately oversold while heating oil was somewhat overbought, as given by the 14-day calculation period. The entry prices are the closing prices for that day, 2.359 and 15.517. Remember that these are back-adjusted futures, so these prices are not the actual prices that occurred on that day.

On the following day, the natural gas momentum rises slightly, and the heating oil momentum drops considerably, resulting in a net momentum difference of –0.53. An exit is triggered because the momentum difference is above the threshold of –10. Most of the profit is due to heating oil, for a net gain of $32,040.

The position size for this trade was determined from the volatility calculation, which is the 14-day average true range. We use the same period as the stochastic calculation for consistency and in order not to introduce an additional parameter. At the time of the entry signal, June 9, 2006, natural gas had a average daily dollar range of $2,837 and heating oil a range of $2,424. With a lower volatility, heating oil will get more contracts than natural gas, in this case –12 to 10.

The second trade on June 14, 2006, is much more volatile. Natural gas is now overbought with a stochastic of 82.80, and heating oil is oversold at 14.52. The volatility is nearly the same as three days prior, so we buy 10 natural and sell 12 heat. However, on the first day, natural gas jumps 3.85% while heat only gains 0.02%, for a net loss of $62,641. After that, the two markets work their way back in the right direction for a net gain on the trade of $43,919 when the momentum difference goes negative. This is a trade that shows how difficult it is to use a stop-loss order, which would have exited the trade at the worst time, locking in the large loss. Remember that the natural profile of performance is to have a few large losses and more smaller profits.

INFLATION SCARES

The first decade of the 21st century included the end of the tech bubble that sent NASDAQ to nearly 5000, the subsequent drop of 75%, the attack of September 11, 2001, real estate hyperinflation leading to the subprime collapse, a run in crude oil to $150/barrel and related panic over impending inflation, a worldwide government takeover of financial institutions, record unemployment, record corporate bonuses, and a smooth rally in the equity markets in 2009 in anticipation of more stable times to come. We live in interesting times.

News of these events can be confusing. Too many of us watch the financial news programs, which, because of the need to make everything

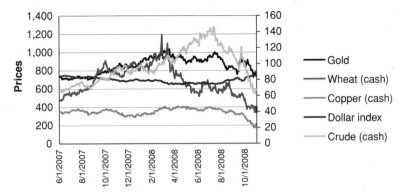

FIGURE 4.1 Inflation-related commodities: the dollar index, gold, crude oil, copper, and wheat. The relationships are strongest when the economy is under stress.

sound urgent, tend to make minor events into something newsworthy and of great importance to the viewers. Without this high-profile coverage, most market fluctuations would most likely be little blips of noise.

The year with the most extreme price moves was 2008. In Figure 4.1, we can compare the bull (and bear) markets in oil with other key commodities. From late 2007, there is a clear upturn in gold, wheat, and crude oil, with a smooth decline in the Dollar Index. Although the rally in prices is somewhat out of phase, the decline that began after crude peaked was remarkably uniform. Was it a reaction to a false alarm in inflation? Not likely. Again, we would argue that it was mostly caused by investors pulling money out of every market at the same time. Commodity index funds had gained in popularity during the bull market in wheat, and everyone had been concerned that the price of bread was going to double or triple. With wheat dropping, followed by a collapse in the crude market, the dollar gaining strength, and gold falling from its highs of $1,000/ounce, investors saw their profits disappearing. Once the liquidation started, it became contagious.

In this chapter, we'll look at the periods where these markets all seem to have moved together and see if there were profits to be made—at a reasonable risk. But first we'll focus on the energy markets, which have gained tremendous interest during the past two years.

Setting Up the Trade

For pairs trading using stocks, we started with a basic unit size of 100 shares for leg 1, the first stock of the pair. The size of the second leg was larger or smaller, depending on its volatility, in order to make the risk of both legs equal. For futures, the starting size will be 10 contracts for the first leg, and the second will then be adjusted in the same way as with stocks. Using 10 contracts does not give us the accuracy of 100 for sizing the second leg, but 10 contracts of futures can be a large investment and is enough to show the effect of adjusting position size to volatility.

Margin and Leverage

Consider that each contract of crude oil is 1,000 barrels (bbl), currently selling at about $75/bbl. The contract size is then $75,000, the minimum trading unit. Of course, you don't need to invest $75,000 to buy one contract of crude; you only need to put up a *margin* deposit of about $7,500, or 10% of the contract value.

If you buy a contract and the price of crude goes up $1, you gain $1,000. Your deposit is $7,500, giving you a return of 13.3%. That can easily happen in one day. On the other hand, if the price drops by $1 you lose 13.3%. If the price rises by $10/bbl to $85 (not out of the question), you have earned 133%. But if it drops by $10 (equally possible), you have lost your $7,500, plus you must pay the broker the remaining $2,500 within 24 hours. If you want to continue to trade you must deposit more money.

In reality, it doesn't quite happen that way. Based on the volatility of the market, your deposit should be high enough to cover most normal moves, so doubling or losing all your money in one day should not happen. On the other hand, you may be required to deposit $25,000 and only trade one crude contract. That protects the broker from the possibility of uncovered losses. If you start to lose so much that your deposit is eroding, the broker will ask you to restore your account to its original value or will liquidate your positions for you. There is no such thing as losing more than you have and then borrowing to cover your losses—only the big banks can do that.

TRADING ENERGY PAIRS

For simplicity, we will trade energy pairs using only the four primary U.S. energy markets, crude oil (symbol CL, also known as WTI for West Texas Intermediate), its products, heating oil (HO) and reformulated blendstock for oxygenate blending (RBOB or RB), gasoline, and natural gas (NG). The gasoline contract, which used to be called *unleaded gas* changes often because of environmental regulations, so it's best to keep watching the volume for any noticeable, permanent declines. Low volume will tell you that there is another, more active contract.

As mentioned before, the crude contract is 1,000 barrels, heating oil is 42,000 gallons, unleaded gas is 42,000 gallons, and natural gas is

10,000 million British thermal units (Btus). The contracts are sized this way because of commercial needs. An oil refiner typically buys three contracts of crude and produces two contracts of gasoline and one of distillate (heating oil). The crack spread, which gets favorable margin from the exchange, is a spread that buys crude and sells RBOB and heating oil in the ratio 3:2:1, although this is not exact. If producing margins are too low, the refiner has the option of doing a reverse crack, in which it sells crude and buys the products. In our trading, we will only spread pairs and decide the relative position sizes using volatility. It is generally unproductive to trade the crack and try to compete with commercials at their own game.

If the price of crude oil moves from \$75 to \$76, the profit or loss from trading each contract is \$1,000. If heating oil moves from \$2.25/gallon to \$2.26/gallon, the profit or loss is \$420, and the same for unleaded gas. If natural gas rises from \$6.500 mmBtu to \$6.600 mmBtu, the gain or loss is \$1,000. Therefore, the minimum move (smallest decimal move) for crude is worth \$10, for heating oil and unleaded gas \$4.20, and for natural gas \$10.

Trading Hours

For us to be able to test these pairs correctly, the data must be posted at the same time. In the energy markets, that is no problem because all four futures markets have a pit session that opens at 9:00 A.M. and closes at 2:30 P.M., Eastern time. It is unclear whether the pit session refers to open outcry trading or if it is just the primary electronic session. If it is not all electronic, it will be soon. There is also an electronic session for all markets that opens at 6:00 P.M. (18:00) and closes the next day at 5:15 P.M. (17:15).

The London Intercontinental Exchange (ICE) also trades similar products: Brent crude oil, a close proxy to our WTI, and gas oil (similar to our heating oil). The ICE is only electronic, with hours from 20:00 to 18:00 the following day (22 continuous hours), Eastern time. Although the closing prices are only 45 minutes later than the U.S. electronic counterpart, it would be necessary to capture prices at exactly the same time in the U.S. and London to have accurate data to trade pairs with one leg on each side of the pond.

As we will see from looking at the equity index and interest rate market pairs that span the U.S. and Europe, there is greater opportunity trading markets that respond to the same fundamentals but are applied to different economies. It is likely that energy pairs that have one U.S. leg and one London leg will be more profitable than the combinations of U.S. markets tested here, but that will be an opportunity that readers must pursue on their own. There is no viable arbitrage between the U.S. and European energy markets, but global macro events seem to keep both markets moving in the same way.

More Fundamental Background

There are some fundamentals that we should discuss ahead of seeing results, as a way of setting expectations. It was already mentioned that heating oil and natural gas have overlapping markets, home heating, but most users cannot change from one to another because of equipment. Some commercial plants have that ability to use both sources, but it is not common. Heating oil is also diesel fuel, used for trucks and an increasing number of cars, especially in Europe. However, there is no practical arbitrage for heating oil. That is, the price of heating oil in Europe, called gas oil, would need to be much higher than the price in the U.S. to make loading and shipping from the U.S. to Europe, or the other direction, a profitable transaction.

Heating oil and gasoline are the refined products of crude oil and are produced in different percentages as the seasons change in North America. The production of heating oil is increased beginning in the early summer to build inventories, and gasoline production is increased in April in anticipation of the driving season, which officially starts on Memorial Day (the end of May) in the U.S. Prices of gasoline tend to increase during the high-demand summer season, and heating oil can increase at the beginning of winter, or anytime between December and March, in expectation of any sustained cold spell that would affect demand.

Crude oil does not have any clear seasonal pattern, being the netting of the products, gasoline and heating oil, which are both seasonal. It does make extreme moves due to geopolitical risk, such as attacks on the pipelines in Iraq or Nigeria or labor strikes in Venezuela. Crude prices are also manipulated by OPEC, which sets production limits for its participating members. This has had mixed success over the years, but they keep trying. In the final analysis, any country in need of money will try to sell more oil.

Crude oil also follows the change in the U.S. dollar because it is quoted in dollars worldwide. For example, if the dollar declines against the euro from 1.35 to 1.40, about 3.7%, we should see a similar rise in the price of crude oil, everything else being equal. Oil maintains what we would call a *global value*. That holds true for commodities as well. In Figure 4.2, the vertical price scales have been extended to fill the chart, giving both crude and the EURUSD the same relative volatility and showing remarkable similarity. Although crude moved much further measured as a percentage, the overlapping patterns show an undeniable relationship since March 2007. Oddly enough, it appears that the EURUSD started up in the first quarter of 2007 before it was joined by crude. This looks like an opportunity, but the daily correlation is only .33, measured beginning in 2007.

Despite the different fundamentals, energy prices move together. When crude oil spikes up during the winter, heating oil is the primary focus,

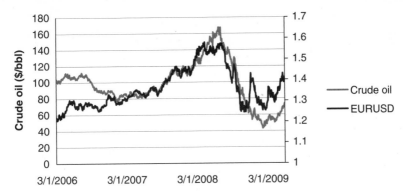

FIGURE 4.2 Crude oil and the EURUSD show a remarkable correlation from 2007.

but gasoline prices must be dragged higher as well. In the spring and early summer, it is the opposite, with gasoline leading the way. You can't expect a big move in any of the energy markets without all the others showing some proportional reaction. It's the lead and lag in these moves that provides trading opportunities.

REVISITING MOMENTUM WITH ENERGY MARKETS

Energy markets have been the focus of rising costs for the past two years, topping with crude oil at $150/bbl and taking the products, gasoline and heating oil, along with it. Natural gas moved higher then lower, along with crude, as did all sources of energy (even firewood), although very few users are able to use heating oil and natural gas interchangeably. The equipment needed to use one or the other is not readily interchangeable. Figure 4.3 shows a chart of crude oil, heating oil, and natural gas from 1990 through January 2010. Heating oil tracks crude because it is derived from crude, and natural gas starts to shadow the movements of crude in 1996, but only when the moves are larger.

Opportunity and Risk

The interesting part about natural gas and heating oil is that the traders create strong correlations during periods of stress. During a crisis, it is always money that moves the market, not common sense. Although the big picture of natural gas and heating oil price moves, Figure 4.3 shows a general, smooth downtrend of natural gas prices, compared with a general rise

FIGURE 4.3 Energy prices, 1990–January 2010, log scale. There is a similarity in natural gas, but there are also large differences.

in heating oil prices into 2008; during the times when crude price moved up faster than normal, natural gas followed. The most extreme example was the peak of 2008 shown in Figure 4.4.

During the 14 months that included the peak crude oil price on July 14, 2008, natural gas moved in step with crude oil and especially heating oil. Once prices came back down in late 2008, the similarity of price movement disappeared. Figure 4.5 shows the prices of heating oil and natural gas from March 2009 through the end of 2009. You can find short bursts of similarity in the prices, but overall the picture is one of heating oil rising and natural gas falling. These differences can offer both opportunity and risk.

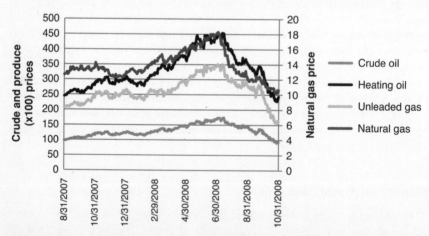

FIGURE 4.4 NYMEX energy prices, August 31, 2007–October 31, 2008. Natural gas tracks crude oil and heating oil during times of stress. At the peak of crude oil prices, in mid-2008, natural gas tracked crude oil as though it were a product.

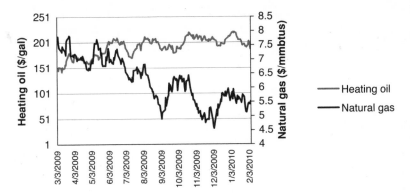

FIGURE 4.5 Heating oil and natural gas, from March 2009 through January 2010, following the peak in crude oil. Arbitrage would have provided more risk than reward.

The correlations during the three periods may give a more exact picture. Table 4.2 shows the three intervals:

1. All data from 1990 through 2009.
2. Peak crude oil price move, September 2007 through October 2008.
3. After-the-peak price moves, March 2008 through December 2009.

In the top panel of Table 4.2, we see the normal, long-term relationship of the three markets. Unleaded gas is omitted because it has a very similar relationship to both crude and natural gas, as heating oil. The left side of the table used the price differences to find the correlations, and the right side used the percentage changes. Normally we would want to use the percentage changes, but most futures long-term data is *continuously back-adjusted* from individual futures contracts. In the worst cases, where there is a significant price gap between the contract that is expiring and the next contract to be used, the aggregate back adjusting can cause the oldest prices to become negative, or near zero. For those markets, percentages don't work. For commodity prices such as energy and metals, cash prices offer a good alternative; however, using differences will give similar results if you stay aware of the data problems.

Heating oil and unleaded gas are always highly correlated to crude prices, which is to be expected because they are both products of crude. During the three periods shown in Table 4.2, the correlation of heat to crude stays over .90. It is not higher due to the seasonality of the products. During the spring and summer months, the product prices are driven by unleaded gasoline, and heating oil becomes a secondary market, causing a less direct relationship.

TABLE 4.2   Cross-correlations of crude oil, heating oil, and natural gas during the three intervals: all data from 1990 through 2009 (top panel); the peak crude period, September 2007 through October 2008 (center panel); and the after-the-peak period, March 2009 through December 2009 (bottom panel).

Difference in Prices				Percentage Change in Prices		
	CL	**HO**	**NG**		**CL**	**HO**	**NG**
CL	1	0.904	0.351	CL	1	0.893	0.317
HO	0.904	1	0.403	HO	0.893	1	0.349
NG	0.351	0.403	1	NG	0.317	0.349	1
Peak Crude Period				**Peak Crude Period**		
	CL	**HO**	**NG**		**CL**	**HO**	**NG**
CL	1	0.933	0.557	CL	1	0.941	0.548
HO	0.933	1	0.536	HO	0.941	1	0.533
NG	0.557	0.536	1	NG	0.557	0.533	1
After the Peak				**After the Peak**		
	CL	**HO**	**NG**		**CL**	**HO**	**NG**
CL	1	0.935	0.295	CL	1	0.931	0.268
HO	0.935	1	0.318	HO	0.931	1	0.292
NG	0.295	0.318	1	NG	0.268	0.292	1

A long-term correlation of 0.351 for crude and natural gas shows some correlation, but it is not clear whether they would be profitable for pairs trading; the risk may be too high. However, during the peak period for crude prices, the correlation with natural gas jumped to 0.557 for crude and 0.536 for heating oil, making it a likely candidate. After the peak, those correlations dropped to below the long-term values, so this opportunity would have increased in risk.

In this chapter, we will look at pairs trading in futures markets that have a long-term history of being fundamentally related, as well as more limited, shorter-term opportunities. Sometimes the best trades are those that spring from special situations.

Trading Energy Pairs

We've looked at the changing correlations in the most active energy futures, and now it's time to see if they can be traded profitably as pairs. The

TABLE 4.3 Correlations of pairs, 10 years beginning 2000.

Leg 1	Leg 2	Corr
Crude	Unleaded	0.837
Crude	Heating	0.883
Unleaded	Heating	0.812
Crude	Natural gas	0.391
Unleaded	Natural gas	0.368
Natural gas	Heating	0.411
Average	Crude & products	0.844
Average	Natural gas	0.390

four futures contracts are crude (CL), heating oil (HO), unleaded gasoline (RB), and natural gas (NG). Both Brent and gas oil, traded on the IPE or ICE, are also candidates but won't be considered here. The data will be the past 10 years, beginning January 2000.

We can first set our expectations by looking at the correlations of the six pairs, shown in Table 4.3. It is immediately clear that the pairs made up of crude and its products have a very high correlation, and those using natural gas are much lower. Because this period included the very volatile run-up in crude to $150, the current correlations with natural gas are toward the high part of the range seen in Table 4.2. The two groups provide very different expectations. The high correlations make it certain that divergences in the momentum will produce a trade that quickly corrects, but the absolute price differences may be too small to be profitable after we subtract our cost of $25 per contract for each round-turn. Because of the lower correlations, natural gas pairs are likely to be more profitable but with much higher risk.

The rules for trading will be exactly the same as in Chapter 3, except that we charge a round-turn cost of $25 per contract. We calculate the stochastic momentum values of the two futures markets separately over the same time period, subtract the two values, and test that difference against an entry threshold. When we tested stocks using calculation ranges from 14 to 4, we found that the smaller momentum periods emphasized market noise, which is to our advantage, and increased the number of trades. The entry threshold was from ±60 to ±40, but the lower value of ±40 generated the most trades. The entry thresholds also affect the size of the individual trade profits (and risk), which is the negative part of the trade-off. Getting enough profits per trade was the biggest problem.

In Table 4.4, the results of these tests are shown for all six pairs, separated into those without natural gas (part a) and those with natural gas

TABLE 4.4	Results of energy pairs varying the calculation period and entry threshold. The stochastic momentum calculation period is on the left and the entry threshold along the top axis.

(a) Results show the information ratio for energy pairs combining crude oil, heating oil, and unleaded gas in all combinations

	Crude and Products			
	Entry Threshold			
Period	60	50	40	Avg
14	−0.222	−0.351	−0.231	−0.268
10	−0.306	−0.250	−0.303	−0.286
8	−0.058	−0.168	−0.135	−0.120
7	−0.167	−0.312	−0.355	−0.278
6	−0.104	−0.399	−0.476	−0.326
5	−0.349	−0.477	−0.614	−0.480
4	−0.528	−0.637	−0.653	−0.606
Average	−0.248	−0.370	−0.395	

(b) Results show the information ratio for energy pairs using natural gas as one leg and crude, heating oil, or RBOB as the other

	Natural Gas Pairs			
	Entry Threshold			
Period	60	50	40	Avg
14	0.173	0.097	0.302	0.191
10	0.561	0.521	0.458	0.513
8	0.538	0.389	0.261	0.396
7	0.458	0.161	0.160	0.260
6	0.459	0.327	0.341	0.376
5	0.258	0.122	0.134	0.171
4	−0.076	−0.099	−0.135	−0.104
Average	0.339	0.217	0.217	

(part b). The test period was January 2000 through March 2010. It is immediately evident that the pairs made up of crude and its products all fail to generate profits after costs. On the other hand, the natural gas pairs were all successful, net of costs, for all combinations of calculation periods and entry thresholds except the fastest, 4 days. We can understand that the shortest calculation periods result in the fastest trades and the smallest returns per trade. In this case, 4 days was too fast.

The natural gas pairs show a consistent pattern of improvement as values move from the bottom right to the top left, which is also from faster to slower, peaking at a calculation period of 10 days. Keeping it in perspective, the range of periods, from 4 to 14, is considered a fast range and not suitable for trend following.

It is often the case that the best ratio is among the fastest trading models, and we find that the profits per contract are marginally large enough to offset costs. That doesn't seem to be the situation here, but then the successful pairs are those with natural gas, and the correlations are fairly low. We can expect these markets to move apart often but come back together because the energy complex has underlying similarities and will react to much of the market news in the same way.

It's likely that some traders will choose a different combination of parameters. They might try to maximize the number of trades or the profits per contract. They may want the combination that is out of the market most often, as a way of avoiding price shocks. And we didn't test combinations of exit thresholds, where a short trade is entered at a momentum difference of 60 and exited at 10 rather than 0. That would increase the number of trades, increase the percentage of profitable trades, but decrease the size of the per contract returns. There is no *best* choice, only trade-offs and trader preference. Those options are left to the reader.

In this example, the best choice will be the parameters that produced the highest ratio, a calculation period of 10 and an entry threshold of ±60. Table 4.5 shows some of the statistics for that choice. There are only 10 trades per year, but the profits per contract are sufficiently large to give us confidence that we can absorb any surprising slippage. The reasonably equal distribution of profits per contract between leg 1 and leg 2 is also good, showing that both markets are moving. Annualized returns averaged only 6.7% but will be higher when this is mixed in a portfolio and diversification reduces the risk. These values are all based on an annualized volatility (standard deviation) of 12%, as are all results shown in this book.

TABLE 4.5 Individual energy pairs' performance using momentum period 10, entry threshold ±60, from January 2000.

					Per Contract		
Leg 1	Leg 2	Trades	Total PL	AROR	Leg 1	Leg 2	Ratio
Crude	Natural gas	102	933692	8.6	189	1106	0.717
Unleaded	Natural gas	110	823201	5.7	509	367	0.471
Natural gas	Heating	98	1110179	5.9	404	486	0.494
Average		103	955691	6.7	367	653	0.561

TABLE 4.6 Results of crude-product pairs with a period of 10 and entry threshold of ±60.

					Per Contract		
Leg 1	Leg 2	Trades	Total PL	AROR	Leg 1	Leg 2	Ratio
Crude	Unleaded	18	−301051	−9.4	354	−2734	−0.787
Crude	Heating	9	−39010	−3.1	−1639	1508	−0.259
Unleaded	Heating	21	71750	1.6	218	154	0.129
Average		16	−89437	−3.6	−355	−357	−0.306

For completeness, we also show the results of the crude-product pairs in Table 4.6. First, the number of trades is very small because the correlations are high. It is rare that the two closely related markets diverge enough to generate a trading signal. The only pair that netted a profit was unleaded–heating oil, which have opposite seasonality and are most likely to move apart. The ratio of 0.129 shows that the performance was very erratic, and you would need to take nearly 8 times the risk for each unit of reward. That's not an attractive profile.

A MINIPORTFOLIO OF NATURAL GAS PAIRS

Selecting the three natural gas pairs, we can combine the profit and loss streams into a portfolio to see how much diversification we gain. This will be the same process that we use for any group of pairs in the same sector. We can later combine multiple sectors for further diversification. As we will see with futures, we have the ability to choose our level of risk and vary our leverage. It is one of the great advantages of trading futures.

The process begins with either the three streams of daily profits and losses or the cumulative profits shown in Figure 4.6. You start with the cumulative profits, then simply subtract each day's value from the previous day to get the change in profits. As you can see in the chart, heating oil appears to be more volatile than either crude or unleaded gas. The process of adjusting to a target volatility will equalize the volatility of the returns of each of the three pairs.

Step 1: Calculation of the Daily Profit or Loss

Each day it is necessary to calculate the daily profit or loss, less the round-turn commission when the trade is closed out. Table 4.7 shows the data

FIGURE 4.6 Cumulative profit and loss streams for the three natural gas pairs, from 2000.

needed to calculate the profits and losses, along with the momentum difference to confirm that an entry or exit has occurred.

The first trade is entered at the close on February 9, 2000, selling 10 contracts of crude at 63.11 and buying 7 natural gas at 20.317 based on current volatility. Note that these prices are back-adjusted futures but work accurately for these examples. On the next day, February 10, 2000, the price of crude rises by $0.66, and natural gas also rises by $0.052. The conversion factor for crude is $1,000 for a 1.00 move and $10,000 for a 1.00 move in natural gas, then 10 contracts of crude generate a loss of $10 \times \$0.66 \times \$1,000 = \$6,600$, and 7 contracts of natural gas generate a gain of $7 \times \$0.052 \times \$10,000 = \$3,640$. That gives a net loss for the day, as well as a cumulative loss, of $2,960.

On the next day, February 11, 2000, crude gains $0.01 and natural gas drops $0.022, both losses for the pairs trade, netting a daily loss of $1,640 and a cumulative loss of $4,600. The calculations continue in the same way, but with prices going in a favorable direction until the trade is closed out on February 17, 2000. On that day, the daily profit or loss is reduced by an additional $25 for each contract, or $250 for crude and $175 for natural gas, giving the final trade a profit of $765.

There are no trades for the next three days; therefore, the daily profit/loss column shows zeros.

The next trade is entered on February 23, 2000, and is also short crude and long natural gas. This time, the volatility of natural gas has dropped, and the position sizes are equal. If we follow the same calculations, we show a large gain on the final day of the trade, February 28, 2000, resulting in a cumulative profit.

The Net PL column, second from the right, will be used to continue the portfolio construction.

TABLE 4.7 Calculating the daily profits and losses for the crude–natural gas pair.

Date	Closing Price		Mom Diff	Crude Position		Natural Gas		Daily PL		Net PL	Cum PL
	Crude	Nat Gas		Ctrs	Entry	Ctrs	Entry	Crude	Nat Gas		
2/7/2000	62.79	20.339	52.12	0	0	0	0	0	0	0	0
2/8/2000	62.36	20.272	53.26	0	0	0	0	0	0	0	0
2/9/2000	63.11	20.317	72.75	-10	63.11	7	20.317	0	0	0	0
2/10/2000	63.77	20.369	59.13	-10	63.11	7	20.317	-6600	3640	-2960	-2960
2/11/2000	63.78	20.347	53.37	-10	63.11	7	20.317	-100	-1540	-1640	-4600
2/14/2000	64.59	20.318	76.95	-10	63.11	7	20.317	-8100	-2030	-10130	-14730
2/15/2000	64.52	20.395	41.46	-10	63.11	7	20.317	700	5390	6090	-8640
2/16/2000	64.66	20.341	62.17	-10	63.11	7	20.317	-1400	-3780	-5180	-13820
2/17/2000	63.88	20.444	-5.15	0	63.11	0	20.317	7550	7035	14585	765
2/18/2000	63.78	20.410	-4.70	0	0	0	0	0	0	0	765
2/22/2000	64.25	20.292	57.74	0	0	0	0	0	0	0	765
2/23/2000	64.72	20.307	70.26	-10	64.72	10	20.307	0	0	0	765
2/24/2000	65.30	20.322	60.83	-10	64.72	10	20.307	-5800	1500	-4300	-3535
2/25/2000	65.68	20.383	19.74	-10	64.72	10	20.307	-3800	6100	2300	-1235
2/28/2000	65.46	20.452	-8.78	0	64.72	0	20.307	1950	6650	8600	7365
2/29/2000	65.76	20.527	-10.38	0	0	0	0	0	0	0	7365

Step 2: Align the Profit/Loss Streams

There are three daily profit/loss streams that must be aligned by date. For markets that all trade on the same exchange in the same country, this is not usually a problem. Pasting them into Excel should be all that's necessary. However, dealing with pairs that have one leg in the U.S. and one leg in Europe requires an additional step.

When the data are aligned by date and one market is closed, it is necessary to enter a zero in the cell if that cell represents returns, or copy down the previous cell if the stream is the cumulative profits/losses.

Step 3: Target Volatility and Investment Size

To generate the daily returns, we need to decide on an investment size and a target volatility. For example, we will invest $100,000 but only want a 2.5% chance of losing 24% of the investment. We choose 2.5% because it represents one side of a 2 standard deviation distribution. Because it is 2 standard deviations and the annualized volatility is based on 1 standard deviation, we know that a target volatility of 12% will satisfy our needs.

If we know what our target volatility should be, then we can arrive at these results with a few steps. We use 12% annualized volatility as the industry standard for risk.

To find the investment size needed to have 12% volatility,

- Find the standard deviation of the profits and losses for the entire performance period.
- Multiply that value by the square root of 252 to get the annualized volatility in dollars.
- Divide the annualized volatility by the target volatility (0.12) to get the investment size for this market (the *market investment*).
- Repeat the process for each market.
- Add the market investments to get the portfolio investment.
- Scale all values to your actual investment size.

Alternatively, if you know your investment size, you can adjust all the returns to your target volatility:

- Convert cumulative profits to daily profits and losses for each series by subtracting the value on day $t-1$ from the value on day t.
- Calculate the returns, r_t, by dividing the daily profits and losses by the investment.
- Find the standard deviation of the returns for the entire series.

- Multiply that value by the square root of 252 to get the annualized volatility in dollars.
- Divide the target volatility (12%) by the annualized volatility to get the *volatility adjustment factor*, VAF. Note that we must always lag the use of VAF by one day to replicate trading.
- Calculate NAVs starting at 100, with each subsequent

$$\text{NAV}_t = \text{NAV}_{t-1} \times (1 + r_t \times \text{VAF}_{t-1}).$$

- All NAV series are now adjusted to 12% volatility. You can now combine them into a portfolio using your allocation percentages.

Table 4.8 shows the steps using the first set of rules. The three daily profit streams are in the columns under the heading "Daily Profits/Losses." They begin on January 1, 2000. Below those columns are three additional values marked "Annualized volatility," calculated as shown in the previous steps. The market investments based on the target volatility of 0.12 are shown below that. The sum of the three market investments is $4,331,319, but remember that this is based on trading 10 contracts of crude all the time. The investment could be smaller if the number of crude contracts is reduced, but we lose the ability to accurately balance the risk of both legs. In the long run, that might not matter, but then it might.

Step 4: Calculate the Portfolio Returns

The next panel shows the market returns, which are the daily profits or losses divided by the total portfolio investment. The daily returns for the three markets are added to get the portfolio returns, shown in the last panel.

Finally, the portfolio NAVs are calculated in the same way as before, starting with 100, and then each subsequent value for day t is

$$\text{NAV}_t = \text{NAV}_{t-1} \times (1 + R_t)$$

Next, calculate the annualized returns through day t (which begin with 100) as

$$\text{AROR} = \left(\frac{\text{NAV}_t}{100} \right)^{\frac{252}{\text{total days}}} - 1$$

The result is a return of 6.73%. We then calculate the annualized volatility of portfolio returns and get 10.19%, lower than the target of 12% due to a modest amount of diversification. The information ratio, which is the annualized return divided by the annualized risk, is then 0.66. Most traders

TABLE 4.8 Calculation of market investment and portfolio investment (on left) and market returns, portfolio returns, and portfolio NAVs (on right).

Date	Daily Profits/Losses			Daily Returns at 12% Vol			Portfolio	
	Crude	HO	RBOB	Crude	HO	RBOB	Returns	NAVs
6/3/2009	−5177	−10550	−27315	−0.00120	−0.00244	−0.00631	−0.00994	184.66
6/4/2009	−23237	−14645	−20783	−0.00536	−0.00338	−0.00480	−0.01354	182.16
6/5/2009	8530	11606	9249	0.00197	0.00268	0.00214	0.00678	183.40
6/8/2009	−7908	−12781	−6595	−0.00183	−0.00295	−0.00152	−0.00630	182.24
6/9/2009	−19200	−16581	−12894	−0.00443	−0.00383	−0.00298	−0.01124	180.19
6/10/2009	−15115	−12742	−22831	−0.00349	−0.00294	−0.00527	−0.01170	178.09
6/11/2009	5235	13813	2830	0.00121	0.00319	0.00065	0.00505	178.99
6/12/2009	972	−959	1163	0.00022	−0.00022	0.00027	0.00027	179.03
6/15/2009	41004	41148	29508	0.00947	0.00950	0.00681	0.02578	183.65
6/16/2009	0	0	0	0.00000	0.00000	0.00000	0.00000	183.65
	Annualized volatility						Ann Vol	AROR
	132,671	218,382	168,705				10.19%	6.73%
Target	Market investment						Ratio	0.66
0.12	1,105,593	1,819,853	1,405,873					
	Total Investment		4,331,319					

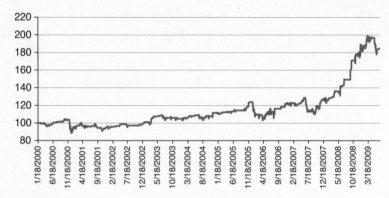

FIGURE 4.7 Returns for the three natural gas energy pairs and the equally weighted portfolio, at 10.2% volatility, 10 years from 2000.

would like this ratio to be greater than 1.0, but then the S&P passive ratio is closer to 0.10 over the past 10 years. When we combine energy pairs with other sector pairs, these results will improve.

In addition to being directionally neutral on price moves, a benefit of pairs trading is that most pairs are in the market less than 50% of the time, often closer to 25%. That means you are less exposed to price shocks and general market risk. No matter how good the system, the only way to avoid price shocks is to be out of the market. It's an important benefit.

Figure 4.7 shows the final portfolio NAVs as calculated using the steps just explained. The method gains steadily over the 10 years, but as we have discussed before, choosing the right time to trade will make a difference. With higher oil prices, volatility is likely to remain high and opportunities will be better.

Energy Summary

Although we found only three pairs that we would trade, it is a good sign that we accomplished that using the exact same method and could have used the same parameters as the original examples using stocks. Not many trading methods hold up across different markets, especially moving from stocks to futures. However, we needed to explain how we could justify removing the three pairs that included only crude and its products.

Market experience must play a role. The relationship between crude oil and its products, heating oil and gasoline, is called the *crack spread*. It is intended to simulate the process of cracking crude oil (breaking its hydrocarbon chain) into its products. Based on the amount of product that can be extracted from crude oil, crack spreads are most often done in the ratio 3:2:1, buying 3 contracts of crude and selling 2 gasoline contracts and 1 heating oil contract. It is also done in the ratio 5:3:2. To be done properly, the products should be traded one or two months out from the crude contract to give the correct delivery relationship, for example, February crude oil produces products that are ready for delivery in March or April. Trying to arbitrage the crack spread using our pairs trading method is the same as an amateur competing with professionals. It's a difficult game to win. Figure 4.4 showed how closely heating oil prices tracked crude oil, and Table 4.3 showed the long-term correlations, with crude and heating oil at .90, crude and gasoline at .86, and gasoline and heating oil at .84. There is no percentage for us to trade those relationships. We need to look at markets in which there is a fundamental relationship, or a psychological one, and the correlations are less than 0.80.

Heating Oil and Natural Gas

When we began looking at energy pairs, our choice would have been heating oil and natural gas because they both serve the home heating market. In the end, that pair was very profitable, but not nearly as good as the crude–natural gas pair, which had higher average profits per contract, as well as a higher information ratio, shown in Table 4.5.

We can conclude after the fact that a sloppy correlation in markets that are fundamentally related can result in more opportunity. Figure 4.6 also shows that returns are much better when prices and volatility are higher, which we've seen since mid-2007, when the oil crisis began. In fact, returns prior to that period were very small.

If we could only limit our trading to periods with exceptional moves, our returns would be outstanding. That leads us to our next main topic, trading inflation pairs, those markets that get the most attention from the financial news networks and newspapers under the headline of *inflation*.

THE INFLATION PAIRS: CRUDE, THE EURUSD, AND GOLD

If only we could trade during the extreme market moves and avoid the other times. It's possible that volatility is the key to identifying price regimes, but the reality is that it takes time to recognize a change in the market structure. With a lag at the beginning and a lag at the end, we've usually given up more than we gain by regime switching. One good example is trend following. The key to profits in trend following is the *fat tail*, the occasional very large profit from an extremely long trend that offsets many small losses that came before. If you use a stop-loss with a long-term trend, you exit the trade with expectations of saving money, but the trend is not over; that is, it hasn't changed direction, and it may only have taken a mid-trend correction. If you're wrong and the trend stays intact and eventually becomes one of the few big winners, you've lost your chance at net profits. Many of these strategies win by diversification and persistence. The performance doesn't look perfect because it's not perfect, but it will make money if you play by the rules.

Another opportunity seems to be in those markets perceived as causing inflation, representing inflation, or being a hedge against inflation, namely, crude oil, EURUSD, and gold. Although the U.S. government measures inflation without food and energy, energy prices have an impact on everything we buy. Because the price of energy is embedded in many other costs, the government thinks it would be double-counting to include raw energy prices in inflation calculations.

We'll take a simpler approach. Everyone knows that doubling the price of crude oil would have a material effect on all commodity prices, as well as disposable income. It also seems clear that the relationships between these three markets become stronger when inflation is in the news. Perhaps someday we will measure the number of square inches devoted to inflation on the front page of the *New York Times* or *Wall Street Journal* to determine when the time has come to trade the inflation pairs.

The U.S. dollar started to weaken against the euro at the beginning of 2006 and so far has moved from 1.20 to 1.50, a loss of about 25%, before recovering back to 1.20. Futures prices in Figure 4.8 show the relationship between the euro, crude oil, and gold, although it is somewhat different from the cash prices that we see on the news each day because they represent both future expectation, the cost of carry, and backward adjustment. But

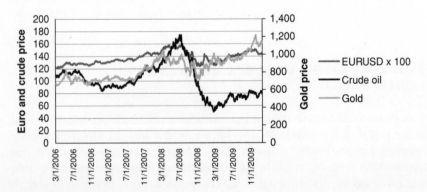

FIGURE 4.8 Components of inflation. EURUSD, crude oil, and gold prices using back-adjusted futures.

we will trade futures, so it's best to look at that data. All three markets peak in mid-2008, drop quickly, and then rally through the end of 2009. We won't try to decide if the relationship is led by crude oil or by the expectation of large U.S. debt, the result of the financial market bailout, diluting the dollar. Is there enough of a relationship to profit from trading these as pairs?

To find out if we should trade these markets, we need to answer some basic questions:

- Would pairs created from these three markets have made money using our strategy during the past three years?
- Could we have known when to start trading them?
- What parameters would we have used?

Different Values, Different Volatility

Remember that these three markets have very different contract sizes and, therefore, different risk. A futures contract in the EURUSD has a face value of $125,000, crude oil is 1,000 bbls × $80 = $80,000, and 100 troy ounces of gold × $1,200 = $120,000 at the current price in May 2010. The volatility, expressed in dollars per day (the easiest way to put them all into the same common terms), must be used to determine the position size in order to equalize the risk on both sides of the pairs trade. Table 4.9 shows the imbalance between crude oil and gold in September 2008 during the subprime crisis. Both markets were volatile, but crude was more so, as shown by the smaller position, 10 contracts, compared with 17 gold contracts. The Net PL column also points out the very large equity swings from day to day, even though this trade netted a profit. Be sure to remember that these prices are the result of continuous back-adjusting of data, so they will not be the same as either the cash prices or futures prices on those days.

Different Holidays

When we discussed trading futures at the beginning of this chapter, we pointed out that these markets can have different hours and may not be open on the same days. Because this is a systematic program, we need a rule that tells us not to trade when one market is open and the other is closed. This can be done in two ways:

1. If the data are omitted, that is, one date does not appear in one of the markets.
2. If today's data are identical to yesterday's data, we assume it was forward filled because there was no trading. Some data services will repeat the data on a holiday.

TABLE 4.9 Trade in the crude-gold pair during high volatility.

Date	Closing Price		Momentum			Volatility		Crude		Gold		Trade Profit/Loss			
	Crude	Gold	Crude	Gold	Diff	Crude	Gold	Ctr	Entry	Ctr	Entry	Crude	Gold	Net PL	Cum PL
9/17/2008	125.20	861.70	21.69	83.17	−61.48	5214	3038	10	125.20	−17	861.70	0	0	0	0
9/18/2008	125.78	908.20	25.06	84.43	−59.36	5216	3544	10	125.20	−17	861.70	5800	−79814	−74014	−74014
9/19/2008	130.99	875.90	43.65	67.08	−23.43	5392	3960	10	125.20	−17	861.70	52100	55441	107541	33527
9/22/2008	137.61	920.20	93.58	90.87	2.71	5059	3971	0	125.20	0	861.70	66200	−76038	−9838	23689

When either of these situations occurs, no trades are entered or exited. If only one market is closed, then the profit or loss is calculated for the market that is open.

Results from 2007 through 2009

We've been consistently looking at results that use similar momentum periods and entry thresholds. If we continue to do the same, we get the results shown in Table 4.10.

These tests include the range of momentum calculations from 14 to 5 days, but only one entry threshold, ±50. Our previous tests included ±50 as the middle of the 40–60 range, but here we will look at varying the exit threshold. An exit threshold greater than zero means that we exit shorts sooner. For example, if the crude-EURUSD pair shows a stochastic difference of 55, we sell crude and buy EURUSD. If the exit threshold is 20, then the stochastic difference needs to drop only below 20, not to zero as in our previous tests, to exit the trade. The trade-off is that we exit sooner and avoid the risk associated with holding a position longer, but we will also have smaller profits. However, we might get more trades because the stochastic value can then increase again to above 50, generating a new signal. We would be taking advantage of market noise.

To avoid too much complication, only the entry of ±50 is used. If the results of using ±50 are poor, then it's not likely that we would be trading these pairs. In addition, Table 4.10 includes a breakdown of the results of each pair, as well as the average of all three.

Normally, we use the average of all pairs to decide the success of a group of related markets, but with these inflation pairs, it's not clear that they are related in the same way as, for example, energy markets. We have chosen three very different markets that we believe are used as an inflation hedge. The results will tell us how closely they track each other.

If we base our decision on the average of all pairs, shown in Table 4.10a, we find there were 15 of 18 profitable tests, and all the losing combinations used the longest calculation period of 14 days. Longer calculation periods imply longer holding periods for the trade, which decreases the advantage of noise; therefore, it is consistent with our concept. Our initial thought is that these pairs are good. The best ratios are at the faster end of the test, a 5-day calculation period. The exit threshold of ±10 is very good, with a ratio of 0.728, but the exit of ±20 is marginally lower and would get us out sooner. Therefore, we expect to trade these pairs with a momentum of 5, an entry of ±50, and an exit of ±20.

Fortunately, we also summarized the results of the individual pairs in parts b, c, and d. All three pairs had very different performance, and the average does not represent the sum of the parts.

TABLE 4.10 Test results in terms of the information ratio for three inflation pairs: (b) Crude-EURUSD, (c) crude-gold, and (d) EURUSD-gold, plus (a) the average of those pairs.

(a) All pairs, entry ±50, exits 0–±20

Period	0	±10	±20	Average
14	−0.230	−0.193	−0.201	−0.208
10	0.236	0.315	0.253	0.268
8	0.449	0.573	0.625	0.549
7	0.283	0.325	0.603	0.404
6	0.473	0.651	0.492	0.539
5	0.469	0.728	0.679	0.625
Average	0.280	0.400	0.409	

(b) Crude-EURUSD, entry ±50, exits 0–±20

Period	0	±10	±20	Average
14	0.302	0.301	0.490	0.364
10	0.912	0.921	0.555	0.796
8	0.389	0.436	0.409	0.411
7	0.909	0.648	0.704	0.754
6	0.509	0.598	0.467	0.525
5	0.641	0.677	0.661	0.660
Average	0.610	0.597	0.548	

(c) Crude-Gold, entry ±50, exits 0–±20

Period	0	±10	±20	Average
14	−0.717	−0.756	−0.792	−0.755
10	−0.627	−0.435	−0.280	−0.447
8	−0.300	−0.286	0.114	−0.157
7	−0.523	−0.135	0.223	−0.145
6	−0.486	−0.060	−0.138	−0.228
5	−0.598	−0.052	−0.023	−0.224
Average	−0.542	−0.287	−0.149	

(d) EURUSD-Gold, entry ±50, exits 0–±20

Period	0	±10	±20	Average
14	−0.279	−0.126	−0.301	−0.235
10	0.425	0.460	0.485	0.457
8	1.259	1.569	1.353	1.394
7	0.464	0.462	0.883	0.603
6	1.396	1.417	1.147	1.320
5	1.366	1.559	1.399	1.441
Average	0.772	0.890	0.828	

- *Crude-EURUSD* is the most consistent, with profits in every combination and ratios varying from 0.301 to 0.909. The row showing the detail for the calculation period of 10 is the best, but it looks as though it's an outlier because, without that row, the information ratio increases smoothly from the larger periods to the smaller. We prefer to pick anything in the lower part of the table. A momentum of 5 and exit of 10 seem reasonable and somewhat typical.
- *Crude-gold* is overall a poor performer, with only two profitable combinations out of 18. Even though we thought this could be a good pair, we need to eliminate it. By including these results in the average, we might have distorted those values so that any choice based on the average would also be poor.
- *EURUSD-gold* has the widest range of performance, from negative to very positive, and also has the highest average ratios. It also seems inconsistent because the rows for calculation periods 10 and 7 are much lower (but still profitable) than most of the others. Choosing the momentum period 5 and exit 10 from the lower section seems the safest.

That wasn't too difficult, but it was all hindsight. We picked the same parameters for the two pairs that seem to work. The cumulative profits for the period from 2007 through 2009 are plotted in Figure 4.9. The EURUSD-gold pair is consistently profitable; the crude-EURUSD pair has a fast, steady run-up, followed by a period sideways, before volatility and profitability returns.

The answer to our first question is *yes*, we could have made money during the period when these markets were considered an inflation hedge by the public. The second question is more difficult.

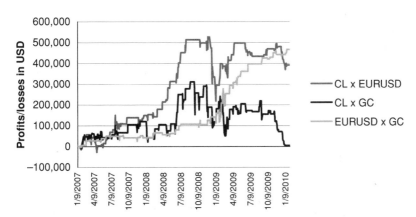

FIGURE 4.9 Cumulative PL for the three inflation pairs, crude-euro, crude-gold, and euro-gold, from 2007.

Could We Have Known When to Start Trading These Pairs?

We know that the subprime crisis caused unprecedented volatility. We can measure that volatility using the formula most often used by the financial industry:

$$\text{Annualized volatility} = \text{Stdev (returns)} \times \sqrt{252}$$

In order to recognize a change in volatility, we calculate a *rolling* standard deviation using the past 10 days. We've discussed before that using only 10 days and annualizing the value will occasionally cause annualized volatility to be greater than 100%. Because our interest is the relative difference in volatility, that won't cause any problems.

In Figure 4.10, the annualized volatility of the three futures markets is seen to change in late 2007, synonymous with the spike in crude oil but a full nine months before the subprime crisis. Had we started trading these pairs at that time, we would have captured the big moves in all three markets. By September 2009, the volatility of the EURUSD and gold had dropped back to previous levels. Crude followed in December 2009. Had we stopped trading when the volatility returned to normal, we might have netted profits in all three pairs.

Using volatility seems to be a simple way to qualify trading in inflation pairs. The volatile periods generate higher correlation between the markets and also increase liquidity. More investors who would not normally trade these markets are attracted to them during periods of high volatility. They are also pushed along by the commentators on the financial news

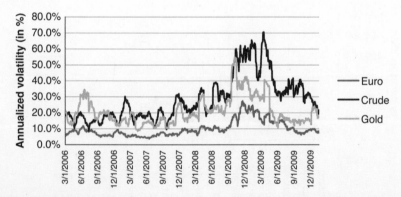

FIGURE 4.10 Annualized price volatility of the euro, crude oil, and gold shows spikes during the subprime crisis.

networks, who manage to convince the public of correlations (and so-called contagion) before they occur.

How Do We Decide, in Advance, Which Parameters to Use?

The most difficult question of the three is how to determine, in advance, which parameters to trade. The easiest answer is to find another period in the past when inflation and volatility were in the news and test that data. Certainly, the early 1980s would qualify, when gold rallied to $800/ounce and interest rates topped at 21%. But we would have to trade the Deutsche mark instead of the euro, which didn't exist at that time, and oil wasn't a factor because the price was so low between the oil shortage in the mid-1970s and the Iraq-Iran War in the mid-1980s that cost wasn't significant. Gold has also been an unreliable gauge of inflation. After the famous run to $800 in 1980, it came steadily down until it reached its low in September 2000. Buying gold at any price during those 20 years would have produced only steady losses.

We could not have found a similar situation using the same three markets, but there may have been other pairs that would show improved returns, and higher correlations, during volatile periods. If we look back at Chapter 3, the use of a low-volatility filter identifies similar situations, although much shorter time periods. It shows that pairs trading does best during periods of higher volatility.

For now, we'll be satisfied with using the past three years to identify the parameters, but if we can show that some other period had the same results, our confidence would increase tremendously. On the other hand, if we had no previous periods with the same profile, then we must base our decision of what parameters to use on the belief that higher volatility will generate the profits we need. There is often a point in developing a trading system when you must make a leap of faith after you've done as much work as possible. Tying performance to volatility seems to be a very small leap.

A Last Word about Inflation Pairs

Trading during periods of high volatility can be very risky, but we expect pairs trading to profit during high volatility because prices move apart quickly and correct just as fast. During periods of low volatility, prices may not move enough to generate profits in excess of costs. Markets that have caught the interest of the general public can offer great opportunity, triggered by a clear increase in volatility.

Having decided which of these markets reflects the most public interest, experience seems to be the key. When we looked at the changing

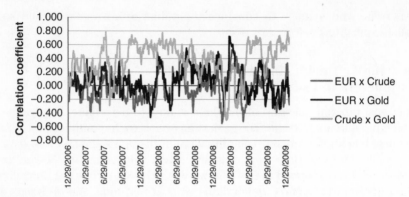

FIGURE 4.11 Rolling 20-day correlations of three inflation pairs. Crude-gold, which shows the highest correlation, had the worst performance.

correlations in the energy markets, we found that the dramatic rise in crude prices corresponded to increased correlations between all energy futures. We could attach a fundamental reason for that change; however, the inflation pairs are much more deceptive. Figure 4.11 shows the rolling 20-day correlations during the same period as the annualized volatility in Figure 4.10. With volatility, we saw a clear increase at the end of 2007 associated with profitable pairs trading. The correlations show that the crude-gold pair is generally more correlated and has moved to its strongest relationship at the end of 2009. But the crude-gold pair was the worst performer. There is a modest increase in the correlation of the EUR-gold pair from the beginning of 2008 until mid-2009, but afterward that pair is mostly negatively correlated, although by only a small amount. Yet EUR-gold was the most consistently profitable pair. If the correlations don't tell us anything, then we can only conclude that it's the money that moves the market. The pairs are profitable because the public believes these markets should react to inflation news, but their movements with regard to one another are unpredictable, just as price noise is unpredictable but profitable for a mean-reverting trader.

EQUITY INDEX PAIRS

We now come to the equity index markets, which are probably the most interesting for traders. During the past 10 years, these futures markets have seen a tremendous increase in activity from traders around the world. Although most of the European markets have been electronic since their inception, the U.S. markets have been slower to change, but the liquidity is now in the electronic contracts. Electronic trading has facilitated the ability to execute on the CME, EUREX, SIMEX, and nearly any other exchange in the world.

Many of the equity index markets can be traded as ETFs, but they are not as liquid or as efficient as futures markets. They do allow you to sell short with no restriction, and they do not need to be rolled when the contracts expire. The results shown in this section all use the smallest futures contracts traded, normally called *minis*. The commission costs for trading minis are much higher for the noncommercial investor than trading the original, larger contracts, but that's where all the liquidity is, so the increased commission cost may be offset by less slippage. The data start on November 21, 2005, when EUREX moved the close of the trading day to 22:00 European time (10 P.M. in New York) and ends on May 1, 2010. Given the windup needed to perform the calculations, this gives us nearly 4 1/2 years of performance for all markets. That can still generate a lot of trades because we hold positions for only a few days.

The markets used to form pairs will be the S&P, Nasdaq, Russell, Dow, EuroStoxx, DAX, CAC, and FTSE, a total of 8 markets and 28 pairs. Of these pairs, 6 are combinations of U.S. markets, 6 are European, and the remaining 16 are combinations of U.S. and European markets.

If you use the combined sessions for European markets, which means the original pit session followed by the evening session, the data will all end at nearly the same time. In the U.S., the evening session starts the new day for the electronic markets, which then ends at the close of the next pit session. In 2005, the European markets extended their hours to trade alongside the U.S. markets, so that they now close at 10 P.M., equivalent to 4 P.M. in New York. This facilitates pairs trading, even though volume on the European exchanges at the 10 P.M. close is considerably lighter than during European business hours. If Asian markets trade electronically 24 hours, it may be possible to include the Topix, Hang Seng, Nikkei, and others, but those markets won't be included here.

Again, we point out that if either leg of the pair does not trade because of a holiday, then no entries or exits are allowed, but daily profits and losses are calculated for the leg that is open. Futures trading is always marked to market each day. When we combine the results of the different pairs into the final portfolio, we must pay attention to any missing days, where there was no trading in one region but trading in the other. The results must be aligned by date.

We already know from previous discussions that shorter calculation periods are most likely to work because they capture more price noise, an advantage for mean-reversion strategies. In this case, we just test a small range of values to confirm that the same parameters work for the index markets as they did for others. We are hopeful that the concept is robust

TABLE 4.11	Average information ratio for 28 index pairs, from November 2005.		
	Entry Threshold		
Period	**±40**	**±50**	**±60**
4	1.311	1.008	0.685
5	1.169	0.851	0.585

and will produce orderly results. There are only six tests, calculation periods of 4 and 5 days, and entry thresholds of ±40, ±50, and ±60. A commission of 25 currency units (USD, EUR, or GBP) per round-turn per leg was charged to all trades, which is very conservative. Table 4.11 shows the results in terms of the information ratio.

The results do not distinguish between good and bad pairs and are simply the average of all 28. Because of that, we consider these quite good and confirm our expectations that faster trading is better. The final decision will be whether the profits per contract are large enough to offer some comfortable cushion to absorb unexpected slippage above the $25 commission cost. We know from experience that the fastest parameters, a period of 4 and short entry threshold of 40, will have the smallest unit returns but the best ratio. We'll look at those results in more detail.

Table 4.12 shows the basic statistics for the fastest parameters, 4 × 40. Only 4 of the 28 pairs show net losses; three of those pairs are combinations of U.S. markets, and the other is Nasdaq–EuroStoxx. If we try to classify the pairs into U.S. versus Europe and relate that grouping to the performance, we find some consistency. For example, the higher the correlation between the two legs, the lower the ratio and performance. If we sort Table 4.12 by the correlation column and then create a scatter plot of the correlations against ratios, we get the results in Table 4.13 and Figure 4.12.

Figure 4.12 is most descriptive. At the top left, the information ratio is greatest and the correlation smallest. At the bottom right is the opposite combination, high correlation and low performance. There seems to be a break in the chart at the horizontal line representing an information ratio of 1.0. Below that line, the values are spread out and less orderly; above the line, they form a clear pattern up and to the left. We can now look back at Table 4.13 and understand which pairs are most likely to succeed.

Starting from the top of Table 4.13, we can see that most of the combinations involve one U.S. index market and one European index market. The correlation of 0.431 between the Russell 2000 and the FTSE shows that these markets have only a modest relationship; that is, they move apart due to very different fundamentals but revert to the mean because all

TABLE 4.12 Results of all index pairs using a calculation period of 4 and entry threshold of ±40.

Leg 1	Leg 2	Corr	Trades	TotPL	AROR	Vol	Unit1	Unit2	Ratio
S&P	NASDAQ	0.859	26	−5168	−1.5	12	472	−331	−0.129
S&P	Russell	0.956	46	281772	5.8	12	−220	439	0.487
S&P	DJIA	0.949	5	−8896	−6.4	12	−90	−23	−0.530
S&P	EuroStoxx	0.823	26	57933	12.3	12	218	47	1.026
S&P	DAX	0.791	39	42844	5.4	12	333	−490	0.453
S&P	CAC	0.577	75	592602	31.5	12	118	580	2.624
S&P	FTSE	0.513	85	694970	35.0	12	153	655	2.917
NASDAQ	Russell	0.783	86	298294	14.7	12	−131	4330	1.229
NASDAQ	DJIA	0.812	34	−90395	−13.6	12	21	−258	−1.136
NASDAQ	EuroStoxx	0.708	56	−5590	−1.4	12	34	7	−0.116
NASDAQ	DAX	0.697	54	13152	0.9	12	−51	418	0.071
NASDAQ	CAC	0.488	101	278850	17.6	12	126	222	1.468
NASDAQ	FTSE	0.424	108	442334	27.7	12	70	502	2.308
Russell	DJIA	0.933	50	84366	7.0	12	352	−227	0.580
Russell	EuroStoxx	0.797	67	144825	11.1	12	499	−297	0.928
Russell	DAX	0.760	84	218840	17.8	12	501	−1072	1.482
Russell	CAC	0.458	114	724317	38.4	12	225	569	3.197
Russell	FTSE	0.431	123	797608	41.9	12	338	515	3.493
DJIA	EuroStoxx	0.797	33	5345	0.6	12	−52	102	0.049
DJIA	DAX	0.774	43	28210	4.0	12	190	−286	0.335
DJIA	CAC	0.563	82	530034	27.3	12	141	507	2.271
DJIA	FTSE	0.506	88	543157	28.3	12	145	564	2.356
EuroStoxx	DAX	0.955	3	2082	0.7	12	−430	2200	0.058
EuroStoxx	CAC	0.754	27	216085	28.8	12	−76	1066	2.397
EuroStoxx	FTSE	0.637	45	256891	30.5	12	26	807	2.543
DAX	CAC	0.728	38	955236	21.4	12	2	754	1.784
DAX	FTSE	0.620	74	1785002	34.7	12	198	788	2.895
CAC	FTSE	0.759	8	56673	20.0	12	−267	1247	1.670
Average		0.709	58	319335	15.7	12	102	476	1.311

TABLE 4.13 Index pairs in Table 4.12, sorted by correlation, highest to lowest.

Leg 1	Leg 2	Corr	Unit1	Unit2	Ratio
Russell	FTSE	0.431	338	515	3.493
Russell	CAC	0.458	225	569	3.197
S&P	FTSE	0.513	153	655	2.917
DAX	FTSE	0.620	198	788	2.895
S&P	CAC	0.577	118	580	2.624
EuroStoxx	FTSE	0.637	26	807	2.543
EuroStoxx	CAC	0.754	−76	1066	2.397
DJIA	FTSE	0.506	145	564	2.356
NASDAQ	FTSE	0.424	70	502	2.308
DJIA	CAC	0.563	141	507	2.271
DAX	CAC	0.728	2	754	1.784
CAC	FTSE	0.759	−267	1247	1.670
Russell	DAX	0.760	501	−1072	1.482
NASDAQ	CAC	0.488	126	222	1.468
NASDAQ	Russell	0.783	−131	4330	1.229
S&P	EuroStoxx	0.823	218	47	1.026
Russell	EuroStoxx	0.797	499	−297	0.928
Russell	DJIA	0.933	352	−227	0.580
S&P	Russell	0.956	−220	439	0.487
S&P	DAX	0.791	333	−490	0.453
DJIA	DAX	0.774	190	−286	0.335
NASDAQ	DAX	0.697	−51	418	0.071
EuroStoxx	DAX	0.955	−430	2200	0.058
DJIA	EuroStoxx	0.797	−52	102	0.049
NASDAQ	EuroStoxx	0.708	34	7	−0.116
S&P	NASDAQ	0.859	472	−331	−0.129
S&P	DJIA	0.949	−90	−23	−0.530
NASDAQ	DJIA	0.812	21	−258	−1.136

index markets react to global economic factors. Even more important than the global factors is the way traders buy and sell these markets, forcing them into similar patterns. While the economy of the U.K. may be perceived as quite different from that of the U.S., when the U.S. economic reports show unexpected strength or weakness, the FTSE reacts to that information. Similarly, there is a smaller but noticeable reaction in other countries if the Bank of England is the first to lower or raise interest rates after a period of stable rates.

Within Europe, the most profitable pairs are between the British FTSE and the German DAX or the EuroStoxx. These represent the widest difference in fundamentals within Europe, with the U.K. not part of the EU and seen as a weaker economy at the moment. But with most of the total trade

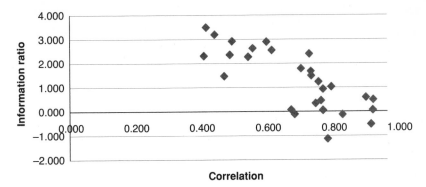

FIGURE 4.12 Scatter plot of index pairs showing the relationship between the correlation of the two legs and the ratio of the performance.

occurring between these two regions, their economies are clearly linked, and their equity index markets must reflect that relationship.

The only pair of U.S. equity index markets to make the cut is the Russell-Nasdaq, showing the highest correlation, 0.933. All of the U.S. equity index pairs show very high correlations, making the unit returns necessarily small. At the bottom of the performance list are three U.S. pairs. Although none of the same companies are part of the S&P 500 and Russell 2000 (large cap and small cap), they move in the same way and provide no opportunity for profit.

A clear example is the S&P-DJIA pair. Of course, all 30 stocks in the DJIA are also in the S&P, and because the DJIA stocks have the largest cap, they represent a disproportionate part of the S&P. The correlation is shown as 0.949 in Table 4.13. Figure 4.13 shows the momentum difference,

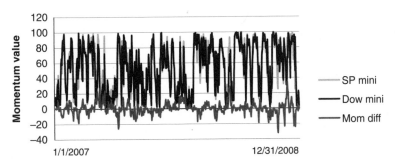

FIGURE 4.13 Momentum values for the S&P and Dow minicontracts during 2008 and 2009 using a calculation period of 8. None of the momentum differences reaches ±40.

the basis for the pairs signals, based on a calculation period of 8 days. While the two individual momentum values range from 0 to 100, the momentum difference reaches near 40 only once since 2000 and peaks over 20 only a few times during the entire period. Table 4.12, which has the detail for the 4-day momentum, shows that there were only five trades over the past five years, and those did not generate enough profit to overcome costs.

Pairs using the S&P futures contract are a typical example of results. In Figure 4.14, we see the NAVs of the seven pairs. The calculation of the NAVs will be given in the next section. For now, Figure 4.14a shows the best results are for the FTSE and CAC, with correlations against the S&P of 0.513 and 0.577, compared with the EuroStoxx and DAX with correlations of 0.823 and 0.791. However, all four results could be combined into

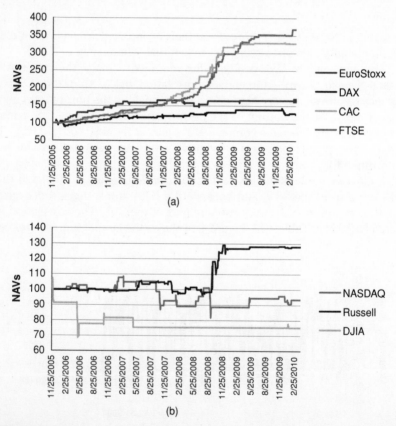

FIGURE 4.14 (a) Sample PL for S&P pairs (4 × 40) with European equity index futures, converted to USD, and (b) sample NAVs for S&P pairs with U.S. equity index futures.

a profitable portfolio. Note that the intervals with horizontal lines indicate there was no trading.

Figure 4.14b shows the results of the U.S. equity index pairs. The DJIA, the bottom line, shows long periods of no trading, confirming the high correlation exhibited in Figure 4.13. In the middle, Nasdaq has trades but can't overcome the commission cost, and at the top, the Russell shows positive returns, but all based on one distortion during September 2008. We would not want to base our expectations on having to repeat a 50% drop in the stock market.

Portfolio Diversification

Combining performance into a portfolio shows the value of diversification. To make this a manageable example, we will use only the four S&P pairs with the European index futures, the CAC, DAX, EuroStoxx, and FTSE, shown in Figure 4.14a. We start with the daily profits and losses and combine them, first adjusting each to a target volatility and then adjusting the final portfolio to a target volatility. Each step is explained in the following.

Step 1. Align the Daily Profits and Losses Table 4.14 starts on the first day of available data. The first pairs trade is initiated on December 8, 2005, and doesn't show a profit or loss until the close of the next day. In the left panel, the daily profits and losses are aligned by date. When using U.S. and European pairs, there will be many days when one or the other market doesn't trade, but the alignment process affects the signal generation rather than the profits and losses shown in the table.

Step 2. Normalize the Volatility and Find the Investment Size To give each pair an equal chance to contribute to the portfolio profits, we need to equalize the volatility of each pair. First calculate the standard deviation (volatility) of the return streams (not the cumulative profits) of each of the four pairs, and multiply each by the square root of 252 (the nominal number of business days in a year) to get the annualized volatility. Note that the profits and losses have first been converted to U.S. dollars using the daily spot exchange rates for the euro and sterling.

Once we have those values, shown in Table 4.15, we take the target volatility of 12% and divide that by the annualized volatility of each pair to get the investment size that would make the profit and loss changes equal to 12%. The total portfolio investment is the sum of the individual investments, $1,280,915. We could also have started with an investment size and converted the daily profits and losses to returns using that value, but we will cover that method later.

TABLE 4.14 Constructing a portfolio with an annualized volatility of 12% from daily profits and losses.

Date	Daily Profits and Losses				Daily Returns from Total Investment					NAV
	EuroStoxx	DAX	CAC	FTSE	EuroStoxx	DAX	CAC	FTSE	Portfolio Return	
11/25/2005	0	0	0	0						100.00
11/28/2005	0	0	0	0	0.0000	0.0000	0.0000	0.0000	0.0000	100.00
11/29/2005	0	0	0	0	0.0000	0.0000	0.0000	0.0000	0.0000	100.00
11/30/2005	0	0	0	0	0.0000	0.0000	0.0000	0.0000	0.0000	100.00
12/1/2005	0	0	0	0	0.0000	0.0000	0.0000	0.0000	0.0000	100.00
12/2/2005	0	0	0	0	0.0000	0.0000	0.0000	0.0000	0.0000	100.00
12/5/2005	0	0	0	0	0.0000	0.0000	0.0000	0.0000	0.0000	100.00
12/6/2005	0	0	0	0	0.0000	0.0000	0.0000	0.0000	0.0000	100.00
12/7/2005	0	0	0	0	0.0000	0.0000	0.0000	0.0000	0.0000	100.00
12/8/2005	0	0	0	0	0.0000	0.0000	0.0000	0.0000	0.0000	100.00
12/9/2005	0	0	3198	0	0.0000	0.0000	0.0061	0.0000	0.0061	100.33
12/12/2005	0	0	1207	0	0.0000	0.0000	-0.0023	0.0000	-0.0023	100.20
12/13/2005	0	0	1111	-1824	0.0000	0.0000	0.0021	-0.0035	-0.0014	100.13
12/14/2005	0	0	4534	-1348	0.0000	0.0000	0.0087	-0.0026	0.0061	100.46
12/15/2005	1783	2914	0	-1971	0.0034	0.0056	0.0000	-0.0038	0.0052	100.74
12/16/2005	7587	8021	0	6941	0.0145	0.0154	0.0000	0.0133	0.0432	103.08
12/19/2005	-2142	-3375	0	0	-0.0041	-0.0065	0.0000	0.0000	-0.0106	102.49
12/20/2005	-1599	-807	-1376	-1540	-0.0031	-0.0015	-0.0026	-0.0030	-0.0102	101.93
12/21/2005	-3623	-3348	-7701	-4568	-0.0069	-0.0064	-0.0148	-0.0088	-0.0369	99.91
12/22/2005	2904	2339	3319	1822	0.0056	0.0045	0.0064	0.0035	0.0199	100.98
12/23/2005	-1041	-1556	-801	250	-0.0020	-0.0030	-0.0015	0.0005	-0.0060	100.65
12/27/2005	-7791	-9599	-7795	0	-0.0149	-0.0184	-0.0149	0.0000	-0.0483	98.05
12/28/2005	1857	508	2983	0	0.0036	0.0010	0.0057	0.0000	0.0103	98.59
12/29/2005	-4166	-3624	-4658	-4746	-0.0080	-0.0069	-0.0089	-0.0091	-0.0330	96.84
12/30/2005	3694	3250	6151	909	0.0071	0.0062	0.0118	0.0017	0.0269	98.24

TABLE 4.15 Annualized standard deviation and corresponding investment needed to have an annualized volatility of 12%.

	EuroStoxx	DAX	CAC	FTSE
Ann StDev	13,000	19,733	58,395	62,582
Investment	108,335	164,439	486,624	521,516
		Total Investment		1,280,915

Step 3. Calculate the Returns for Each Pair   The second panel of Table 4.14, Daily Returns from Total Investment, is simply the daily profits and losses in the first panel, divided by the total investment size, the sum of the individual investments.

Step 4: Create the NAVs   The final NAVs must reflect our target volatility, the amount of risk we are willing to take. When we calculate the annualized standard deviation of the portfolio return column, we get 0.2236, more than 22%, an unacceptably high number. To adjust to our 12% target volatility, each return must be multiplied by 0.537. Then the NAVs begin at 100 and each subsequent NAV is

$$NAV_t = NAV_{t-1} \times (1 + R_t \times 0.537)$$

The final NAV stream at 12% volatility is shown in Figure 4.15. Although the performance flattens out in 2009, a portfolio of more pairs would add diversification and consistency. All pairs using the S&P are likely to have similar performance.

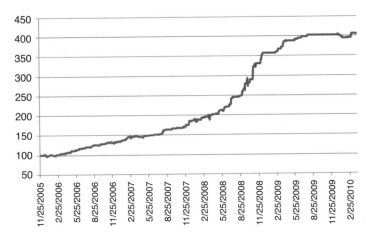

FIGURE 4.15   Portfolio of four S&P pairs adjusted to 12% volatility.

An alternative approach to constructing this portfolio, and one that will be useful when using diverse sectors, is to assign an arbitrary or an actual portfolio investment size. In this case, we can still use the sum of the investment sizes calculated using our current method, $1,280,915. We then

- Calculate the returns of each pair by dividing the daily profit or loss by the investment size, the same as the returns shown in panel 2.
- Next, find the annualized volatility of the returns of each pair. Only the one with the highest volatility, the FTSE, will show 12%. The others are

	EuroStoxx	DAX	CAC	FTSE
Volatility	0.0249	0.0378	0.1120	0.1200
Factor	4.8139	3.1715	1.0717	1.0000

- The *factor* in the table is the multiplier that changes the volatility to 12% for each return's stream.
- We calculate the portfolio returns by using Excel's sumproduct function, which multiplies each daily return by the factor and adds them together to get a portfolio return for that day.
- Again, we find the annualized standard deviation of the new portfolio returns and get 0.025. Dividing the target volatility of 0.12 by 0.025 gives a new return factor of 4.863.
- The final NAVs are created using the last formula given, but the return factor is 4.863 instead of 0.537.

You might think that this second method is unnecessary because it gives the same results as the simpler method shown first. However, when dealing with portfolios composed of diverse sectors, such as interest rates, equity index, and foreign exchange (FX), you must have each sector adjusted to the same volatility before you combine them into the final mix. For example, if you are allocating to these three sectors equally, and the interest rates have an annualized volatility of 5%, the equity index markets 20%, and FX 25%, then your risk exposure is 10% for rates, but 40% for index and 50% for FX. The profits and losses from interest rates will have only a small impact on the total portfolio. To maximize diversification, you must have all sectors adjusted to the same risk level before you apply your portfolio allocation percentage.

LEVERAGING WITH FUTURES

During the construction of the futures pairs, a target volatility of 12% was used. That means we have the ability to vary the number of futures contracts that we trade without increasing the portfolio investment size. There is a limit to the amount of leverage you can get using futures, but most investors should expect that their exposure (the face value of the futures contracts being traded) can be 4 to 6 times their investment. That's not possible with pairs using only stocks, where the cost of trading is the number of shares times the price per share. We don't consider stock margining, in which you borrow part of the funds.

We have discussed that margin in futures is very different from equities. Margin is a good faith deposit, where you are obligated to invest on average about 10% of the face value of the purchases. For example, if you buy one contract of crude oil at $80, you own 1,000 barrels, a value of $80,000. Typically, you need only a deposit of $8,000 unless you are a qualified commercial trader (in the oil business, a hedger), in which case your margin might be only 5%, or $4,000. Commercials are often able to provide a bank letter that guarantees any losses; therefore, it is not clear how much they put up as margin or what leverage they get.

Spreads are also given preferential margin. The exchange recognizes that buying one oil product and selling another related product has less risk than an outright position; therefore, the margin is also less, perhaps 5%. For exact amounts and which combinations of spreads qualify, you will need to refer to the exchange web sites, as well as contact your broker. Brokerage firms must conform to the exchange minimum requirements for margin, but they may choose to ask for more if they feel that the risk is higher.

Cross-market spreads, such as the S&P–DAX may not get lower margins, although some exchanges have cross-margin agreements. But let's use energy pairs as an example of leveraging.

Leverage Example

An example will make this clearer. Going back to the crude–natural gas pair, we calculate the annualized volatility of the daily profits and losses using the standard method: the standard deviation times the square root of 252. We get $132,671. An investment of $1,105,593 is needed to give that performance a volatility of 12% of the portfolio. However, with stocks we found that the amount needed as an investment was fixed, based on the number of shares times the share value. That's not the case for futures. Table 4.16 gives the necessary calculation.

For the pairs trade in crude–natural gas, we often took positions of 10 contracts in each leg; therefore, we will use that quantity here. The first column of Table 4.16 is the current price of crude and natural gas, followed by the size of the contract and the total value per contract. If we buy or sell 10 contracts, we are trading $800,000 worth of crude oil and $500,000 in natural gas, at total exposure of $1,300,000. The exchange considers a spread in two related markets as having less risk and will give lower margin

TABLE 4.16 Calculations needed to understand leverage in futures markets.

	Price	Contract	Value	Size	Total	Margin	Needed
Crude	80.00	1,000	80,000	10	800,000	0.05	40,000
Natural gas	5.000	10,000	50,000	10	500,000	0.05	25,000
Totals					1,300,000		65,000

requirements, for example, 5%. The last column shows that the amount needed to buy 10 crude and sell 10 natural gas is only $65,000.

If we could invest only the margin, our leverage would be 20:1. The volatility of $132,671 would be more than 200% rather than our target of 12%. However, brokerage firms require more than margin, although the exact amount varies from firm to firm and is also based on the net worth of the client and the amount of trading activity expected. Ironically, a good client, such as a hedge fund that trades in a large number of contracts, will have lower requirements, and those deposits might be a small amount of cash plus a credit note or some other form of collateral. As with Long-Term Capital Management, the bigger you get, the more you can negotiate, regardless of the exposure to risk.

But let's say you are an ordinary investor and the brokerage firm requires 4 times the margin as your deposit. That would change the $65,000 margin to a minimum investment of $260,000 and reduce the 200% volatility to a fourth, or 50%. Therefore, the amount required in your investment account for trading futures determines the amount of leverage you can achieve. In this case, $260,000 to buy $1.3 million in energy futures gives you a leverage of 5:1.

Varying the Leverage

In trading the crude–natural gas pairs, we varied the number of contracts but averaged no more than 10 per leg. Most investment managers target 12% volatility, or less, the same level we have been using in our examples.

Starting with the volatility of 50% based on a margin of 5% and brokerage requirements of 4 times the margin, we can reduce the annualized volatility of the portfolio to 12% by dividing the current volatility of 0.50 by the target volatility, giving a factor of 4.16. Then the investment needed to trade an average of 10 contracts of each leg is 4.16 × $260,000 = $1,083,333. The less you invest, the greater the leverage and the greater the risk. Remember that an annualized volatility of 12% means that there is still a 16% chance of seeing a loss greater than 12% in one year, and a 2.5% chance of having a loss greater than 24%. And if you don't see that loss in your first year, the chances are greater that you'll see it in the next year. By anyone's standards, that can be a lot of risk.

LONDON METALS EXCHANGE PAIRS

The six nonferrous metals traded on the London Metals Exchange (LME) are another group of futures markets that seems natural for arbitrage. This group of markets consists of aluminum, copper, lead, nickel, tin, and zinc. In different ways, each of these markets is related to each of the others through commercial and individual home construction, copper for plumbing, others for stainless steel. It is said that the floor traders will arbitrage any combination of these markets because, during an expanding economy or real estate boom, they all move in the same direction. Figure 4.16 shows that the six markets have similar movements, although nickel seems to be out of phase with the others.

Trading on the LME is different from trading on other exchange-traded futures markets. First, trading occurs during four sessions, when each metal is traded for a relatively short period in turn. The traders aren't standing in a pit yelling and using hand signals; most often, they are directors of large metals firms sitting in a circle, called a *ring*. Although there could be a lot of active trading when prices are moving quickly, it could also look more like a poker game during quiet times. Contract sizes are large, and delivery dates are designated during trading; they do not need to be on specific dates set by the exchange but can correspond to the commercial needs of the trader. For convenience, we can choose a delivery date

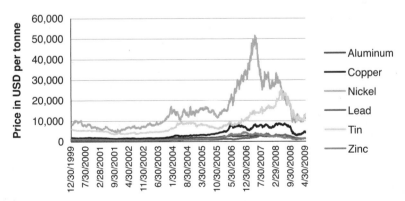

FIGURE 4.16 LME nonferrous metals, from January 2000 through April 2009, quoted in USD per tonne. There is similar movement in all markets, but nickel seems to be out of phase with the others.

for copper, for example, that corresponds to the same delivery date as the NYMEX copper contract, but any delivery date is acceptable when trading. For these tests, we use the rolling three-month contract, so that any position entered will deliver three months from the entry date. That gives enough time to exit the trade without the need to roll forward or be forced out because of contract expiration and delivery.

Using the same parameters and rules we have for other markets, we tested the six LME metals from January 2000 through April 2009. The results, shown in Table 4.17, are dismal. Not one combination was profitable. As we noticed in the price chart, Figure 4.16, nickel has the lowest overall correlation to the other metals, but the pairs aluminum-copper, aluminum-zinc, and copper-zinc all have reasonably good correlations. We would have expected them to be profitable. There is always something to be learned by looking at more detail. Sometimes you find a relationship that can make the entire process, including the good results we've already seen, even better—often by reducing the risk. With that end in mind, we will look at the pair of the two most liquid markets, aluminum and copper, at the top of the table.

To understand the price relationship between the aluminum and copper, we need a more accurate view of prices, found in Figure 4.17. The

TABLE 4.17   LME pairs results, January 2000 to April 2009, using parameters ±50 x 10.

Pair							PL/	
Leg 1	Leg 2	#Tr	Total PL	NAV	AROR	Corr	Share	Ratio
Aluminum	Copper	46	−26403	74.5	−3.1	.723	−3.91	−0.259
Aluminum	Nickel	80	−32356	80.6	−2.3	.478	−3.74	−0.191
Aluminum	Lead	80	−135901	48.6	−7.4	.491	−5.57	−0.621
Aluminum	Tin	83	3845	95.1	−0.5	.384	0.36	−0.045
Aluminum	Zinc	65	−75043	57.4	−5.8	.614	−5.47	−0.482
Copper	Nickel	79	−264212	62.6	−4.9	.535	−28.60	−0.409
Copper	Lead	75	−422762	45.9	−8.0	.534	−11.97	−0.670
Copper	Tin	85	−607503	40.5	−9.3	.450	−45.77	−0.772
Copper	Zinc	64	−105715	69.3	−3.9	.674	−5.07	−0.323
Nickel	Lead	92	−4094386	40.8	−9.2	.416	−18.92	−0.764
Nickel	Tin	82	−2502113	65.1	−4.5	.388	−66.31	−0.376
Nickel	Zinc	89	−225199	87.7	−1.4	.496	−1.60	−0.116
Lead	Tin	92	−108849	70.7	−3.7	.342	−10.06	−0.305
Lead	Zinc	72	−9304	89.4	−1.2	.549	−0.75	−0.100
Zinc	Tin	88	−360127	44.3	−8.4	.383	−32.25	−0.697

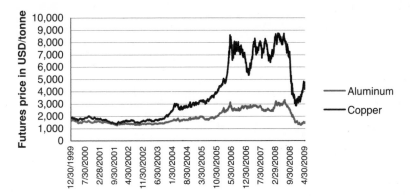

FIGURE 4.17 Price moves in aluminum and copper have many similarities that would make them a good candidate for pairs trading.

two metals have very similar moves, although copper is significantly more volatile. The bull market that started in 2003 first peaks in 2006 but doesn't collapse until the subprime crisis in 2008. While the copper price drop in 2007 is not seen in aluminum, many of the other moves are similar. Given volatility adjustments for position size, these two look as though they are a good candidate for pairs trading.

The returns, however, don't reflect what we think should be true. Profits were generated steadily through late 2006, followed by a large drawdown, and finally another profitable period beginning in late 2007, shown in Figure 4.18. What happened to cause the large losing period? Our first thought is to look at volatility.

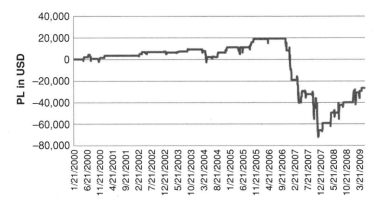

FIGURE 4.18 Cumulative profits/losses for the aluminum-copper pair. Profits drop sharply beginning in October 2006 and then rally in late 2007.

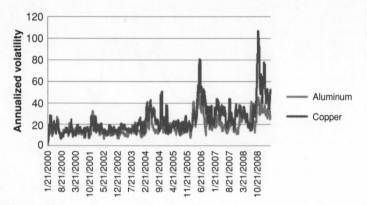

FIGURE 4.19 Volatility of aluminum and copper as measured by the annualized standard deviation.

The standard calculation for volatility is the standard deviation of returns times the square root of 252. Although 20 days is standard for option volatility, we use 14 days to correspond to the same period as the stochastic indicator used for momentum. Using 14 days rather than 20 will be a little less stable; that is, fewer days will tend to show more volatility. In Figure 4.19, we see that copper has been much more volatile than aluminum, spiking to about 80 in 2006, when aluminum reached only 40, and peaking at almost 110 in 2008, when aluminum reached about 45. However, neither of these spikes corresponds to the problem dates seen in the cumulative profits and losses. In fact, when the subprime crisis drove the price of copper sharply lower, the pairs trade was adding steady gains to the total returns. But when a pairs trade has a large imbalance in the position size, then there is potential risk and potential loss. For example, if we had 20 contracts of aluminum and 5 of copper, then we can say that copper is four times more volatile. Because volatility is measured over only 14 days, that value can change quickly. If aluminum became volatile and copper quiet, we would be exposed to large swings in returns. We can say that it would be prudent to limit the trades entered when there is a large position imbalance.

Dangers of High Leverage

As a side note, the large discrepancy between the position sizes means that we have assumed much greater leverage in one market based on relatively low volatility. This situation is similar to what happened in the hedge fund industry in 2010 for those trading interest rates.

As yields fell to unprecedented low levels, they also showed excep-tionally low volatility. If rates are only one of a number of sectors in the hedge fund portfolio, then the returns of that sector must be leveraged up to have the same impact as other sectors and provide both comparable returns and diversification. Then, as interest rate volatility fell, positions got bigger, and at some point they were disproportionally large compared with other sectors. This poses a real threat of disaster due to event risk. A price shock that moves the market against you can wipe out all your gains—and perhaps your entire investment.

The only way to avoid this is to cap your leverage, that is, put a limit on the size of the position you can take based on low volatility. That would reduce the risk, but capping one sector or asset puts the portfolio out of balance. Interest rates would not contribute the right amount to the diversification of the portfolio, and the hedge fund has reduced its diversification.

If maintaining the diversification is most important (and it is an important way to control risk), then all positions in the portfolio must be reduced in the same ratio when the interest rates are capped. That way, the shape of the portfolio remains the same. Unfortunately, potential returns are reduced along with the risk, but you can't have both. Keeping the integrity of the shape of the portfolio at the cost of lower returns and lower risk is the best choice for the investor.

Alternate Way of Calculating Pairs Risk

We are now concerned that large differences in the annualized volatility, combined with equally different position sizes in the legs of the pairs trade, can result in unacceptably large risk. But the position size is calculated using the average true range (ATR), so we need to see if that tells us anything. Figure 4.20 shows that a structural change took place in early 2006

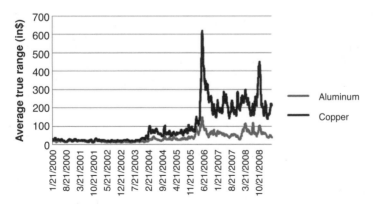

FIGURE 4.20 Volatility of aluminum and copper as measured by the average true range.

that may correspond to the drop in performance. Copper volatility spiked above $600/tonne while aluminum reached only $150/tonne, a ratio of 4:1. Although the change in volatility looks clear, we might also find an imbalance before 2006, possibly at the beginning of 2004, when copper volatility touched $100/tonne and aluminum was well down, near $30/tonne. Using the ATR instead of the traditional annualized volatility measure gives us much more information.

To distinguish between high volatility and extreme volatility, we will create a rule that combines both the annualized standard deviation and the average true range.

Do not enter a new position, and exit any existing trade, if both of the following two factors hold:

1. The ratio of the position sizes is less than the position ratio threshold (this can be written as min(size1/size2,size2/size1) < position ratio threshold).
2. The annualized volatility of leg 1 > annualized volatility threshold or the annualized volatility of leg 2 > annualized volatility threshold (called the "high" filter).

To see if our premise works, and to find the value of the thresholds, we run a series of tests on values of both thresholds. For the annualized standard deviation, the choices are 15% through 30% in varying small steps of 5% or less (the high filter), and for the average true range, we test from 0.20 through 0.90, in steps of 0.10. The results are given in Table 4.18. The pattern of improvement is consistent for the ATR, but much narrower for the annualized volatility (STD). We also looked at trading only when the volatility was high—that is, removing trades below the threshold—as shown in the part of the table marked STD Low. Results were actually more consistent than STD High, but the number of trades was very small. If we look at the cumulative profits and losses of the best filter tests, compared with no filters and with both filters, we can see the results in Figure 4.21.

Can we use these results? The ATR and the ATR plus the STD low filter look good, and the result is just what we wanted. The statistics for the combined filters, STD 30 (low) and ATR 35, had 31 trades, $47,071 in profits, 6.5% annualized return, and a ratio of 0.539. There was no trading during the period of loss in 2006 and 2007, and the cumulative profits move steadily higher. That's all good.

On the negative side, we have clearly fitted the results. It's good that the ATR had progressively better performance and consistent ratios, but the positive results from the annualized standard deviation were in a very narrow range, and the best results used the most volatile prices when we

TABLE 4.18 Test results showing the comparison of filter thresholds for aluminum-copper.

Filter	Threshold	Trades	Total PL	AROR	Ratio
No filter	0.00	46	−26403	−3.1	−0.259
STD Low	0.15	31	−42866	−4.7	−0.389
	0.20	15	3930	−0.2	−0.014
	0.25	8	1882	−0.4	−0.033
	0.30	5	22117	5.5	0.462
	0.35	1	11194	7.5	0.624
STD High	0.15	4	−2912	−3.4	−0.280
	0.17	10	6617	3.4	0.287
	0.20	16	13477	4.6	0.385
	0.22	19	−11413	−3.0	−0.249
	0.25	26	−6229	−1.8	−0.149
	0.30	32	−33371	−4.6	−0.384
ATR	0.25	40	−30991	−3.8	−0.313
	0.35	27	34518	5.1	0.427
	0.45	19	16731	4.6	0.383
	0.55	14	9242	3.8	0.314
	0.70	9	8808	4.1	0.339
	0.80	5	6979	4.5	0.379
	0.90	3	3470	2.2	0.189

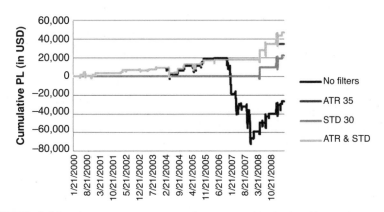

FIGURE 4.21 Aluminum-copper cumulative PL with volatility filters.

were trying to filter those periods. For that reason, we would reject the annualized volatility results (both STDs) and use only the ATR filter. In Figure 4.21, the combined filters results are identical to the ATR filter results except at the very end, where the use of the STD adds some value.

Distortion Filter

In Chapter 3, we introduced the high-distortion filter, or distortion ratio. This is a simple way of recognizing when two markets are acting very differently based entirely on the relative position sizes needed to equalize the volatility of the two legs. The implication is that when the two legs have very different volatilities, then:

- The leg with the lower volatility and the larger position may have an unusually big move, causing an unusually large profit or loss relative to the other leg.
- Or the leg with the lower volatility and the larger position may not move at all, thus not providing the market-neutral effect that we are trying to achieve.

The distortion ratio is simply the minimum of the leg 1 position size divided by the leg 2 position size or the leg 2 size divided by the leg 1 size, so that the distortion increases as the ratio gets smaller. For example, if the leg 1 size is 10 contracts and the leg 2 size is 7 contracts, then the distortion ratio is 0.7; or if leg 1 is 7 and leg 2 is 10, the ratio is also 0.7. In Table 4.19, the distortion ratio is tested against both the 14- (left) and 4-day (right) momentum results of the aluminum-copper pair. In both cases, the results are significantly improved by choosing trades that have similar volatility (higher ratios); however, these levels are different for each of the calculation periods. The position sizes are based on the same calculation periods as the momentum, so it should not be surprising that these levels are different. By fixing the period for determining position size, rather than using the same period as the momentum calculation, these results will be more uniform and interpreted as robust.

It is equally important to view the results of using the distortion filter. Figure 4.22 makes this clear. The filter does exactly what it is intended to do: remove trades that could present higher risk, and keep those trades with more balanced positions. The 4-day momentum produces twice as many trades as the 14-day, so there are more remaining after the filter is applied. As we can see from the horizontal lines in the figure, there are long periods of time with no trades, although fewer with the 4-day momentum. Our conclusion is that the filter works, but we're not interested

TABLE 4.19 The distortion ratio applied to both the 14- and 4-day momentum results for the aluminum-copper pair.

	14-day Calculation Period					4-day Calculation Period				
	Threshold	Trades	Total PL	AROR	Ratio	Threshold	Trades	Total PL	AROR	Ratio
No filter	0.00	46	−26403	−3.1	−0.259	0.00	83	41750	3.1	0.257
Filter	0.90	3	4970	3.4	0.282	0.90	2	4753	5.1	0.426
	0.80	5	10084	6.6	0.550	0.80	10	11374	5.9	0.489
	0.70	9	14981	7.1	0.591	0.70	14	15355	6.7	0.555
	0.60	13	14865	6.1	0.509	0.60	24	24306	5.6	0.467
	0.50	17	−6064	−2.2	−0.181	0.50	36	41964	8.9	0.745
	0.40	23	2041	−0.3	−0.027	0.40	47	59471	10.0	0.837
	0.30	35	−23218	−2.7	−0.228	0.30	62	71723	8.0	0.663
	0.20	42	−63499	−5.5	−0.415	0.20	77	30190	2.1	0.172

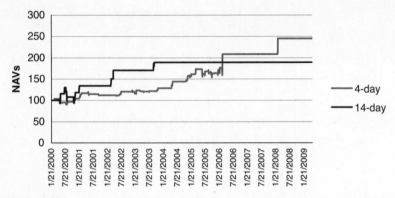

FIGURE 4.22   Net performance of the aluminum-copper pairs after applying the distortion filter.

in trading it because there is not enough activity. We have learned two important points:

1. The distortion filter has merit.
2. We can find a way of turning a loss into a profit.

But have we just completed an exercise in overfitting? We could go on to test if the filter works on other LME pairs, but the overall results of pairs trading are poor. In the next chapter, we will change our approach and look at trends in these pairs, but before moving on, there is another example of volatility distortion that makes this distortion index more relevant.

Lead and Zinc

If we think of this as an in-sample test, we now want to know if using the ATR as a filter works for the other pairs. We've rejected the use of the annualized standard deviation. We choose to look at lead-zinc because it has an average number of trades (72), average correlation (0.549) compared to the high correlation for aluminum-copper (0.723), and poor performance, shown in Figure 4.23. Returns follow the same pattern as aluminum-copper, gaining small, steady profits until 2006, then dropping precipitously before a recovery begins. Given the same pattern, we would like the exact same solution to work. Unfortunately, that's not the case. While the original test with no filters had 72 trades, a loss of $9,304, and a ratio of –0.100, the ATR filter of 0.35 had 61 trades, a loss of $26,354, and a ratio of –0.178. Why are the results so different?

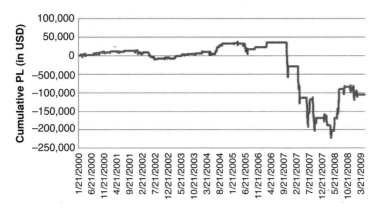

FIGURE 4.23 Cumulative PL for lead-zinc shows the same general pattern as the aluminum-copper pair.

Because we are filtering volatility, a look at the relative volatility of lead and zinc, compared with aluminum and copper, should show why our filter didn't work. In Figure 4.24, the annualized standard deviation is much the same for the two markets, unlike the extreme volatility of copper. We see that lead was more volatile in late 2008, but zinc had been more volatile in mid-2006. Overall, there is not enough of a difference to distinguish one from the other. But then, we are no longer using the annualized volatility.

On the other hand, the ATR in Figure 4.25 again shows that it's a better measure of volatility. In 2006, zinc spikes well above lead, much more than copper above aluminum. With its peak at about 270 and the corresponding peak in lead at about 60, zinc is more volatile by a factor of 4.5. Unlike

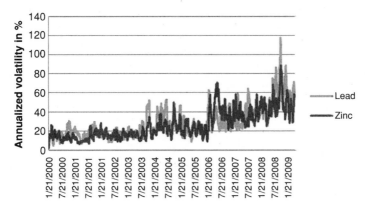

FIGURE 4.24 The annualized volatilities of lead and zinc show that they are very similar and would not be useful to distinguish risk.

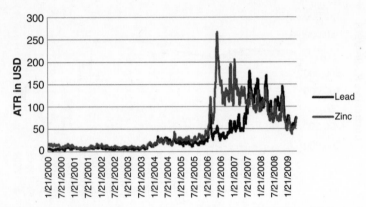

FIGURE 4.25 ATR volatility comparison of lead and zinc shows a different pattern from aluminum and copper.

copper, which remained more volatile than aluminum, zinc fell back into its previous pattern and even trades marginally below the volatility of lead.

Is there a threshold value that turns lead-zinc losses into profits? To find that answer, it is necessary to run tests on various values of the ATR threshold, actually the ratio of the position sizes calculated using the ATR. Those results can be seen in Table 4.20. If you look back at the copper tests in Table 4.18 (the bottom panel), the returns jumped from a large loss to a large gain when the threshold increased from 0.25 to 0.35. Here we started from 0.35 because that value showed a loss, then moved up. As the threshold becomes larger, the relative difference between the position sizes that will cause the filter to be activated will become smaller. For this pair, the trigger value is 0.50, where one position is twice the size of the

TABLE 4.20 Test of the ATR filter for lead-zinc shows profits once past the 0.50 threshold (twice the position size).

Filter	Threshold	Trades	Total PL	AROR	Ratio
No filter	0.00	72	−9304	−1.2	−0.100
ATR	0.35	61	−26354	−2.1	−0.178
	0.40	59	−25918	−2.1	−0.176
	0.45	55	−28091	−2.2	−0.186
	0.50	53	86280	4.7	0.395
	0.55	49	86407	4.8	0.402
	0.60	45	80854	4.5	0.373
	0.65	38	64461	3.7	0.307
	0.70	29	22539	1.0	0.084

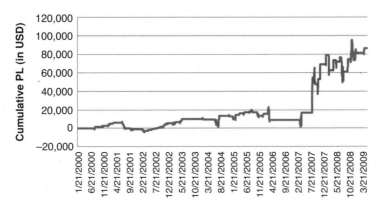

FIGURE 4.26 Cumulative PL for lead-zinc using the ATR filter of 0.50.

other. Any trade with one leg twice that of the other will not be entered, and if at any time during the trade, the volatility of the two legs is such that one is more than twice the other, that trade will be exited.

Using the ATR threshold of 0.50, the cumulative profits are shown in Figure 4.26. Again, it is similar to the filtered results of aluminum-copper. It avoids trades during the highly volatile period in 2006, then begins trading again when the relative volatility of the two legs comes back to normal. It seems reasonable. Should you be comfortable trading this method? No.

VOLATILITY FILTERS

This chapter gives a simple solution to a basic pairs trading concept. We enter when the two prices are relatively far apart. We exit when they come back together. We adjust the two legs so that we have equal risk and equal opportunity. That worked well for the housing sector and the equity index markets, where all pairs used exactly the same parameters.

We then found that the metals markets do not work well under extreme volatility. It is clear that the metals pairs we observed had very similar patterns and could be solved by creating a volatility filter—that is, a relative volatility filter—to identify when one of the legs was much more volatile than the other. We reason that the more volatile leg could overwhelm the profits and losses, or that the less volatile leg has the potential of becoming much more volatile (possibly due to event risk), causing our risk balancing to fail. Although the same situation occurs with each pair, the volatility threshold would also be different for each one. Is that an acceptable solution?

You may rationalize the results and say that we should expect those differences and that if the threshold is only shifted up or down by some small amount, then the answer is still valid. It may not be possible for anyone to say whether that is right or wrong. The market will tell you. For now, let us say that the better solution is when the parameters and rules are identical for all pairs.

INTEREST RATE FUTURES

There are many similarities between equity index and interest rate futures. There are at least four exceptionally liquid markets in the U.S. (Eurodollars, 5-year notes, 10-year notes, and 30-year bonds), and there are comparable futures markets in Europe (Euribor, Eurobobl, Eurobund, British long gilt, and the short sterling). As you would expect, there are stronger correlations between interest rate markets than between equity index markets. Our experience says that with high correlations, profits would be very small and survival would depend on extremely low transaction costs, the venue of the professional traders. That does not turn out to be entirely true. There is opportunity trading interest rate pairs when one leg is a U.S. interest rate and the other is European.

Rather than include those markets in this chapter, we will look at them in Chapter 7, "Revisiting Pairs Using the Stress Indicator." Readers are encouraged to try these pairs using the momentum difference method covered in Chapters 3 and 4.

SUMMARY

Although the rules were clearly specified in Chapter 3 and the same parameters were used for all examples in this chapter, the purpose was to show how a simple method can be used in different markets to create trading opportunities. No rules or calculations have been omitted, but some of the test statistics were summarized and not shown in detail.

To implement this, you will need to put this into a spreadsheet or computer program and verify all the results. You cannot rely on anyone else's numbers when it's your money that is at risk. You will need to understand the process, do the calculations, and place the orders with precision. To help you, there are sample spreadsheets available at www.wiley.com/go/alphatrading.

CHAPTER 5

Risk-Adjusted Spreads

N ot all trading that removes directional risk is mean reverting. There are times when two related markets move steadily apart, with one product more desirable than another or one company doing better than another. There are many examples in the stock market. One classic case was Dell and Compaq. Compaq was the early success story in personal computers and the first company to use MS-DOS (the first product of Microsoft) in the early 1980s. In a sign of the evolution of small computers, Compaq acquired Digital Equipment Corporation in 1998, the most prestigious minicomputer company. In another turn of the tables, Dell's new business model, selling computers with no retail outlets, rapidly overwhelmed other manufacturers, and by 2002 Compaq was forced to merge with Hewlett-Packard. Even the Compaq name didn't survive for long.

DELL AND HEWLETT-PACKARD

For the past 10 years, Dell and Hewlett-Packard share prices have flip-flopped, with Dell leading for the first five years and HP overtaking Dell in 2006, as shown in Figure 5.1. An investor normally takes advantage of these broad moves by studying the fundamentals of both companies. If they are clever enough to realize that Dell's business model worked brilliantly when profit margins were high but would suffer as price competition became more intense, they could have sold Dell short and bought Hewlett-Packard, netting a hefty gain. But our focus is on systematic, algorithmic trading.

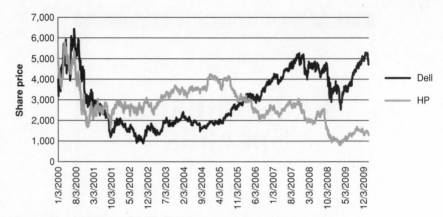

FIGURE 5.1   Dell and Hewlett-Packard share prices from 2000.

A basic way to track these markets is to use the standard 200-day moving average. The only thing special about the 200-day moving average is that many traders watch it and it has taken on the role of a significant indication of market trend. We might have expected a 250-day, a 125-day, or a 63-day average to be more interesting because they are multiples of calendar quarters (in business days), and stocks report earnings quarterly. However, it's never a good idea to fight the market, so we'll stay with 200 days. Figure 5.2 shows the 200-day averages for Dell and HP from 2000. The trends are very clear and remain intact for months and years at a time. Simply buying when the trend turns up and selling short when the trend turns down would have been a successful strategy.

However, following the trend of these two stocks independently means that from 2003 through mid-2005, you would have been long both companies and, during 2001 and from 2008 through mid-2009, you would have been short both. During those periods, amounting to about half the data, you would be exposed to directional risk. The purpose of this book is to avoid directional risk; therefore, we'll only look at positions where we are short one stock and long the other.

If we're patient, we could trade only when the two trends are going in opposite directions. That would actually give us hedged positions, some of which would be held for a long time. It also would create a lot of small trades, many of which will be losses. Even though the moving averages look smooth, and we take our positions from the direction of the moving average, the eye can deceive us. During the sideways period in 2002, the Dell trend wiggled up and down, causing false signals. Figure 5.3 shows the spread trades by posting a +1 when we are buying Dell and selling short HP, a –1 when we are selling Dell short and buying HP, and a 0 when we

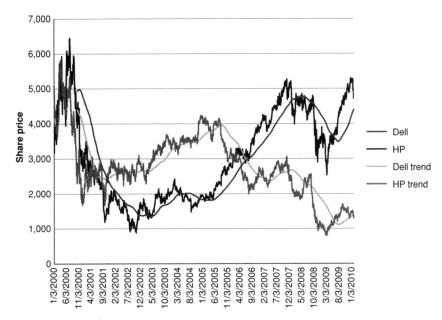

FIGURE 5.2 The 200-day moving averages applied to Dell and Hewlett-Packard.

have no position (both trends are moving in the same direction). We want the chart to have continuous horizontal lines at +1 or −1, which means that we held the trade for a long time, as we did from about September 2005 through April 2007. Unfortunately, that is the only sustained position. From mid-2001 through April 2005, the lines going up and down indicate positions that have been closed out and reset. When more positions are reset, there are more losses.

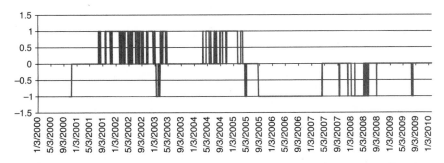

FIGURE 5.3 Dell-HP trades when their trends are going in the opposite direction.

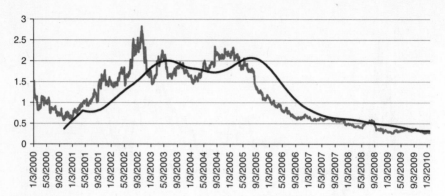

FIGURE 5.4 The Dell/HP ratio with a 200-day moving average.

The better way to look at the Dell-HP trade is by using the ratio of their prices, in this case Dell divided by HP. Some analysts use the difference in prices, but that creates a very different picture. For example, when Dell and HP were both $25, the ratio would be 1.0 and the difference would be zero. If Dell moved to $50 while HP remained at $25 then the ratio would be 2.0 and the difference $25. The ratio indicates that Dell is twice the price of HP, even if Dell was $100 and HP was $50. At that point, the difference would be $50. We would need to remember the starting value of $25 to know that we had doubled the difference. As prices got higher, the differences would also get larger, reflecting higher volatility. But the ratio remains a percentage measurement and offers more consistency.

Figures 5.4 and 5.5 show the ratio and difference, each with a 200-day moving average. Both of the trends are smoother than the trends of the two

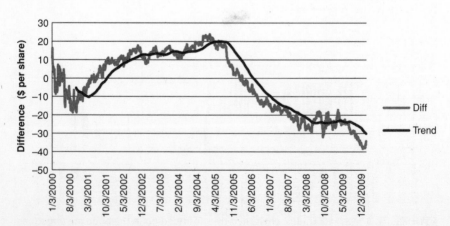

FIGURE 5.5 The Dell-HP difference with a 200-day moving average.

stocks separately, as seen in Figure 5.2. The ratio shows a few sustained, smooth trends, while the trend of the differences has two periods where it reversed direction numerous times, during 2003 and 2004 and then again in 2008 and 2009. Strictly from a practical view, the ratio performs better. To show this clearly, we calculated the number of trades for each method, where a trade is based only on the direction of the moving average line and not triggered by the price penetrating the moving average. The trend of the ratio had only 6 trades based on the changing direction of the 200-day trend line, while the trend of the differences had 60 trades over the same period, of which 17 were reversed after only one day. Without calculating the performance of the differences, the net returns using differences are likely to be a large loss.

To trade the ratio, we buy Dell and sell HP short when the trend of the ratio is up, and sell Dell short and buy HP when the trend of the ratio is down. As we did for pairs trading in the previous two chapters, the positions must be balanced according to their volatility. This maximizes diversification and reduces risk. In this case, the volatility was calculated using the average true range over the past 120 days, and the size of the positions were not changed during the length of the trade. Table 5.1 shows the six individual trades for the Dell/HP ratio. In 2001, HP was more volatile than Dell; consequently, it has only 79 shares compared with Dell's 100. During the next few years, as Dell showed more success than HP, it shows more volatility and smaller positions than HP. Overall, the percentage returns over less than nine years were greater than 11% per annum. More important, the big picture satisfies our general concept of when we would go long and short these two stocks, given a strategic approach to trading. And, of course, there is no directional risk.

TRADING BOTH LONG-TERM (HEDGED) TRENDS AND SHORT-TERM MEAN REVERSION

The trades in this chapter focus on the long-term divergence of two stocks or futures markets. This divergence can occur even while there are short-term opportunities for statistical arbitrage. The reason for this can be found in Chapter 2. If we look at prices over a very short time interval, we see more noise, but over the longer period, the trend is dominant. We can then be arbitraging Dell and HP over 3-day intervals but be long HP and short Dell for the longer-term trade.

In general, any calculation period under 10 days is targeting market noise, and those over 30 days are looking for the trend. Macrotrend strategies typically use trends in the range of 60 to 80 days, but those periods

TABLE 5.1 Trades for Dell and HP using the 200-day moving average of the Dell/HPQ ratio.

Date	Trades						Returns in USD			Returns in %		
		DELL			HPQ		DELL	HPQ	Total	DELL	HPQ	Total
6/25/2001	Buy	100	24.45	Sell	−79	24.14						
6/6/2003	Sell	−100	31.35	Buy	126	19.87	690	337	1027	28.22	13.97	42.19
8/11/2004	Buy	100	33.57	Sell	−136	17.76	−222	−266	−488	−7.08	−13.38	−20.46
7/18/2005	Sell	−100	40.64	Buy	146	23.48	707	−778	−71	21.06	−43.80	−22.74
12/10/2009	Buy	100	13.23	Sell	55	50.06	2741	3881	6622	67.45	165.28	232.72
12/30/2009	Sell	−100	14.79	Buy	55	52.93	156	158	314	11.79	3.15	14.94
1/29/2010	Exit		12.90			47.07	189	−322	−133	12.78	−6.09	6.69
Totals							4261	3010	7271	134.22	119.13	253.35

could be longer rather than shorter. In the previous example we used a 200-day average to base our technical version of a fundamental, or value, trade in order to emphasize the trend and minimize noise.

Balancing Fundamentals and Technicals

There is constant debate over which is better, fundamental (or value) trading or technical analysis. The reality is that both can be good or bad. With fundamental analysis, you take a long position because the stock is undervalued, and if it goes down but there is no new information to say that fundamentals have changed, you simply own the stock at an even better price. Then the risk of a value trade can be very large, and there is no way to put a limit on it by using the same fundamental data.

Technical traders have a different problem. Because they may be following a long-term trend, they could go long Eurodollar interest rates when the price is 99.75 (a yield of 0.25%). The return is severely limited because prices can only go to 100, but the risk can be much greater (understanding that there can also be carry profits). The trend calculation does not know that yields are at historic lows and that the risk/reward of the trade is very unattractive. Some traders would call going long simply stupid and following every system trade naïve.

Why not use the best of both methods? If you have an opinion on the direction of a stock or futures market, then use the technicals for timing. For example, if you have decided that the U.S. dollar is going to decline because of debt and relative Asian economic strength, then you would want to buy the EURUSD or sell the dollar against the Korean won, USDKRW. But you would do this only when the trend of USDKRW signaled a turn down. Then, if you're wrong, the trend will turn up, and you can exit. As long as you believe the dollar will weaken, you don't go long but wait for another short signal. This way, you've put a risk management plan on top of a calculated decision to sell the dollar and buy Asia.

GOLD, PLATINUM, AND SILVER

The relationships between gold, platinum, and silver have been studied for many decades. The gold/silver ratio was traditionally considered normal at 35:1, but then gold was fixed at $35 per ounce and silver was $1 per ounce. It was also said that you could buy a pound of meat for an ounce of silver, but times change. With gold at more than $1,200 per ounce and silver at reaching new highs of $20 per ounce, the relationship seems to have broken down and now sits at 64:1. Is it simply adjusting to a new level, or is it a false concept?

These next comments should be prefaced by saying that everything is clear after the fact. If you don't like this explanation, you can substitute your own. You'll find that the financial news commentators, who are indeed very smart, always sound brilliant when discussing the issues that made the market go up or down yesterday. But these reasons are only clear afterward and never seem to be the same. Our problem is to decide on a profitable position in advance.

Many things have changed, perhaps *evolved*, during the past 50 years. With regard to gold and silver, some countries still hold a store of gold to back their currency, but it is not as formal or as common as in the past. The value of a currency floats based on the perception of the country's economic strength, with only a slight help from an above-average holding of gold reserves. Yet most people still value gold as an internationally recognized store of value. In addition, the consumption of gold has increased with new electronic uses. Gold turns out to be very good for conducting electricity and has been used as a contact point on high-end circuit boards. Reclaiming that gold is a difficult and highly regulated process, so much of it is lost.

Some history of gold trading is also necessary to understand the changes. Gold was fixed at $35 per ounce until the decision at Bretton Woods on August 15, 1971, to allow gold to float and allow Americans to own gold. The impact of that decision was that the value of a country's currency would be determined by its economic strength and not by its store of precious metals that served to back the currency. Following that decision, gold moved steadily higher, settling near $150 an ounce.

In 1970, the Hunt brothers decided to corner the market in silver, and by 1979, they had effectively accomplished that goal. From 1979 to 1980, silver moved from $11 per ounce to $50, peaking in January 1980 before starting one of the greatest collapses in history. Because of the gold-silver relationship, gold paralleled the silver move, peaking at about $800 per ounce and then plunging along with silver. At the peak, the gold:silver ratio was 16:1, indicating that silver was the driving force.

In the same way investors joined the great tech rally in the 1990s, they also kept buying gold and silver during the run-up to 1980. The general public always seems to have the largest position at the worst time. A large number of companies offered to help investors acquire gold to diversify and improve their personal portfolios. Even now, with gold above $1,200, there are firms saying the same thing. When gold and silver collapsed in 1980, investors were badly hurt—not quite as badly as the tech collapse, because gold and silver have an intrinsic value, but still losses that exceeded 75%.

Silver, which for investment purposes is considered the poor man's gold, never recovered. Those investors had long memories. Even gold prices remained low and very quiet for 20 years, until September 2000.

FIGURE 5.6 Gold/silver ratio using nearest futures, from August 1983 through August 2009.

Along with the decline in the economy that paralleled the tech bubble, people started buying gold. It is not surprising that investors would choose hard assets after losing badly in the stock market. But they did not go back to buying silver. Once seems to have been enough.

For those still considering trading the gold/silver ratio, Figure 5.6 shows the wide fluctuations and occasional volatile shifts. This is not what we would consider a tight relationship. There seem to be large intervals where the ratio trends up or down, making it difficult to put rules in place. Some traders may think of this as a challenge, but we will look for markets that are less risky.

THE PLATINUM/GOLD RATIO

Unlike silver, platinum is a precious metal, so the relationship between gold and platinum should be more stable. However, the uses for platinum have also changed over the years, with platinum, or platinum group metals, now the key component in catalytic converters. That increases the similarity between gold and platinum because both have industrial uses and both are still a very desirable store of value, but gold remains more popular as an investment. Figure 5.7 shows gold and platinum continuous futures prices from 2000. We use continuous futures because we will be trading futures. There are significant differences in the delivery months, with gold trading in February, April, June, August, October, and December, and platinum trading in January, April, July, and October. Even with these differences, we have no choice but to use the ratio of the nearest delivery. The main difference will be the carry, or interest rate cost as well as storage, both

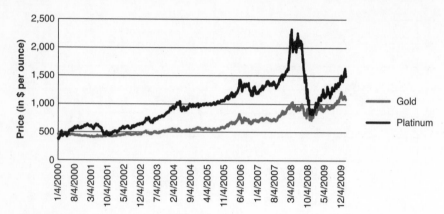

FIGURE 5.7 Platinum and gold prices from January 2000 (from continuous futures). Movement is similar except for the drop in platinum in 2001 and again in 2008. Gold has been more stable in its rise.

based on the number of days until delivery of the contract. That makes the carry different for both metals except when we trade October.

As you can see, prices moved in a very similar pattern most of the time, with notable exceptions in mid-2001 and the relative collapse of platinum in mid-2008. Nearly all commodities dropped precipitously in reaction to the U.S. bailout program and expectations of bad times to come. Because gold only dropped a much smaller amount in 2008, while platinum reflected an anticipated drop in consumer spending for jewelry and automobiles, the platinum/gold ratio collapsed to par.

Is the platinum/gold ratio any better than the gold/silver ratio? We think so. Figure 5.8 shows both the platinum/gold ratio and the gold/platinum

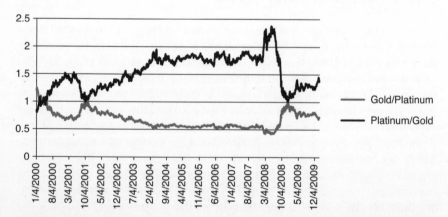

FIGURE 5.8 The traditional platinum/gold ratio, as well as the gold/platinum ratio.

ratio. Traditionally, the higher-priced market is divided by the lower-priced one because values over 1.0 have better resolution and are not limited as when the ratio approaches zero. The chart shows that the variation in the platinum/gold ratio is greater. We prefer the gold/platinum ratio because gold is the primary market, and the difference in the ratios, when used for systematic trading, will be minimal. Nevertheless, we will include the results of both gold/platinum and platinum/gold to show that computers don't really care as long as the numbers have enough decimal places.

The ratios show that, while there are periods where one market gains over the other, there are also three years when the ratio went sideways. The highly volatile period beginning in November 2007 will be our biggest concern. Will spread trading survive the disaster during August and September of 2008?

Trading the Platinum/Gold Ratio

The platinum/gold ratio is easier to trade than stock pairs because there only two components: the trend of the ratio and the position sizes. A simple 60-day moving average of the ratio is calculated; then the spread is bought (long platinum, short gold) when the ratio turns up and sold when it turns down.

As with pairs trading, the volatility of the two legs must be equalized to create a position that is not biased toward one of the two legs. Table 5.2 shows a sample of three trades during the second part of 2009. In this example, platinum is always traded with 10 contracts, and gold is adjusted higher or lower based on its volatility relative to platinum. The position sizes are nearly the same for the three trades because the volatility of the two metals is similar. There are no costs reflected in the profits and losses, but you could subtract $35 per round turn for each leg to be conservative.

The bigger performance picture is more interesting, as shown in Figure 5.9. During the past 10 years, trading the ratio would have yielded losses from 2002 through 2006, then extremely good profits. The NAVs for trading both the platinum/gold ratio and gold/platinum ratio are shown to point out that, while there are differences along the way, the long-term results are nearly the same. The statistics show that the profits per contract were slightly higher using the gold/platinum ratio ($212 versus $194), but the information ratio was slightly higher using the platinum/gold ratio (0.387 versus 0.383).

Using Volatility

It's unrealistic to think that anyone would start trading this ratio in 2000 and still be trading it at the end of 2006 when the losing streak ended. The solution to that problem is the same as the one we looked at in Chapter 4

TABLE 5.2 Same platinum/gold trades.

	Platinum			Gold			PL/GC Ratio	Exit			Profits and losses		
Entry Date	Order	Size	Entry	Order	Size	Entry		Date	Platinum	Gold	Platinum	Gold	Net
7/23/2009	Buy	10	1198.30	Sell	9.39	960.30	1.307	8/28/2009	1256.20	961.50	28950	-1127	27823
8/28/2009	Sell	10	1256.20	Buy	9.99	961.50	1.319	9/11/2009	1331.00	1009.10	-37400	47552	10152
9/11/2009	Buy	10	1331.00	Sell	9.68	1009.10	1.283	10/20/2009	1361.40	1061.30	15200	-50530	-35330

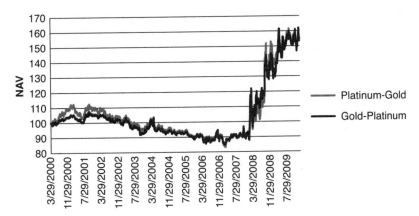

FIGURE 5.9 Performance of trading the platinum/gold ratio and the gold/platinum ratio from 2000.

when we found that inflation scares created volatility that improved performance. There are windows of opportunities that surface during critical economic times, and those opportunities are best recognized by watching the volatility. An abnormal increase in volatility generally signals a stronger correlation between many markets and a potentially profitable trading period.

The opposite of this, a period of low volatility, is often associated with listless price movement. The risk may be very low because price movement is quiet, but that doesn't help if wandering prices do not generate profits and make it more difficult to offset transaction costs.

In the same way we looked at volatility in the previous chapters, we will review both the annualized standard deviation and the average true range as the choices for measuring volatility. Because the annualized standard deviation uses only the change in closing prices, while the average true range uses the highs and lows, we have advocated the average true range as more robust. Figure 5.10 supports that claim.

The annualized volatility shows that platinum is much more volatile than gold most of the time. From 2000 through 2004, gold remains reasonably consistent at 10% while platinum bounces from 10% to 40%. We expect platinum to have a higher volatility when prices are higher than gold, but this variation does not parallel the ratio between the two metals. To show that clearly, we divide the annualized volatility by the price and compare the results in Figure 5.11. The volatilities of the two markets are very close in the past two years but still varied much more than the volatility measure using the average true range, shown in Figure 15.10b. It is also interesting that gold and platinum had the same dollar-value fluctuations throughout

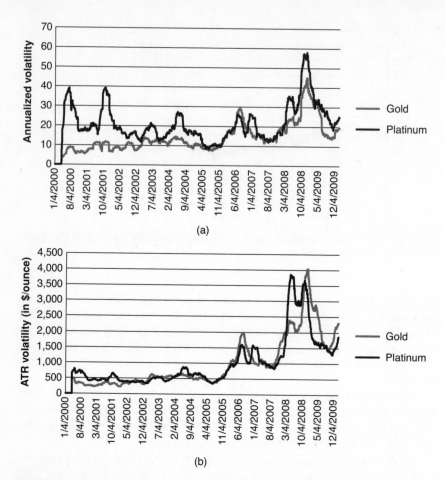

FIGURE 5.10 Volatility measured using (a) the annualized standard deviation method and (b) the average true range method.

the 10 years using the average true range, but not using the annualized standard deviation. This seems to be another strong argument for using the average true range.

If we focus on Figure 5.10b, we see a clear move to higher volatility at the beginning of 2006, when the average true range reached about $850. If we isolate only those trades from the beginning of 2006, we show a return of 10% per annum at 12% volatility. Because trading these metals using the ratio should be uncorrelated to any other trading, the 10% volatility will be leveraged higher when this performance is mixed with others in a portfolio,

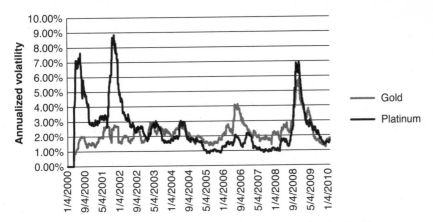

FIGURE 5.11 Comparison of gold and platinum annualized volatility as a percentage of price.

a benefit of diversification. The final results of trading the platinum/gold ratio can be seen in Figure 5.12.

Trading the platinum/gold ratio becomes another special situation rather than an ongoing process. But with markets becoming more complicated and competition keener, waiting for the right time is more the rule than the exception.

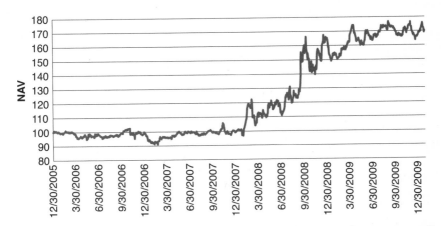

FIGURE 5.12 Performance of platinum/gold from 2006. Even after two years of sideways returns, a NAV of 170 is equivalent to an annualized return of 10% at 12% volatility.

IMPLIED YIELD

Some commodities are pure carry markets because the forward prices always reflect the cost of holding that product. That cost is mostly the interest on the money needed to buy the product, but it may also include insurance, storage, inspection fees, and additional minor costs. The easiest case to understand is gold. Each forward month of gold reflects the basic costs of carry. It always increases, never decreases. This is not the case with most commodities. Copper is known to trade in backwardation, where the deferred contracts sell for less than the nearby. This is generally caused by a combination of falling demand and purchasers (manufacturers and fabricators) who will wait for the last minute to buy, thereby avoiding the carrying charges and holding unnecessary inventory. Crude oil is similar to copper, sometimes going for years in backwardation. We will not address whether there is any manipulation in these markets because we're not able to use that information for making trading decisions.

Because forward gold prices always reflect the cost of carry, traders can keep the term structure in line by arbitraging the various delivery months. For example, if the current price of gold was $1,000 and the price 12 months forward was $1,050, that would reflect a simple carrying charge of 5%. All things being equal, we would expect the price of the 6-month forward contract to be $1,025, reflecting a return of 2.5% for half the period. However, if the 6-month forward was $1,035, then it is too high, given the 12-month forward. It would imply an annualized yield of 7%, much higher than the 12-month contract shows. We could buy physical gold, sell twice as many of the 6-month delivery and buy the 12-month delivery, a trade called a *butterfly* (with one foot in the cash market). At some point, the 6-month and 12-month annualized yields will need to line up. If not, gold will go to backwardation, which is unheard of. However, the term structure does not get out of line by enough to produce a profitable trade because professional arbitrageurs are hovering like vultures for that opportunity.

Table 5.3 shows the forward prices for the electronic Globex and open outcry sessions for CME gold (previously NYMEX and COMEX exchanges) and the corresponding forward prices for CME Eurodollar interest rates. Prices were posted on the CME web site as of March 16, 2010. Some of the calendar months do not have a futures contract; therefore, for the purpose of this example, the missing yields were interpolated from the surrounding prices.

To the right of Eurodollar prices in Table 5.3 is the annualized yield implied from the discounted price, which is simply 100 minus the price. As you would expect, yields increase with time, beginning with the current, very low yield of 0.31% and increasing to 2.22% if held until December 2011, about 18 months.

TABLE 5.3 Forward delivery prices and implied yields for Eurodollar interest rates, Globex gold, and open outcry gold.

	Gold		Eurodollars		Gold	
	Globex	Outcry	Price	Yield	Implied Globex	Implied Outcry
Apr-10	1122.0	1124.2	99.695	0.31%	−0.04%	0.15%
May-10	1122.9	1124.8	99.665	0.33%	0.04%	0.20%
Jun-10	1122.9	1125.3	99.640	0.36%	0.04%	0.25%
Aug-10	1123.7	1126.5		0.50%	0.11%	0.35%
Oct-10	1125.0	1127.6		0.64%	0.22%	0.46%
Dec-10	1126.0	1128.8	99.220	0.78%	0.31%	0.56%
Feb-11	1128.1	1130.4		1.26%	0.50%	0.72%
Apr-11	1129.4	1132.3		1.74%	0.61%	0.87%
Dec-11	1145.0		97.785	2.22%	2.00%	

Alternatively, you could buy physical gold and sell Dec 11 futures of an equivalent quantity (each contract is 100 ounces). Then you would be buying at the spot price of $1,122.50 and hedging by selling short the Dec 11 contract at $1,145.0 for an implied interest rate return of 2.00%. Figure 5.13 shows that the implied yield from both Globex gold futures and open outcry sessions parallel Eurodollar yields, although somewhat lower.

Why would someone take 2.00% interest out of gold (or less after costs) rather than the equivalent return in government debt? When you buy U.S. debt, you are subject to variations in the U.S. dollar because when you buy

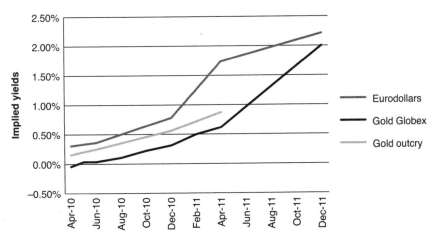

FIGURE 5.13 Comparison of implied yields from Eurodollars and gold (Globex and open outcry) as of April 2010.

U.S. interest rates you also buy the U.S. dollar. If you are a European investor and the EURUSD rises from 1.400 to 1.428, a relatively small amount in terms of forex fluctuations, you have effectively lost your 2% return when the money is repatriated back into euros.

Counterparty Risk

Although bank CDs (certificates of deposit) always pay more than government treasuries, the risk of bank failure became a reality for many investors in 2008. Although they had considered Lehman Brothers bonds a AAA investment, their money was backed only by the strength of the company, which disappeared before anyone could withdraw their funds. Since then, advertisements for corporate bonds and CDs are followed by the disclosure "backed by the strength of the institution."

ETFs have enjoyed tremendous acceptance and liquidity by the public, but they have various risks that are not well publicized, although probably appear somewhere in the fine print. Some of these risks include:

Counterparty risk. ETFs are similar to mutual funds in that you have some direct ownership in the stocks or bonds held in the ETF. But in many cases, the agency has short-sale repurchase agreements with other companies who might not be able to fulfill their end of the arrangement under a worst-case scenario, such as Lehman Brothers.

Label risk. The shares or futures held in the ETF may not be the ones that you expect.

Tracking risk. The agency will try to use fewer stocks to duplicate an index or sector. This might not always work.

Spread risk. Stocks and futures are changed and rebalanced. These transactions are subject to the cost represented by the bid-asked spread and tend to be larger when the ETF is larger.

Fees. Although ETFs can be very efficient, there is a fee paid to the agency that reduces the ETF price, most often applied daily.

If you buy an ETF directly from an agency rather than through the exchange, then you rely entirely on the integrity and financial strength of the issuing company. When you trade through an exchange, you are guaranteed delivery of what you buy—that is, the shares are delivered to you—but the exchange does not guarantee the solvency of the company, nor does it review its financial statements for potential risk that could threaten the shareholders. The exchange is simply a vehicle for share transfer.

A sector ETF is a collection of shares held by the agency issuing the ETF. For a gold ETF, we have a more complicated problem. If the position is created using exchange-traded futures, then it is guaranteed, and there is little risk. If it uses forward contracts (which might be issued by a gold dealer), then there is no guarantee. For example, if you buy physical gold (a bar of gold), then you have no risk; however, if you buy a gold certificate from a bank, you do not own gold, you own the bank's debt, denominated in gold. This is similar to a bank CD in which you own the bank's debt denominated in some currency, such as U.S. dollars or euros. A gold ETF may claim to have physical gold inventoried, but there are no audit procedures that assure how much gold is held. In addition, if the company issuing the ETF goes under, it is not clear that the investors in the ETF have first claim on the gold, if any. This should not be surprising. Even for stocks listed on the New York Stock Exchange, the exchange itself has no responsibility for financial misrepresentation, as we saw with Enron.

Exchange-traded futures are guaranteed by an independent clearing house with enough funds to cover most losses. Excessive losses, which have never happened, are guaranteed by the members and the value of their memberships. The exchanges make sure that all traders holding positions have adequate funds to cover losses, based on a fiscally conservative expectation of volatility. If there are insufficient funds to cover these anticipated losses, the trader must deposit additional money within hours of a margin call, or his or her positions will be liquidated at the market by the exchange. Extracting implied yields from futures contracts has less risk than other forms of interest income and has been used more actively during the past two years by large hedge funds and high-net-worth investors.

The same distinction needs to be made between exchange-traded derivatives and over-the-counter derivatives. One is guaranteed, and the other is not. Most notable are credit default swaps, a vehicle that has been very actively traded but is attributed with the collapse of the mortgage market and the Greek economy. Of course, taking a position to profit if something goes wrong does not cause the collapse, but the publicity of someone (especially a large hedge fund) profiting from someone else's misery can bring about countless Senate hearings and threatened regulation. The biggest issuer of credit default swaps was AIG, and had the government not bailed it out, it would have defaulted on all of them; those institutions holding large profits would have lost all their gains, as well as any money on deposit with AIG.

The lesson to be learned is to be aware of counterparty risk. Don't assume that everything is fine. In the history of financial risk, other than the sovereign debt of the major industrialized countries (which is now not quite as secure as we thought), exchange-traded futures have been the most secure.

THE YIELD CURVE

Interest rates are the target of many strategies used by investment banks and hedge funds, so there may not be much room for the armchair trader. Normally, the areas that are still open for exploitation require longer holding periods and greater risk. That turns out to be the case with yield-curve trades, with the added restriction that there are fewer opportunities.

The yield curve is also called the *term structure of interest rates*. As you move from shorter maturities to longer—for example, fed funds; 3-month T-bills or Eurodollars; 1-year bills; 2, 5, and 10-year notes; and finally, 30-year bonds—the yields form a relatively smooth curve. Based on various economic events and central bank policy, the curve can steepen (shorter-term rates move down and/or longer-term rates move up relative to the other end of the curve) or flatten (shorter-term rates move up and/or long-term rates move down). During 2009 into 2010, the economy remained depressed, and continued economic news seemed only to add to the dismal view of the future, causing the short maturities to go to near zero, while the long end held steady or began to rise in expectation of better days and future inflation due to extreme debt. When the view of the recovery dimmed, longer term rates declined, flattening the curve.

These changes in the yield curve appear to be an opportunity for a directional profit rather than a mean-reversion approach. Mean reversion is the source of large commercial profits, mainly the arbitrage of small abnormalities in the smoothness of the yield curve using various techniques, including 4-legged spreads (for example, buying the 3-month maturities, selling the 6-month, buying the 9-month, and selling the 12-month). However, the profits are very small, and costs must be near zero for this to be viable. But the risks are also very small.

Noncommercial traders can't compete with the banks using a mean reversion or stat-arb strategy, but there may be opportunities looking for shifts in the yield curve that last for a few days. We're going to use a short-term moving average applied to the differences between the U.S. 30-year bond, 10-year note, and 5-year note, three very liquid futures markets.

Trading the Short-Term Trend

The first step is to create the data using continuous, back-adjusted futures. Because we will be using only a few days of data at a time, it could be done with individual contracts rather than a continuous series; however, this gives us the opportunity to conveniently backtest our method.

Being careful that the three data series, the U.S. 30-year bond (US), 10-year note (TY), and 5-year note (FV), always roll on the exact same day, we create three series, US-TY, US-FV, and TY-FV. We can't use the ratio because the back-adjusted prices can become very distorted as you go further back in their history due to compounding of the price gap on the roll dates.

Using the difference series, we apply a very short-term moving average to see what happens. No costs are applied because these may vary considerably for each trader and for spreads. We will stay aware that the profits per contract must cover costs and slippage. Results are converted to NAVs at 12% volatility, our normal benchmark, to make comparisons easier. Before starting, we test the correlations between the three series of price differences from the beginning of 2000 through May 2010 and find that they are very high, reducing our expectations of success.

Series	Corr
30yr–5yr	0.872
30yr–10yr	0.939
10yr–5yr	0.961

To make the trading system more responsive, the entry rules are:

- If the closing price moves above the moving average, then *buy*.
- If the closing price moves below the moving average, then *sell*.

The results are shown in Table 5.4. There are a large number of trades, good returns, and good ratios, but the profits per contract are too small for our costs. An experienced analyst might ask if using a longer calculation period would increase the size of the profits, but as it turns out, shifts in the yield curve occur over short periods of time, and longer trends perform worse. Even in the test of 2, 3, and 4 days, the performance seems to peak at 3 days, and the profits per contract decline in the 4-day test. Results generally conform to the correlations, with the TY-FV pair showing the highest correlations and the smallest unit profits.

Increasing Unit Profits with a Volatility Filter

It should be no surprise by now that our next step is to introduce a low-volatility filter. For this application, it makes even more sense because we want to only trade when there is a significant change in the yield curve, not just the odd wiggle. There were a large number of trades, and isolating the more volatile ones might work.

TABLE 5.4 Result of trading three yield-curve series using a simple moving average strategy.

	2-Day Moving Average			3-Day Moving Average			4-Day Moving Average		
	Trades	AROR	PL/Unit	Ratio	Trades	AROR	PL/Unit	Ratio	Trades	AROR	PL/Unit	Ratio
30yr–5yr	1256	9.0	11	0.749	680	12.8	28	1.067	598	6.1	17	0.506
30yr–10yr	1241	11.8	13	0.985	675	10.7	22	0.893	583	7.3	19	0.612
10yr–5yr	1225	5.7	4	0.478	671	1.6	2	0.130	581	1.9	3	0.162

The volatility filter will be a multiple of the average true range, the same method we have used before. The period of the calculation will be the same as the moving average period, also the same technique that has been used throughout the book. We define the filter,

A trade is only entered if the current day volatility > average volatility × factor.

The results are shown in Table 5.5, with the volatility factor ranging from 0.50 through 2.00. As we would like to see, there is a clear pattern from faster to slower moving averages (left to right) and from smaller to larger filters (top to bottom). The number of trades gets smaller as we go to the right and down, and the profits per contract get bigger. In the lower right box, the profits are very good, but there are only 24 trades in 10 years, less than 3 per year. Because the trades are held for only a few days, we have a very inactive trading strategy.

The best compromise seems to be in the middle, a 3-day moving average and a volatility factor of 1.5. That gives 118 trades for the 30-5 combination, and profits of $109 per contract. Even with less than 12 trades per year, the returns are 12.8% per annum. The 30-10 combination has smaller per contract returns but may still be acceptable; however, the 10-5 combination generates only 15 trades over 10 years and is not interesting. Although we can look at interest rates in other countries, such as the Eurobund and Eurobobl, the U.S. is the only country with a 30-year futures contract, and the Eurobund and Eurobobl are similar to the 10- and 5-year U.S. notes, which did not produce large enough profits.

If we look at the pattern of profits in the 30-5 pair, shown in Figure 5.14, we see that the interval of very low interest rate volatility, from 2005 through 2007, as the equity index markets began their rise, produced no trades. On the other hand, the subprime crisis during late 2008 was so volatile that the method was able to capture large, consistent gains. The short interval at the end again shows no trades, not because of low volatility, but because of declining volatility, which causes the filter to read positive.

For our purposes, the yield curve spread is another example of an event-driven market. When the volatility is high, then large profits are produced quickly. When volatility is low, there are no trades. From 2000 through most of 2004, there was a normal market generating small but steady returns. On its own, this may not seem exciting, but when combined in a portfolio with many other strategies, it could be excellent diversification.

TABLE 5.5 Tests of three yield-curve differences using a low-pass volatility filter.

		2-Day Moving Average				3-Day Moving Average				4-Day Moving Average			
		Trades	AROR	PL/Unit	Ratio	Trades	AROR	PL/Unit	Ratio	Trades	AROR	PL/Unit	Ratio
Filter 0.5	30yr-5yr	870	9.4	17	0.781	676	12.9	28	1.072	597	6.0	17	0.504
	30yr-10yr	845	9.1	15	0.758	670	10.7	22	0.894	582	7.4	19	0.614
	10yr-5yr	843	1.5	2	0.128	546	2.1	4	0.178	485	2.6	5	0.213
Filter 0.75	30yr-5yr	712	8.6	18	0.715	562	13.1	34	1.094	516	5.2	17	0.437
	30yr-10yr	688	7.9	16	0.661	554	10.7	26	0.893	507	6.1	18	0.509
	10yr-5yr	396	0.0	1	−0.001	316	0.6	3	0.053	292	1.7	5	0.139
Filter 1.0	30yr-5yr	501	8.8	24	0.732	398	11.5	40	0.961	369	3.4	15	0.286
	30yr-10yr	489	7.0	19	0.580	393	10.6	34	0.880	362	5.9	22	0.491
	10yr-5yr	194	−1.3	−2	−0.105	145	2.8	12	0.234	121	0.1	3	0.010
Filter 1.5	30yr-5yr	174	9.7	56	0.807	118	12.8	109	1.065	110	8.1	76	0.671
	30yr-10yr	178	7.7	43	0.646	116	8.0	68	0.665	119	8.2	69	0.680
	10yr-5yr	30	3.0	39	0.253	15	1.9	43	0.158	18	0.6	19	0.052
Filter 1.75	30yr-5yr	77	9.6	98	0.799	55	12.5	175	1.045	45	5.4	81	0.447
	30yr-10yr	86	6.7	66	0.554	53	9.1	119	0.755	44	1.2	25	0.099
	10yr-5yr	16	3.3	63	0.278	11	3.1	82	0.261	6	3.0	139	0.249
Filter 2.0	30yr-5yr	40	8.5	154	0.707	26	10.2	191	0.853	24	10.5	228	0.872
	30yr-10yr	43	4.4	71	0.363	22	5.0	115	0.420	26	5.0	103	0.421
	10yr-5yr	11	4.3	106	0.356	7	2.3	98	0.189	2	2.2	277	0.180

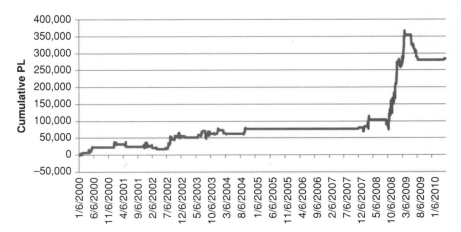

FIGURE 5.14 Results of trading the 30-5 interest rate difference using a 3-day moving average and a volatility factor of 1.5.

Skewness in Volatility Filters

One point needs to be discussed before moving on. In Figure 5.14, we had the case where the volatility filter worked when volatility was rising but not when it was falling. On the back side of the price rise, in mid-2009, decreasing volatility caused trades to be skipped, even though the absolute level of volatility was very high. That situation should be corrected.

One approach is to use an absolute level of volatility; that is, we trade when the dollar value of volatility, measured by the ATR, is some multiple of our costs, or above an absolute level of, say, $250.

Another approach is to calculate the volatility over a much longer time period, perhaps 1, 2, or 3 years, so that a run-up and the following decline in price lasting three months will all be recognized as high volatility. It might help to lag the volatility measure by one to three months, so that any surge in volatility is not included in the current measure. Otherwise, volatility is always chasing you.

TREND TRADING OF LONDON METAL EXCHANGE PAIRS

As stated at the beginning of this chapter, there are markets that are correlated yet do not mean revert; that is, there may be a series of long-term shifts in the way the public values each company. The first example was Dell and Hewlett-Packard. This can also happen in commodities markets.

The London Metal Exchange (LME) base metals are all tied together through the construction industry. The average correlation of all the LME pair combinations was .45 from 2000 through 2009. In Chapter 4, we used these relationships to show that the LME pairs could be traded with a short-term, mean-reversion strategy, but the results were only marginal. That is, after commissions and slippage, profits were small.

We're now going to look at relative trends in these LME metals. Consider tin and zinc, which are both noncorrosive metals used in plating steel. Stainless steel is coated with tin and galvanized steel is coated with zinc. Tin cans are actually made of a combination of aluminum and steel, brass is a product of copper and zinc, and bronze is made from copper and tin. Copper is also the choice for hot-water pipes. Uneven demand for a specific metal may drive one price more than another, or a problem with supply may cause one to become more expensive for prolonged intervals. If this turns out to be true, we can capitalize on the trends while, at the same time, hedging one against the other to take advantage of their long-term correlation. By buying one and selling the other, we still maintain a neutral position with regard to price direction. Both metals could be rising or falling, and we would be long one and short the other. This type of trade, a *directional spread*, offers important diversification in a broad trading portfolio.

When we looked at price noise in Chapter 2, we concluded that a long-term view of prices emphasized the trend, while a short-term view increased the effects of noise. This can be seen by first looking at a daily chart of the S&P and then converting that to weekly data. The trends will appear much clearer. Now change the daily chart to an hourly chart, and you won't be able to see any trends, only noise. In Chapter 4, we used mean reversion, holding the trade for only a few days. In this chapter, we'll take a much longer view to give the trend every opportunity to develop.

Creating the Trend Trade

Trends are simple to calculate, and the most popular method is a simple moving average. We've mentioned before that a typical macrotrend system, one that attempts to profit from trends that align themselves with economic fundamentals apply calculation periods from about 40 to 80 days, sometimes longer. It isn't necessary to overcomplicate a trend strategy. Some have different risk and reward profiles, but all of them make money when markets are trending and lose when they are going sideways. For that reason we won't look any further than a moving average to identify the trend.

There are two choices in the way the data are constructed: the ratio of prices and the price difference. Because we are using back-adjusted

TABLE 5.6 The information ratio for six moving average calculation periods and 15 LME pairs.

Ratio			Moving Average Calculation Period					
Leg 1	Leg 2	Corr	3	5	10	20	40	80
Aluminum	Copper	0.672	0.307	0.402	0.430	0.449	0.673	0.383
Aluminum	Nickel	0.431	0.405	0.408	0.322	0.549	0.672	0.445
Aluminum	Lead	0.455	0.546	0.095	−0.128	0.142	0.438	0.370
Aluminum	Tin	0.349	0.482	0.691	0.074	0.518	0.230	0.504
Aluminum	Zinc	0.550	0.815	0.506	0.615	0.478	0.313	0.402
Copper	Nickel	0.502	0.636	0.252	0.325	0.537	0.534	0.056
Copper	Lead	0.494	0.199	0.057	0.271	0.905	0.904	0.380
Copper	Tin	0.398	0.722	0.494	0.539	0.569	0.446	0.473
Copper	Zinc	0.604	0.614	0.289	0.827	0.651	0.140	0.337
Nickel	Lead	0.394	−0.255	0.185	0.518	0.402	0.196	0.367
Nickel	Tin	0.341	0.320	0.117	−0.085	−0.254	0.017	0.339
Nickel	Zinc	0.467	0.218	0.344	0.017	0.297	0.504	0.219
Lead	Tin	0.307	0.367	0.240	0.452	0.407	0.847	0.512
Lead	Zinc	0.502	0.658	0.495	0.605	0.634	0.435	0.124
Zinc	Tin	0.344	0.533	0.483	0.586	0.378	0.588	0.728
Average		0.454	0.438	0.337	0.358	0.444	0.462	0.376

data, we'll choose the differences. Data begins in 2000 and ends at the end of 2009.

Table 5.6 shows the information ratio from six tests where a moving average is applied to the series of price differences created from 15 LME pairs. Table 5.7 shows the corresponding profits per contract for the same combinations. Results do not reflect any commissions.

The first thing we notice in the tables is that nearly every test is profitable. We then believe that there are trends that can be exploited in the way the metals move in relationship to one another. The average ratios at the bottom on Table 5.6 show a slight tendency to get larger as the calculation periods get longer. The highest ratio, 0.462, occurs for calculation period 40.

Distribution of Tests

Notice that the calculation periods chosen essentially doubled for each test. Doubling these values is a fast way of getting a good sample over a wide range of values without many tests. If we were to test every period from 3 days to 80 days, we would find that the greatest difference in

TABLE 5.7 Profits per contract for the same tests shown in Table 5.6.

Markets		Moving Average Calculation Period					
Leg 1	**Leg 2**	**3**	**5**	**10**	**20**	**40**	**80**
Aluminum	Copper	1.14	1.97	3.37	5.41	15.06	15.07
Aluminum	Nickel	3.04	4.00	5.37	13.20	29.45	26.37
Aluminum	Lead	1.33	0.46	−0.33	1.35	4.44	5.24
Aluminum	Tin	3.25	5.88	1.56	10.62	8.23	43.16
Aluminum	Zinc	2.03	1.76	3.05	3.81	3.62	6.20
Copper	Nickel	12.03	7.22	13.53	32.67	70.26	15.18
Copper	Lead	1.24	0.73	2.89	13.10	24.85	19.70
Copper	Tin	11.65	11.14	19.55	34.01	37.63	85.60
Copper	Zinc	3.18	2.20	8.26	9.29	4.49	14.17
Nickel	Lead	−1.02	1.65	6.37	8.65	7.48	20.82
Nickel	Tin	11.74	8.02	−1.73	−18.87	12.94	105.65
Nickel	Zinc	1.82	3.71	1.09	7.22	18.87	13.13
Lead	Tin	3.73	3.36	8.75	12.38	32.60	41.42
Lead	Zinc	2.89	2.84	5.47	8.55	8.91	4.18
Zinc	Tin	5.84	7.31	12.38	14.40	30.28	98.40
Average		4.26	4.15	5.97	10.39	20.61	34.28

performance came when we moved from 3 to 4 days, an increase of 1/3, while the smallest difference was from 79 to 80 days, a change of only 1.3%. If we then averaged the results of all tests, we would be heavily weighting them toward the long end. By doubling the values, all the changes are equal at 100%, and we get a much fairer sample.

Pattern of Results

Table 5.7 shows the profits per contract for the same calculation periods as Table 5.6. The averages show an increase from $4 to $34 per contract. This is the right pattern when the calculation period increases, but $34 is not large enough to be comfortably above the cost of trading. If we look more closely at the results of the individual pairs, we could select five that might have per contract returns large enough to trade. But we were expecting more.

Is there anything that can be done? In the past, we have used volatility filters to select the trades that have a greater chance of larger returns. We can try to do the same thing here. But first we want to look at a sample of the NAVs. Figure 5.15 shows the results of four pairs chosen arbitrarily, lead-tin (PB-SN), aluminum-copper (AL-LP), copper-nickel (LP-NI), and nickel-lead (NI-PB). They all show that there was very little activity

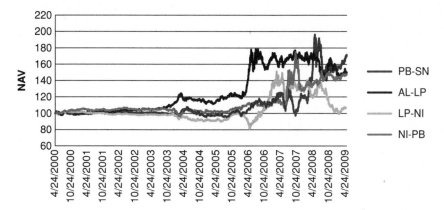

FIGURE 5.15 Sample NAVs for four LME pairs show little activity up to 2005.

through 2003 followed by low volatility of returns for another two years. From 2005 on, the returns are much more active.

If we consider the data beginning in 2005 and see that the markets are currently performing at a much higher level, we can rerun the 80-day moving average test from 2005 to get the profits per contract that we can expect under current market conditions. Table 5.8 shows that the results

TABLE 5.8 Return statistics for LME trend pairs from 2005 through 2009.

Leg 1	Leg 2	Corr	Trades	AROR	PL/Ctr	Ratio
Aluminum	Copper	0.707	31	5.4	33.29	0.450
Aluminum	Nickel	0.493	35	8.8	70.68	0.737
Aluminum	Lead	0.547	13	13.3	117.25	1.108
Aluminum	Tin	0.427	23	9.2	147.68	0.769
Aluminum	Zinc	0.676	29	12.3	48.10	1.024
Copper	Nickel	0.550	32	3.0	71.29	0.247
Copper	Lead	0.582	27	7.4	62.95	0.616
Copper	Tin	0.470	20	9.0	365.81	0.747
Copper	Zinc	0.729	30	8.7	54.92	0.722
Nickel	Lead	0.450	37	7.8	90.13	0.647
Nickel	Tin	0.407	38	6.6	311.93	0.551
Nickel	Zinc	0.540	36	6.1	55.56	0.509
Lead	Tin	0.403	22	9.6	142.58	0.804
Lead	Zinc	0.635	35	3.5	16.82	0.292
Zinc	Tin	0.425	17	13.2	359.23	1.098
Average		0.536	28	8.3	129.88	0.688

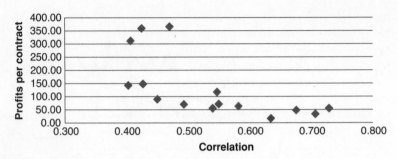

FIGURE 5.16 Lower correlations generate higher profits per trade for trending LME pairs after 2005.

for all pairs are far better. The number of trades was reduced by about two-thirds, but those removed were mostly losses because trends between these pairs do not appear to have been as strong. The average rate of return of 8.3% and the average ratio of 0.688 would come out much higher when these pairs are combined into a portfolio and the benefits of diversification increase leverage. It is also reassuring that every pair was profitable, and the smallest ratio was for copper-nickel at 0.247. Remember that these results do not reflect costs, but an average per contract return of $129 should be enough to retain reasonable profitability.

If you look carefully at Table 5.8, you will notice that the profits per contract seem to be inversely related to the correlation between the two legs of the pair. The largest per contract return was for the copper-tin pair, $365, which also has a correlation of 0.470 in the total range of 0.403 to 0.729 for all pairs. Figure 5.16 is a scatter diagram of correlations versus unit profits, showing that correlations over 0.60 have marginal unit returns and correlations under 0.50 have the highest values.

We can conclude that the LME nonferrous metals move in a way that can be exploited using trends where the two legs are volatility adjusted to equalize risk. But in many of the other situations we've looked at, more recent price movement, which reflects higher volatility, generated much better performance. We might have been able to introduce the usual volatility filter and systematically remove the quiet period before 2005, but that did not seem necessary because these markets transitioned into a better trading period. If volatility declines, it would be necessary to stop trading when returns dropped below costs, but that is not a current problem.

SUMMARY

Stat-arb trading, which buys and sells abnormal differences in related markets, profits from prices returning to relative normal. It is a trading approach that has withstood the test of time and evolved into one aspect of high-frequency trading. But while we can profit from these distortions in the short-term, there may be a major shift going on in the long term.

We know that noise dominates price in the very short time frames and trends surface when we look at the same prices over a long time period. Up to now we have focused on the short term, but this chapter looked at the longer term and larger moves that could occur when two fundamentally related markets diverge. Examples of this were Dell and Hewlett-Packard, gold and platinum, and the LME nonferrous metals. By going long and short according to the trend of the price ratios or price differences, and equalizing the risk of the two legs, we removed the directional risk.

Most of the opportunities in this chapter, and some in previous chapters, seem to have increased in recent years with the higher volatility associated with economic crisis and market stress. Perhaps that's the primary consequence of more competition. Yet, if we continue to scan these markets, there always seems to be a place that will produce profits.

To implement these strategies, you will need to put this into a spreadsheet or computer program and verify all the results. You cannot rely on anyone else's numbers when it's your money that is at risk. You will need to understand the process, do the calculations, and place the orders with precision.

We did not look at fixed-income markets in this chapter. Our experience says that they are too highly correlated. Profits would be very small, and survival would depend on extremely low transaction costs, the venue of the professional traders. However, there is a combination of interest rate markets that will work for us and is discussed in Chapter 7.

The next chapter will introduce a different relative value measurement, the *stress indicator*, that will correct some of the problems we faced in Chapters 3 and 4.

CHAPTER 6

Cross-Market Trading and the Stress Indicator

C hanging times and improved technology allow more versatile trading solutions. In this chapter, we look at the stress indicator, which will allow us to identify buy and sell levels with greater flexibility than the momentum difference method used in the previous chapters, and we will apply it to some of the previous pairs. It also gives us the ability to trade across very different markets, combining physical commodities with stocks that are highly dependent upon those products.

In previous chapters, we have discussed the classic method of statistical arbitrage (stat-arb), pairs trading. Pairs trading is based on a strong fundamental relationship between the stock prices of two companies in the same business, affected by the same events in similar ways. The correlations between their price movements may vary from as low as 0.30 to above 0.90. At the low end, there are more opportunities but at greater risk. At the high end, we need to be selective about which trades are taken because they track each other so closely that the potential profit might be too small to overcome costs.

The stat-arb represented by pairs trading has become more difficult. The method is widely known, even though there are many traders, especially novices, who do not balance the risks correctly. They can squeeze out the opportunity for others without profiting themselves.

Because of the small margin of profit in stocks, we also looked at pairs of U.S. and European index markets, pairs relating to inflation hedges, and LME metals. Some of these were quite promising; others appeared successful, but the unit returns were too small to realistically expect a profit.

The method used to trigger signals is called *relative value trading*. Using a stochastic indicator, we calculated the value of each leg over the same time period and then looked to see how often the indicator values moved far enough apart to offer a profit opportunity. Overall, the results were good. In this chapter, we introduce a different way of identifying the trigger points using the *stress indicator*, which seems to be a more general and robust way of identifying the buy and sell points when trading pairs. With this indicator, we look at other interesting trading opportunities.

THE CROSSOVER TRADE

The market is filled with opportunities, and it's up to us to uncover them. One of these, the most interesting one we'll discuss in this chapter, crosses over from stocks to commodities.* There are many brokerage firms that give access to different investment vehicles, but not as many as a year ago. The consolidation of the industry in 2008 was followed by a review of both the profitability and the risk of various divisions, the result being a narrower focus for some firms, creating a less accommodative service for clients. Nevertheless, there are still firms, such as Interactive Brokers, that can facilitate trading across a wide range of markets from a single investment account.

The first step is to identify a business whose primary input is a commodity. The obvious ones are the major oil-producing companies, mining operations, and agribusiness complexes. It's important to avoid companies that are too diversified because we're looking for a dependency on the price of the underlying commodity. For example, if the gold price increases, we want that to be reflected in the share price of Barrick Gold Corp (ABX). Because we are concerned with company profits and losses, the airlines might also be candidates for this method, based on the stock price reaction to the price of crude oil (refined into jet fuel). However, this may be a temporary situation, complicated by other economic factors such as a decrease in travelers related to changes in disposable income or just an increase in fares. As the relationship between the commodity and the share price becomes less direct, the risk of the trade will increase. That's not always bad, nor is an opportunity that lasts for only six months. In Chapter 4, we saw that fear of inflation causes markets that previously had a loose relationship to move together in a way that allowed profitable pairs trading.

---

*This method was first introduced in the January 2009 *Futures* magazine, "Crossover Relative Value Trading," by Perry Kaufman.

Trading Hours

It is very important to know that futures and stock prices do not close at the same time. This was discussed in the Chapter 4, "Pairs Trading Using Futures." The main points are:

- There will be trading signals that are generated but not tradable when markets close at different times. If the S&P makes a move after the close of EuroStoxx, then the stochastic based on different closes will appear to be different, but the opening of the EuroStoxx will gap to correct that difference. There is no profit opportunity. It turns out that the European exchanges have all aligned their trading times with the U.S. trading hours, so this is no longer a problem.
- For markets such as gold and Barrick Gold, the markets close at much different times, although the after-hours gold market continues to trade and can be captured at 4 P.M. when the stock market closes. For convenience, we will use the commodity closing price, even though it is a different time. When we studied the relationship between the U.S. and European index markets before hours were aligned, we found the results were very similar. There may be a few false trades due to the difference in closing times, but we believe the results will be representative of the performance when prices are posted at the same time.
- In real trading, you must capture prices at the same time, while both markets are open, to assure a correct signal.
- Capturing prices at multiple times during the day, especially following an economic report in either time zone, will increase the number of signals and the ultimate profitability. For example, capturing prices at 8:45 A.M. in New York, 15 minutes after the jobs release, should take advantage of a volatile move in the U.S. index and interest rate markets, while there is a less certain reaction in Europe.
- We believe that the pair trading concept is sound and will profit as expected from real distortions in price movement that are reflected in the momentum calculations.

We will come back to this at different points during our analysis.

THE STRESS INDICATOR

We can think of stress as a rubber band. As we stretch it farther and farther out of shape, it seems to pull harder to return to normal. In the previous chapters, we measured our opportunity in pairs trading by calculating two stochastic indicators, one for each leg of the pair, subtracting the indicator value for leg 2 from the corresponding value of leg 1 and then found the threshold levels based on the difference that worked for entries and exits.

The *stress indicator* goes one step further. When we take the difference in the stochastic values between leg 1 and leg 2, we then use that series of values as the input for another stochastic calculation. There are two advantages to this:

1. There is a single value that varies between 0 and 100.
2. This new value adjusts for volatility in the momentum difference.

By automatically adjusting the volatility, there will be more trades; however, we lose the absolute value of the volatility, so we may want to add a filter that avoids trading when the opportunity is small.

Starting from the beginning, the stress indicator is calculated in the following four steps:

1. Find the *raw stochastic* for leg 1 over an n – day period:

$$\text{Raw(leg 1)}_{\text{today}} = \frac{\text{Close(leg 1)}_{\text{today}} - \text{Low(leg 1)}_{n-\text{days}}}{\text{High(leg 1)}_{n-\text{days}} - \text{Low(leg 1)}_{n-\text{days}}}$$

This is effectively the position of today's closing price within the high-low range of the past n – days, measured as a percentage from the bottom of the range. Note that n – days is the entire n – day period.

2. Find the raw stochastic for leg 2, using the same n – day period:

$$\text{Raw(leg 2)}_{\text{today}} = \frac{\text{Close(leg 2)}_{\text{today}} - \text{Low(leg 2)}_{n-\text{days}}}{\text{High(leg 2)}_{n-\text{days}} - \text{Low(leg 2)}_{n-\text{days}}}$$

3. Find the difference in the two stochastic values:

$$\text{Diff}_{\text{today}} = \text{Raw(leg 1)}_{\text{today}} - \text{Raw(leg 2)}_{\text{today}}$$

Up to this point, we have followed the same process as in the previous chapters.

4. Find the stress indicator, the stochastic value of the differences, *Diff*:

$$\text{Stress}_{\text{today}} = \frac{\text{Diff}_{\text{today}} - \text{Low(Diff)}_{n-\text{days}}}{\text{High(Diff)}_{n-\text{days}} - \text{Low(Diff)}_{n-\text{days}}}$$

Even though the Diff values do not have highs and lows each day, the stress indicator can provide added value. There is also no smoothing involved in this calculation, so there is no lag, as there is in most *trending* indicators.

Spreadsheet Example of the Stress Indicator Calculations

The stress indicator is easily calculated using a spreadsheet. In Table 6.1, there are only four steps needed once the data are loaded. In this example, we pair crude oil prices (continuous futures) with the Conoco Philips stock price. The high, low, and closing prices are loaded; the open is not used. Only 41 days will be used in this example.

In the two columns with the headings mom1 and mom2, we calculate the values of the raw stochastic from steps 1 and 2. For example, the 10-day stochastic, mom1, is written =(D12-min(C3:C12))/(max(B3:B12)-min(C3:C12)). The same formula is applied to the next three columns in order to get mom2. Both start in row 12 because it is the first row with 10 previous values. Column J, the mom diff, is simply H12 – I12. The final column, K, the stress indicator, needs 10 values in column J, so it cannot start until row 22 on February 12, 2007. It uses column J for the high, low, and close in the momentum calculation and is written =(J22-min(J11:J22))/(max(J11:J22)-min(J11:J22)).

The momentum calculations for the first 41 days of data are shown in Figure 6.1. The first 10 days are omitted because they are needed for windup. Values of each indicator range from 0 to 100. Up until February 28, the two markets track fairly closely, but then Conoco prices decline ahead of crude (do they know something?), crude catches up, Conoco rallies to meet crude, and then crude falls ahead of Conoco. These short periods where the two markets are out of phase will create the trading opportunities.

The last step is shown in Figure 6.2, where the difference between the two momentum indicators is combined into the stress indicator. In this example, the momentum difference ranges from about –60 to +60 out of a possible –100 to +100 (–100 when leg 1 is 0 and leg 2 is 100). The stress indicator has a range from 0 to 100. It reaches these extremes because a 10-day calculation is sensitive to change. That is, a 10-day high will be recorded as 100 and a 10-day low as 0. Those values occur much more often with a 10-day calculation than they would with a 30-day calculation.

Rules for Trading Using the Stress Indicator

The trading rules for the stress indicator are very similar to the momentum difference that we used previously. There are still two primary variables, the calculation period and the buying/selling thresholds. We always use symmetrical thresholds, even though some analysts argue that certain markets, such as equity indices, are biased to the upside. We want to give the longs and shorts an equal chance to profit. We could still have an exit

TABLE 6.1 Example of stress indicator calculation.

A	B	C	D	E	F	G	H	I	J	K
	Crude Oil			Conoco Phillips						
Date	High	Low	Close	High	Low	Close	Mom1	Mom2	Mom Diff	Stress
1/17/2007	86.07	83.77	85.87	58.14	56.78	57.62				
1/18/2007	86.39	83.85	84.55	58.47	56.49	56.68				
1/19/2007	86.24	84.22	86.14	58.30	57.03	58.02				
1/22/2007	87.39	84.81	85.32	58.64	57.20	57.45				
1/23/2007	87.89	85.15	87.78	59.38	57.74	59.04				
1/24/2007	88.19	86.40	88.11	59.89	58.52	59.69				
1/25/2007	88.64	86.84	86.97	59.73	57.99	58.13				
1/26/2007	88.32	86.94	88.16	59.18	58.16	58.84				
1/29/2007	88.70	86.49	86.75	59.51	58.53	58.69				
1/30/2007	89.79	86.56	89.71	59.90	58.82	59.72	98.7	94.72	3.95	
1/31/2007	90.94	88.49	90.88	60.71	59.22	60.48	99.2	94.55	4.60	
2/1/2007	91.60	89.84	90.04	61.49	60.41	61.38	78.9	97.53	−18.67	
2/2/2007	91.99	89.79	91.76	61.60	60.59	61.36	96.8	94.55	2.25	
2/5/2007	92.69	91.20	91.48	61.84	60.95	61.11	84.0	82.20	1.76	
2/6/2007	92.73	91.24	91.62	61.93	60.31	60.71	82.5	69.04	13.43	
2/7/2007	92.59	89.99	90.45	61.01	59.84	60.30	63.5	58.63	4.83	
2/8/2007	92.61	90.04	92.45	61.20	59.68	60.94	95.5	73.74	21.77	
2/9/2007	93.54	92.04	92.63	61.40	60.60	61.06	87.1	74.41	12.68	

Date									
2/12/2007	92.52	90.07	90.55	60.83	59.77	60.10	57.2	41.16	16.01	85.74
2/13/2007	92.25	89.96	91.77	61.42	60.22	61.34	65.0	78.23	-13.28	13.34
2/14/2007	91.76	90.00	90.49	62.17	61.27	61.53	18.7	74.30	-55.63	0.00
2/15/2007	90.97	89.03	90.43	61.57	60.25	60.64	31.0	38.55	-7.51	62.17
2/16/2007	91.83	89.99	91.78	60.88	60.23	60.63	61.0	38.15	22.82	100.00
2/20/2007	91.78	89.70	90.77	60.13	59.50	60.06	38.6	20.97	17.61	93.35
2/21/2007	92.55	89.99	91.99	60.84	59.15	60.77	65.6	53.64	11.99	86.19
2/22/2007	93.17	91.53	92.87	61.45	60.08	61.36	85.1	73.18	11.97	86.16
2/23/2007	93.72	92.42	93.06	62.22	61.58	61.68	85.9	82.41	3.52	75.39
2/26/2007	93.67	92.57	93.31	62.92	61.94	62.44	91.3	87.27	3.99	75.99
2/27/2007	94.17	91.98	93.38	62.01	58.49	59.53	84.6	23.48	61.15	100.00
2/28/2007	94.02	91.84	93.71	60.92	59.13	59.80	91.1	29.57	61.48	100.00
3/1/2007	94.41	92.72	93.92	60.82	58.75	60.43	90.9	43.79	47.10	79.16
3/2/2007	94.32	93.08	93.56	60.47	58.99	59.41	82.0	20.77	61.19	99.49
3/5/2007	93.22	91.47	91.99	60.17	58.31	58.97	48.6	14.32	34.30	53.11
3/6/2007	92.72	91.57	92.61	60.44	59.37	60.30	59.3	43.17	16.11	21.72
3/7/2007	94.02	92.56	93.74	63.23	60.19	61.64	77.2	67.68	9.53	10.37
3/8/2007	94.22	93.12	93.56	62.62	61.71	62.05	71.1	76.02	-4.93	0.00
3/9/2007	93.58	91.81	91.97	62.78	61.91	62.28	17.0	80.69	-63.68	0.00
3/12/2007	91.94	90.57	90.97	62.21	61.28	61.72	10.4	69.31	-58.89	3.83
3/13/2007	91.99	90.17	90.36	62.92	61.04	61.07	4.5	56.10	-51.62	9.64

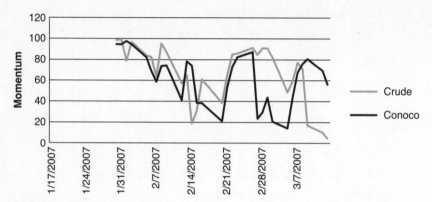

FIGURE 6.1 Starting stochastic momentum calculations for crude oil and Conoco Philips.

threshold, which is nominally set at 50, but could be 55 or 60 for shorts and 45 or 40 for longs.

The main difference between the methods is that the stress indicator will find a relative peak or valley in the price movement that cannot be found using the previous method.

If the indicator is robust, then moving the threshold from 90 to 95 should reduce the number of trades and increase the size of the profits per trade, or unit profits. In the same way, holding the threshold constant at, say, 95, and increasing the calculation period from 10 to 20 should also reduce the number of trades and increase the size of the unit profits. When the threshold is very low, for example, 70, the unit profits are likely to be too small to overcome transaction costs, even though it will vary based on

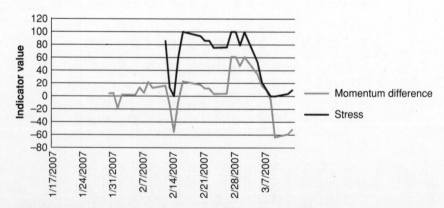

FIGURE 6.2 Momentum difference and the stress indicator.

the volatility of the two legs. Even if there are sufficient profits, there will be many times when you enter based on a 70 threshold and prices continue in the same direction, pushing the indicator value to 90. That represents a sizable risk, even if the final accounting is a profit.

There are also reasons to use exit thresholds, but we have chosen not to use them. Actually, that is not a fair statement. When you exit at a value of 50, you are expecting the two legs to both come back to their relative midpoint price based on the calculation period. That is as much a positive decision as saying that we exit when the short position (entered at a stress value of 90) moves to 60 (not quite neutral) or that the short moves to 40, slightly better than neutral. Some traders would like to take as much as possible from a trade by entering a short at +90 and exiting at +10, the point where you would reverse to long. When you use a short calculation period, the indicator will swing from high to low, yet the market has no obligation to do that. If you get caught selling into a strong market, then the chances of exiting at an indicator value of +50 are far greater than exiting at +10. Risks that are very large but occur infrequently are extremely important to your final success. We can now look at some market examples.

GOLD, COPPER, AND PLATINUM

We start by applying the stress indicator to mining stocks. With gold in the news, the higher prices and volatility are likely to cause mining stocks to move in tandem with the underlying metal. This relationship may be increased because some investors choose to buy a portfolio of gold mining shares rather than the metal itself.

Fundamentally, we would expect a gold mining company to show increased profits when the price of gold goes up. From one day to the next, their cost of mining and fabrication doesn't change as the price of gold changes, so better gold prices should translate into higher company profits. Along with gold, we will look at companies that mine copper and platinum. In that way, we can see if the stress indicator works across a wider range of markets and stocks, rather than just gold.

We can use the Internet to look up those companies that specialize in particular metals, but some of them produce more than one in large quantities. One web site, www.miningnerd.com, gives you a choice of both metals and companies in many countries. We could also find what we wanted on www.yahoo.com. We were able to sort by capitalization and select the largest companies to include in our test.

A well-diversified company will not perform as well as one highly focused on mining one metal. Even so, we won't try to analyze the fundamentals of the company but assume that successful trading means that the metal is of primary importance to the company share price. One of the uncertainties of trading stocks is that, even though a company is dependent on gold or copper, it may be that management, labor and trade contracts, or mining operations overwhelm the impact of gold prices.

Trading Rules

Our test will cover both metals prices and share prices beginning in January 2000, a little over 10 years. We gave the trading rules in the previous section, but briefly:

- The stress indicator takes the metal price as leg 1 and the stock price as leg 2.
- The stress indicator will use a 10-day calculation period.
- We sell the metal and buy the company shares when the stress indicator moves over 95.
- We buy the metal and sell the shares short when the stress indicator falls below 5.
- We volatility adjust the position sizes of both legs in order to have the same risk.
- We exit both longs and shorts when the stress indicator crosses 50.

The Dynamics of Changing Parameters

The parameters used, the 10-day calculation period and the thresholds for entering and exiting, are basic values and not fitted to the best solution. Varying the short entry threshold above and below 95 should result in fewer or more trades in a predictable pattern. For example, moving the threshold from 95 to 98 might cut the number of trades by 20% but increase the unit profits (per contract and per share). Similarly, lowering the threshold would increase the number of trades but lower the unit profits; it should also increase the overall trading risk because trades would be entered earlier and held through more variation in price movement. Lowering the threshold will, at some point, cause the unit profits to fall below the transaction costs.

Changing the exit threshold has a similar dynamic. For shorts entered at 95, exiting at 50 is considered a neutral point, where both legs come back into equilibrium. If we raise the exit point to 55, we reduce the unit returns by exiting sooner, and we may increase the number of trades by a small amount. If the value of the stress indicator falls to 53, allowing an exit, then moves back up to 96, we get another trade. The chances of that happening are smaller when the calculation period is shorter because the stress indicator value will move quickly and has less definition.

The biggest changes to performance come when the calculation period is changed. By shortening the period below 10, the stress indicator will move between 100 and 0 faster, more trades will be generated, and unit returns will be smaller. Increasing the calculation period will do the opposite. But there is another dynamic affecting results—price noise.

Pairs trading is mean reverting; therefore, markets with more noise produce better results. Entering a short on a sudden jump up in gold that has no follow-through is exactly the pattern for profitability. In Chapter 2, we discussed how to measure noise and also that viewing prices over a shorter time period magnified the noise, while longer periods emphasize the trend. Then shorter calculation periods will be better for pairs trading. If we were to use a 60-day period to generate the stress indicator, then we might see only a few buy or sell signals each year and hold that trade for weeks before exiting. We would be fighting the trend, usually unsuccessfully.

This all explains why this chapter looks at trading in a variety of commodities and stocks, all with the same parameters. If you choose to use this method, you should prove to yourself that varying the parameters has a predictable effect on results, and that most choices of parameters will be profitable. A high percentage of profitable results across markets means that you have a robust trading method.

Remember that the stress indicator has no notion of volatility. All peaks and valleys are relative to recent price swings. If prices are quiet for 10 days, the stress indicator will adjust the buy and sell zones to a narrower range. Part of this process will be to apply a volatility filter, a common solution that seems to work well.

Costs

In the previous chapters, no costs have been applied to the results based on stocks, but $25 per round turn was used for futures. Per share returns in stocks were shown so that you could decide if the fees that you pay allow net profits after costs. In this chapter, we use commodities for one leg, and the cost for buying or selling a contract is larger and could change the outcome; therefore, we will charge the commodity leg $25 for each round turn. We assume stocks can be traded for less than 1 cent per share; therefore, no cost is used for the stock side of the trade.

Slippage in trading commodities can be larger than the commission costs if you throw your order into the market as a *stop* or a *market order*. Most professional traders use limit orders; that is, if they want to sell gold at $1,105.50, where the market is currently trading, they place an order to "sell 10 gold 1106," looking to do slightly better. If the order is not filled in a few minutes, they can lower that order to "sell 10 gold 1105.50 or 1105." Some amount of patience is usually rewarded with a good fill. For that reason, and because of trading experience using systematic methods, we have chosen to use $25 for each commodity trade. For some professionals, this cost can be near zero. For the novice, it might be $100.

MINING COMPANIES

The following eight mining companies were selected, mostly by capitalization, but also for the convenience of getting the data:

Symbol	Company	Dependency
ABX	Barrick Gold	Gold
NEM	Newmont Mining	Gold
GG	Gold Corp	Gold
IAG	IAMGOLD	Gold
BVN	Compania de Minas Buenaventura	Gold
FCX	Freeport McMoRan	Copper (and gold)
RTP	Rio Tinto	Copper
SWC	Stillwater Mining Corp	Platinum

The pattern of metals prices can be seen in Figure 6.3, beginning in 1983. Older prices are not the actual cash price at the time because these are back-adjusted futures prices; however, the patterns are the same. Gold declined from its cash peak of $800 per ounce in January 1980 and kept dropping throughout the 1980s and 1990s. Anyone holding gold from the bull market of 1979 would not have recovered their investment until 2003, without including the lost interest income or adjustments due to inflation. Because of that steady decline and the associated low volatility of prices, it would have been difficult to trade gold using any strategy and net a profit (other than holding a short position for 20 years).

Instead, we'll look at the more recent periods, first from the beginning of 2000 and then starting from 2007. It's important that the strategy is successful even during less volatile periods, but more interesting if we focus on the last few years, when inflation has been a concern of investors and volatility has increased. Figure 6.4 shows that although both precious metals and nonferrous metals have received a lot of press coverage during the past few years, prices for the three metals were stable from January 2006 through mid-2007. All three rallied in the first quarter of 2008, but gold was the only metal to recover; copper and platinum are now trading below their

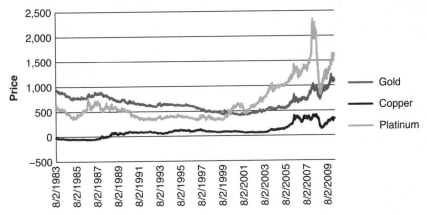

FIGURE 6.3 Prices of gold, copper, and platinum from 1983, back-adjusted nearest futures.

highs. The similarity in patterns, given the very different fundamentals, indicates a global market issue, in this case inflation and the change in the dollar, was driving prices. Investors, concerned about the loss of purchasing power, choose hard commodities and put their money into commodity funds containing all three metals, among others such as crude oil and wheat. By using a short calculation period, pairs trading should be able to focus on short-term market noise and distinguish between these markets, at the same time gaining valuable diversification.

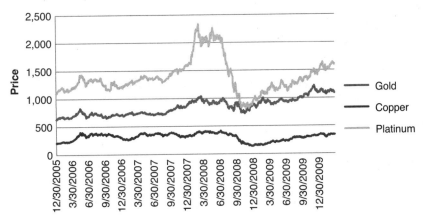

FIGURE 6.4 Prices of gold, copper, and platinum prices from 2006 through March 2010.

The Test

The cross-market strategy was run on the eight share prices and their metal dependencies beginning in January 2000, with a 10-day calculation period, 95 short entry, 50 exit, and a $25 cost per contract for commodity trades. Results are shown in Table 6.2.

Overall results are remarkably good, with an average information ratio above 1.0 and an annualized return of 12.5% at an annualized volatility of 12%. The gold-copper-platinum leg averaged $114 per contract after a charge of $25, but the per share return was a marginal 5.9 cents. A few of the companies, Newmont, Barrick, and Rio Tinto, had returns that were reasonably high, but it would be much better to get the returns per share higher.

There are two ways to solve this problem:

1. Find a time period when volatility was higher.
2. Filter those trades entered when volatility was relatively low.

The more recent years, from 2007, would satisfy the first option, but if volatility were to fall, we might not have a trade for months or years at a time. By applying a volatility filter that varies with price, we gain some flexibility. Even during extended periods where volatility is low, there are bursts of activity that could produce profitable returns.

In pursuing the first option, Figure 6.4 shows that the period from 2007 had higher volatility. Table 6.3 shows the results of using our basic parameters and costs applied to that trading interval. Because the interval was slightly over 30% of the first period, we expect the number of trades to drop proportionally. Instead of 529 trades, there are now 178, 33.6% of the original, close to expectations. The higher volatility apparent from

TABLE 6.2 Results of cross-market mining tests from 2000.

Leg 1	Leg 2	Trades	TotPL	AROR	Std	Corr	Unit1	Unit2	Ratio
Gold	ABX	548	1013215	17.2	12	0.612	117.82	0.083	1.437
Gold	NEM	547	1016481	15.1	12	0.615	92.78	0.163	1.254
Gold	GG	550	661599	11.2	12	0.570	132.95	0.011	0.932
Gold	IAG	368	700841	9.5	12	0.368	102.88	0.029	0.792
Gold	BVN	543	1067740	17.5	12	0.493	84.31	0.067	1.456
Copper	FCX	558	457856	11.6	12	0.374	100.49	0.024	0.968
Copper	RTP	552	428046	10.5	12	0.344	90.25	0.084	0.876
Platinum	SWC	568	1217798	7.3	12	0.270	198.36	0.009	0.612
Average		529	820447	12.5	12	0.456	114.98	0.059	1.041

TABLE 6.3 Results of cross-market mining tests from 2007.

Leg 1	Leg 2	Trades	TotPL	AROR	Std	Corr	Unit1	Unit2	Ratio
Gold	ABX	179	886991	32.2	12	0.672	186.80	0.257	2.687
Gold	NEM	172	912648	29.3	12	0.634	284.77	0.233	2.441
Gold	GG	181	566683	21.4	12	0.668	272.65	0.056	1.786
Gold	IAG	180	662019	18.7	12	0.590	178.50	0.043	1.561
Gold	BVN	186	994221	37.0	12	0.540	196.24	0.239	3.080
Copper	FCX	182	343831	21.1	12	0.559	185.64	0.106	1.760
Copper	RTP	175	212199	11.4	12	0.492	166.20	−0.221	0.948
Platinum	SWC	172	932528	13.1	12	0.386	638.84	−0.014	1.093
Average		178	688890	23.0	12	0.568	263.70	0.087	1.920

the chart translated into much better annualized returns, 23.0% compared with 12.5%. The information ratio also jumped from 1.04 to 1.92, a very large increase, indicating that this trading period yielded higher returns for the same risk. Most important, the profits per unit traded (contracts and shares) increased significantly. The metals returned $263 per contract, up more than 100%; the stocks increased to 8.7 cents per share from 5.9 cents.

One interesting result is that Rio Tinto and Stillwater show losses on the stock side of the trade but ratios near 1.0. That happens when the number of contracts times the unit metal returns is greater than the number of shares times the unit share return. The returns of the commodity metals leg overwhelms the losses of the stock. Returns per share of Barrick, Newmont, and Buenaventura exceeded 23 cents, a very safe margin of profit. Figure 6.5 shows the cumulative profits for each pair from 2007. At the top

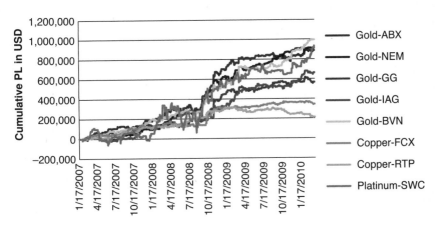

FIGURE 6.5 Cumulative profits for mining companies from 2007.

are gold trading against Barrick (ABX) and Newmont, and platinum with Stillwater. Platinum shows more volatility in returns during 2008 than any of the other pairs during the entire period.

The overall impression that you get from the results in Figure 6.5 is that mining pairs work and continue to generate good returns. Copper pairs post the lowest returns but would help diversification when this is viewed as a portfolio.

Filtering Volatility

Using the average true range for measuring volatility over the same period as the stress indicator, we can filter out trades entered during periods of low volatility. This may not be necessary because the results from 2007 were very good. Still, trading less often reduces your exposure to price shocks and risk in general. If you can achieve the same return by being in the market less often, you are always safer.

Higher volatility improves the performance of most arbitrage strategies. It allows the entry spreads to be larger; therefore, costs become a smaller factor. Using a momentum indicator, such as the stochastic or stress, results in self-adjusting entry thresholds because the concept of high and low is relative to recent price movement. It is not necessary to change anything in the strategy to account for increases in volatility. In addition, the number of shares traded for each commodity futures contract will vary as the two markets change in volatility relative to one another. Of course, risk increases with volatility, but the position sizes will drop to maintain a constant risk level.

Decreasing volatility is another matter. As volatility drops below some very low level, the average profit from a trade will not be enough to offset costs. Before 2006, volatility greatly reduced the rate of return. We can see this by netting the values in Tables 6.2 and 6.3. The returns from 2007 were twice the returns over the entire period from 2000, which means that the returns from 2000 through 2006 must have been very small.

In Figure 6.6, the volatility of gold and Newmont Mining are parallel at low levels from 2000 through the third quarter of 2005. Volatility is measured as the average true range of prices over the past 10 days, the same period as the stress calculation. By reading the chart, we can estimate that volatility less than $500 per day in gold and $1.50 per share in Newmont is too low to trade.

Results Using a Volatility Filter

When we apply the volatility filter, we use a multiplication factor to raise the threshold to a reasonable level. Without that, the use of 1 average true range would eliminate half the trades. To generalize the use of the volatility

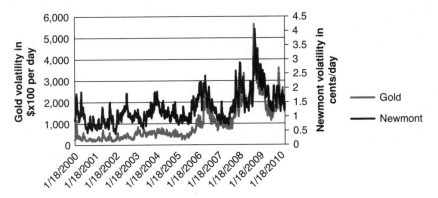

FIGURE 6.6 Comparison of gold and Newmont Mining volatility, January 2000 through February 2009.

filter and avoid overfitting, we use the same multiplication factor for all markets, where the average true range of the price moves is converted to a percentage, ATR%, as follows:

For stocks,

$$ATR\%(S) = 100 \times \frac{ATR(10) \times 1}{S_t}$$

where the ATR is calculated over 10 days, the conversion factor is 1.0 indicating 1 share minimum, and S_t is today's stock price. The value is multiplied by 100 to get a whole percent.

For futures,

$$ATR\%(F) = 100 \times \frac{ATR(10) \times \text{Conversion}}{F_t}$$

the only difference is that the *conversion* is the value that gives you the profit or loss based on a *big point move*. For example, one contract of gold is 100 troy ounces; then the conversion or big point value is 100.

By using a factor and converting the current ATR to a percentage, ATR%, we are able to use the same values for each pair. We will use only the filter factor of 3.0, which means that we will enter a trade only if the current volatility is greater than 3%, as measured previously. In our rules, both the metal prices and the share prices must have a volatility below 3% to filter the trade. In other words, if either the metal or the share price shows a volatility greater than 3%, we take the trade. If both markets have low volatility, the chance is greater that the overall market is quiet and we are not just seeing a small interval of low activity in the metal or the stock.

TABLE 6.4 Mining pairs from 2000 with volatility filter of 3.0.

Leg 1	Leg 2	Trades	TotPL	AROR	Std	Corr	Unit1	Unit2	Ratio
Gold	ABX	141	886278	33.4	12	0.672	208.58	0.350	2.781
Gold	NEM	119	808274	26.6	12	0.634	302.10	0.343	2.221
Gold	GG	159	559763	21.6	12	0.668	248.49	0.106	1.802
Gold	IAG	165	618123	17.6	12	0.590	166.91	0.046	1.463
Gold	BVN	174	958181	35.8	12	0.540	171.32	0.278	2.981
Copper	FCX	171	340478	21.2	12	0.559	200.67	0.090	1.766
Copper	RTP	157	219170	13.0	12	0.492	172.77	−0.144	1.080
Platinum	SWC	169	959475	13.6	12	0.386	660.36	−0.013	1.130
Average		157	668718	22.9	12	0.568	266.40	0.132	1.903

Filtered Results

Table 6.4 shows the results of the mining pairs from 2007, applying the volatility filter with a factor of 3.0. Even though the volatility was higher during the last 3 years, we want to remove lower-volatility trades that would have generated smaller unit profits.

Results are similar to those without the filter, but unit returns for shares increased significantly from 8.7 cents to 13.2 cents. The two pairs, copper-RTP and platinum-SWC, still show losses on the stock side, but their ratios increased slightly. Overall, the information ratio was the same, but the results are more uniform. The average returns for each metals contract remained almost the same, but those values are large enough to net a realistic profit. Figure 6.7 shows the cumulative profits of the eight pairs.

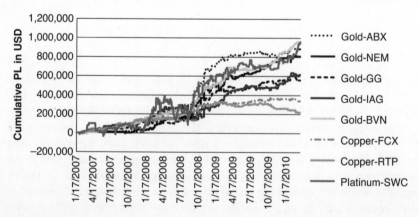

FIGURE 6.7 Cumulative profits from mining pairs from 2007, using a volatility filter.

Alternative Rules

The cross-market strategy as discussed in this section had very little testing. Only a 10-day calculation period was used, and only the 95 short entry and 5 long entry thresholds were tested. We consider the exit at 50 a nonchoice. Essentially, we used a basic set of values applied to all new markets with good success.

You can increase the size of each profit, and also the risk, by waiting until the stress indicator reaches 45 for shorts and 55 for longs, but there will be fewer trades. More trades can be generated by narrowing the entry thresholds to 90 and 10 or 85 and 15, but you reduce the potential profits. Once a trade is entered, the exit zone could be closer—for example, 55 instead of 50 for shorts—to capture more profits, but those profits will be smaller, and it will be more difficult to overcome transaction costs. You can decide to exit the trade if it's not profitable after 3 or 5 days, but that will reduce the percentage of profitable trades and turn some of the profits into losses. Using any stop or exit rule intended to cut losses also puts severe restrictions on the profits. It will require that prices move within a narrow range to satisfy the risk constraints. Markets don't like to do that and seem to know when you've placed a stop so that it can be touched before reversing back in the direction that would have posted a profit.

Mean-reverting strategies require a high percentage of profitable trades to succeed because the few losses can often be quite large. That is a natural pattern in trading. There is no free lunch. Trend-following systems have a large number of losing trades, but a few exceptional gains, called the *fat tail*, make up for all the losses. Mean-reverting methods are the opposite. They have a high percentage of smaller, profitable trades and a few much larger losses. There is no way to change these patterns. If you add a filter that seems to beat the odds, chances are you've overfit the data, and it won't work in real trading. You may even succeed for some time, as did Long-Term Capital, but in the end, the risk is still there.

Volume

Volume can be a simple substitute for volatility or an additional measure that adds stability. When volume increases, so does the opportunity for volatility. Volume can be considered *potential volatility*. In Figure 6.8, the volume of gold is the total volume of all futures contracts, and the volatility is the 10-day average true range. Volume can be erratic and is normally smoothed to see if it's in an uptrend or a downtrend, but the shapes of the two curves are very similar. Volume seems to lead volatility as it moves higher in 2002, it has only a minor setback compared with volatility in 2005, and it clearly starts to decline well ahead of volatility at the end of 2008.

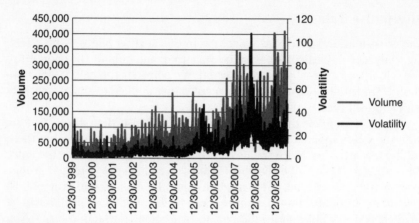

FIGURE 6.8 Comparison of gold volatility and volume.

For those familiar with futures, open interest is also a good measure. Open interest is the number of outstanding contracts. As public interest in a market grows, such as gold during a declining U.S. dollar period, investors enter the futures market by buying a gold contract. They are matched with someone who wants to sell a contract at the same price. If this is a new transaction, it adds one contract of open interest. If the new buyer gets the contract from a person who previously owned a contract of gold, then there is no change in open interest. During inflation periods, there are always more people wanting to buy gold. Investors currently holding gold are not interested in selling. The short-term trader, who believes that gold prices will drop slightly over the next few minutes or hours, will accommodate the new investor by selling a contract of gold, intending to get out of that trade before the end of the day by buying it back.

Open interest is said to have a pattern that confirms the trend. That is, when large numbers of investors are buying gold, then open interest rises. When gold prices suddenly turn to the downside, those investors liquidate their positions en masse, causing open interest to drop. Analysts should consider using open interest as an alternative to volume.

AGRIBUSINESS PAIRS

Agribusiness companies are another group of stocks that are dependent on commodities. These include Archer Daniels Midland (ADM), the biggest public company that crushes soybeans (A. E. Staley and Cargill are both privately held); Purina (part of Nestlé), which uses grain for dog food;

TABLE 6.5 Soybean-ADM pair using the standard parameters, with and without a volatility filter.

	Leg 1	Leg 2	Trades	TotPL	AROR	Std	Corr	Unit1	Unit2	Ratio
No filter	Soybeans	ADM	565	1229597	8.3	12	0.09	33.10	0.067	0.693
Filter 3.0	Soybeans	ADM	335	1223117	10.3	12	0.09	122.31	0.100	0.858

Oscar Mayer (now a division of Kraft) and Swift, which processes mainly poultry; ConAgra, which provides diversified food services; and a score of other companies. Although ADM is quite diversified, it is still highly focused on grain.

Taking soybeans as the dependent commodity, we pair it with ADM and apply the same parameters as mining, beginning in 2000 through March 2010. The first line of Table 6.5 shows the results using these same basic parameters. Results are good, but the returns per contract and per share are marginal, even after deducting $25 for each contract of soybeans traded.

This problem can be overcome by applying the same filter that we used for mining, a 10-day ATR with a factor of 3.0. Results then improved everywhere, while the number of trades dropped by about 40%. The ratio improved nicely, as did the annualized returns. Most important, the unit returns for soybeans rose to $122 per contact, and the ADM returns to 10 cents per share. The cumulative profits for both the nonfiltered and filtered cases are shown in Figure 6.9. The two return streams are nearly parallel, but the filtered stream has intervals when it was out of the

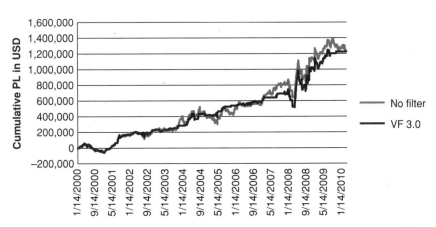

FIGURE 6.9 The soybean-ADM pair from 2000, with and without a volatility filter.

market. These can be seen as horizontal lines on the chart. The trades that were eliminated netted a total return of near zero, which can be seen in Table 6.5, because the TotPL is almost the same, even though the number of filtered trades declined substantially. Fewer trades with the same profits will result in higher unit returns, just what we were trying to achieve.

Although we tested only one stock, the result was similar to our mining results. This adds substance to the robustness of the concept.

THE MAJOR ENERGY PRODUCERS

No cross-market trading method could be complete without looking at energy. In Chapter 3, the pairs were made up only of various major energy companies. Now we'll look at whether the price of crude oil directly affects the share prices of those companies.

We also looked at the increased correlation in certain inflation products, gold, crude oil, and the EURUSD, beginning in 2007. We would expect the relationship between crude oil and the oil companies to increase similarly. We make no attempt to find out how much of their profit margins are dependent on the price of crude because these companies have large downstream operations (refining and retail), as well as exploration and production, or upstream operations. We expect that a significant increase in the price of crude oil will go right to the company's bottom line because there are no costs added to their operations when prices rise.

Of these players, the first pair will be ExxonMobil (XOM) and the crude oil futures contract traded on the New York Mercantile Exchange (NYMEX), now part of the Chicago Mercantile Exchange (CME). Because ExxonMobil is a very large, diverse company, factors other than the price of crude oil will move its share price; therefore, it shouldn't be surprising if an arbitrage with crude is not reliable in a normal market. But with the price of crude moving from $50 to $150 per barrel and back to $30, this market is far from normal. If there was ever a time that Exxon profits would track crude prices, this is it.

In Figure 6.10, we can see that crude oil and XOM prices track reasonably well until the last quarter of 2006. Crude prices take a sharp drop from about $120/bbl (these are back-adjusted futures) to near $80, while XOM continues higher. Then, when crude prices spike in mid-2008, XOM prices have already started lower. It's not clear from this chart that an arbitrage between the two will be consistent, if at all profitable, from the last quarter of 2006; however, they come back together at the end of 2008 and again seem to be tracking closely.

One point to keep in mind is that our trades are held for only a short time. Although we see the big trends in the chart, pairs trading holds

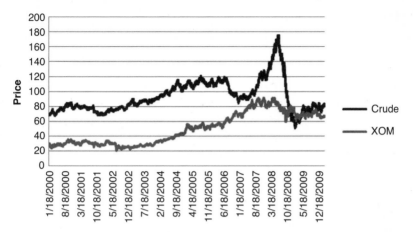

FIGURE 6.10 Crude oil and ExxonMobil prices, January 2000 through March 2010.

positions only a few days, capitalizing on the noise. When using a mean-reverting system, such as pairs trading, holding a trade for a long time would be a disaster when there are sustained moves in opposite directions. Fortunately, when you view prices in the short term, there is a lot of noise.

Relative Value

It would not be easy to find an absolute price level where a stock and a commodity price are both distorted or both normal. Even if there was one point where they appeared to be in equilibrium, everything would change as prices changed. An economist might be able to draw a supply-demand curve to explain the relationship, but econometric analysis has not been particularly dependable and has a time horizon that is far longer than any trader would care to think about. The empirical approach is a much more satisfying and rewarding way to solve this problem.

Stress Indicator for Crude-ExxonMobil

The risk of trading crude against XOM is going to be high because both markets have been very volatile. If we were more demanding with our entry points and faster to exit, we should expect to reduce that risk, even though it would also reduce the size of our individual profits. Up to this point, we have only used a 10-day momentum and entered shorts at a 95 threshold and longs at 5. Exits are only when the stress indicator crosses 50. We will continue to use exactly those parameters and rules because success adds to the robustness of the method, and that's important for longevity.

TABLE 6.6   Results of trading the crude-XOM pair for two different time periods.

From	Corr	Trades	AROR	Unit1	Unit2	Ratio
			Crude-XOM Performance			
2000	0.331	352	14.5	309.46	31.14	1.212
2007	0.441	118	28.0	948.90	53.50	2.337

A \$25 round-turn cost per contract will be deducted from each crude trade to be more realistic about results. Although you could deduct your own costs from the unit returns, the information ratio would be highly inflated if costs were omitted. Still, with stock costs less than 1 cent per share, we have not subtracted any costs on the stock side.

Results trading the crude-XOM pair are shown in Table 6.6. Two periods are compared, 2000 through March 2010 and 2007 through March 2010. When we looked at inflation pairs, for example, gold and the EURUSD, we found that correlations increased, volatility increased, and per unit returns increased when we selected periods when there was more investor activity. The results in Table 6.6 confirm that same expectation. Over the entire 10-year period, results were good. There were a reasonable number of trades, 352, or about 35 per year, with annualized returns of 14.5% and a good information ratio of 1.21. Also important are the unit returns, which indicate the method's sensitivity to slippage and costs. Crude returned about \$309 per contract net of a \$25 cost, and ExxonMobil returned 31.1 cents per share (results are shown as 100 shares). Both are well within our requirements for trading. However, this pair may not be representative of other energy sector pairs, and keeping per unit returns high is an important target of system development.

The second line of Table 6.6 covers only the period from January 2007 through March 2010. The number of trades drops by 66% to 118, but the unit returns for crude jump to \$948, more than three times the original \$309. Profits per share of XOM also increase by 71%, a healthy amount. The information ratio increases to an impressive 2.33. Keep in mind that this period from 2007 to now was selected with hindsight. Because we are in a more volatile market, this could be traded now, but it will eventually revert to the normal volatility. It simply points out that you can be more aggressive about taking positions when the market is more active. After we finish looking at the detail of the trades, we will try to simplify the selection of trades using a volatility filter. Meanwhile, Figure 6.11 shows the cumulative PL for the crude-XOM pair beginning January 2000. Profits didn't begin until 2005; then they increased rapidly. From late 2008, there has been some moderation in the rate of increase, but it remains profitable.

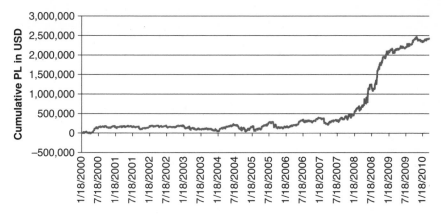

FIGURE 6.11 Cumulative profits from the crude-XOM pair using a calculation period of 10 days and entry threshold (for shorts) of 95.

Trade Detail

Before looking at a broader selection of markets, it would be useful to review the numbers associated with a specific trade. Table 6.7 gives a complete profile of all the calculation results needed to make a trade. Table 6.7a has the data, the stress indicator calculations used for entry and exit signals, and the volatility calculations needed to determine the position size. Table 6.7b shows all of the positions, as well as the profit and loss calculations.

Table 6.7a begins with the date and then the high, low, and closing prices for crude oil (nearest futures) followed by the high, low, and close for ExxonMobil. The high and low are used for both the initial momentum calculations and the volatility, which, in turn, is used to decide the position sizes. Trades are entered on the close, so the open is not needed here. We said earlier that the markets do not close at the same time, but if you enter prices ahead of the crude close, you can trade both markets at that time. Experience shows that signals occurring anytime during the day should produce a good return.

The next two columns show the raw stochastic momentum calculations for crude and XOM. These values range from 0 to 100, as prices go from oversold to overbought. The calculation was shown earlier in this chapter, and it is the same calculation that was used in Chapter 3. All momentum values change quickly because only 10 days are used in the calculation.

Column 10, M1 – M2, is the momentum difference, which becomes the input to the stress indicator, given in the next column. Although the momentum difference can range from −100 to +100, the stress indicator

TABLE 6.7 Crude-XOM pairs trades.

(a) Data and calculations

Date	Crude Oil			ExxonMobil			Crude	XOM			Crude	XOM
	High	Low	Close	High	Low	Close	Mom1	Mom2	M1 – M2	Stress	Vol1	Vol2
12/2/2008	78.97	75.54	75.68	75.92	72.85	75.53	1.45	73.13	−71.68	15.14	4270.0	460.8
12/3/2008	76.82	74.98	75.51	77.36	73.65	76.85	5.45	83.50	−78.05	0.00	4243.0	458.3
12/4/2008	75.99	72.08	72.39	76.92	72.94	74.19	2.46	62.61	−60.15	24.32	4395.0	457.3
12/5/2008	73.19	69.22	69.53	75.90	70.60	74.52	2.00	62.71	−60.71	43.38	4234.0	439.1
12/8/2008	73.42	70.27	72.43	77.98	76.11	77.52	20.74	82.87	−62.14	39.80	4336.0	396.8
12/9/2008	73.29	70.55	70.79	77.55	75.43	76.12	10.14	66.11	−55.97	55.24	3960.0	368.8
12/10/2008	74.89	70.61	72.24	79.63	76.79	77.99	19.51	81.84	−62.33	39.32	3974.0	377.5
12/11/2008	77.63	71.68	76.70	79.84	77.33	77.94	48.32	79.44	−31.12	100.00	4087.0	358.1
12/12/2008	76.16	72.34	74.98	78.92	75.76	78.37	40.79	84.09	−43.30	74.05	4037.0	372.8
12/15/2008	78.81	72.93	73.33	79.42	76.78	77.87	42.15	78.68	−36.53	88.48	4025.0	340.8
12/16/2008	75.40	71.65	72.56	81.56	77.99	81.06	34.83	95.44	−60.61	37.16	4057.0	340.8
12/17/2008	74.84	70.30	70.47	81.16	78.98	78.98	13.03	76.46	−63.43	0.00	4327.0	325.5
12/18/2008	71.50	67.41	67.53	78.90	74.12	74.92	1.05	39.42	−38.36	77.57	4345.0	334.3

(b) Profit and loss results

Date	Crude		XOM		Crude	XOM	Net PL	Cum PL
	Contracts	Entry	Shares	Entry	P/L	P/L		
12/2/2008	0	0	0	0	0	0	0	1955466
12/3/2008	10	75.51	−93	76.85	0	0	0	1955466
12/4/2008	10	75.51	−93	76.85	−31200	24627	−6573	1948893
12/5/2008	10	75.51	−93	76.85	−28600	−3055	−31655	1917238
12/8/2008	10	75.51	−93	76.85	29000	−27774	1226	1918463
12/9/2008	0	75.51	0	76.85	−16650	12961	−3689	1914775
12/10/2008	0	0	0	0	0	0	0	1914775
12/11/2008	−10	76.70	114	77.94	0	0	0	1914775
12/12/2008	−10	76.70	114	77.94	17200	4908	22108	1936882
12/15/2008	−10	76.70	114	77.94	16500	−5707	10794	1947676
12/16/2008	0	76.70	0	77.94	7450	36408	43858	1991533
12/17/2008	10	70.47	−133	78.98	0	0	0	1991533
12/18/2008	0	70.47	0	78.98	−29650	53971	24321	2015855

resets those values to the range 0 to +100. This is the column used to determine a short entry (greater than 95), a long entry (less than 5), and an exit (crossing over 50).

The last two columns are the volatility calculated using the average true range and expressed in dollars. You'll notice that the stocks are based on trades of 100 shares, so when we see the results, it will show unit profits in whole cents rather than in dollars (i.e., a 12 cent unit profit will be shown as 12.00 rather than 0.12).

The first trade shown is a long (long crude, short XOM) taken on the close of December 3, 2008, when the stress indicator drops from 15.14 to 0. That happens when today's low is the lowest of the past 10 days. The entry prices are the close of trading in each market. The position size is always 10 contracts for crude and the number of shares in XOM needed to make the ATR equal for both legs. Remember that we are using stock units of 100, so a position size of –93 is actually short 9,300 shares. We get those shares by dividing the volatility of crude, $4,243, by the volatility of 100 shares of XOM, $458.30, for a position size of 9.258 for each contract of crude. We trade 10 contracts; therefore, the XOM position is 93 (100 share units) or 9,300 shares.

Following the profits and losses for the trade is straightforward. Crude was entered at 75.51 per barrel and XOM at 76.85 per share. The stress indicator rises steadily until on December 9, 2008, it reaches the value 55.24, above the exit threshold of 50, triggering an exit on the close. The exit price for crude is 70.79 for a net loss of 10 contracts × (70.79 – 75.51) × 1,000 per big point for a loss of $47,200 less $25 per contract for a net loss of $47,450. XOM was sold short at 76.85 and bought back at 76.12 giving a profit of 9,300 × (76.85 – 76.12), or $6,789. That nets to a loss on the pairs trade of $40,661. Well, not every trade can be a profit.

On the next trade, the stress indicator jumps to 100 on December 11, 2008, and we sell 10 crude at 76.70 and buy 11,400 shares of XOM at 77.94. On December 16, the indicator value drops to 37.16, and the trade exits at 72.56 for crude and 81.06 for XOM. In this trade, we were short crude for more than a $5 profit and long XOM for more than a $3 profit. The total return on the pairs trade was $76,758.

Visualizing the Pairs Trade

It is always a good check of your work to see the trading signals on a screen. Many careless errors are avoided that way. You can plot the stress indicator, the individual momentum indicators for the two legs, and the corresponding buy and sell points for the trade. Figure 6.12 is a Trade Station Securities chart with the signals given in the top panel along with prices for XOM. Crude oil prices are in the second panel, and the indicators

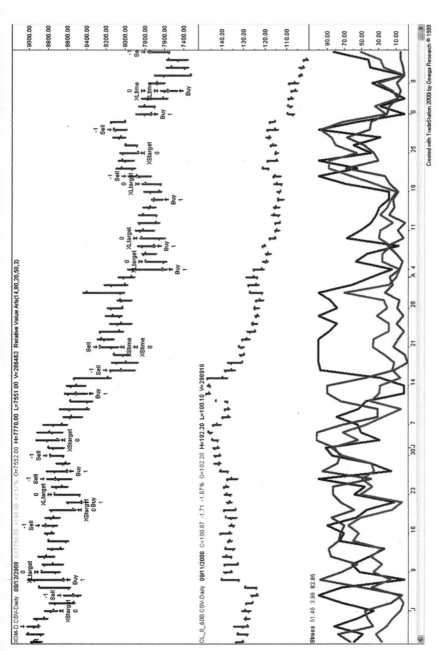

FIGURE 6.12 XOM (top panel), crude oil (middle panel), and the stress indicator (bottom panel), along with the momentum indicators for the two legs.

© 2001–2008 TradeStation Technologies, Inc. All rights reserved.

215

at the bottom. TradeStation is a good candidate for programming this indicator and generating live signals or end-of-day signals. Table 6.2 showed some of the trading signals that appear in Figure 6.6. For each trade, there is only one crude contract traded, and the XOM shares represent the number needed to volatility-adjust the two legs.

A Reminder about Trading Hours

When trading two very different markets, you will find that they often do not close at the same time, although they are both open at the same time for many hours. The crude oil market closes in New York at 2:30 P.M. each day, while the stock market is open until 4:00 P.M. Crude continues to trade in the after-hours market and can be traded 24 hours, although volume is much thinner throughout the evening and night.

The prices used in these examples are captured at two different times. If you wait until after the stock market closes, then calculate the values, you will be using the same prices. But then you would need to trade stocks and crude at about 4:30 P.M. That's not too bad for stocks, but you may start to see low volume for crude.

A professional systematic trader will capture both crude and stock prices shortly before the close of the stock market, run the numbers, then trade on or near the close of the stock market, when most other markets are still reasonably active. For these pairs trades, the best approach is to capture prices before the crude close, when both crude and the stock market are open and trading actively. And it is more likely that a distortion will occur intraday than based on the closing prices. It doesn't matter what time of day you calculate the stress indicator and generate a signal. If prices are distorted at 11 A.M. or at 1 P.M., and the stress indicator is above 95 or below 5, then the timing is good for a trade.

Tracking the Trades

While entries must be executed promptly, exits are not as critical. We enter the trade when the distortion is unusual (and therefore less frequent), but there are many more opportunities to exit when prices return to normal, the most common situation. However, during volatile markets, which have become more frequent, exiting the first time the price moves back to equilibrium (a stress indicator value of 50) removes unnecessary risk.

Other Petroleum Companies

While the crude-XOM pair has shown very good performance during the past three years, it is even more important that the exact same strategy works for other petroleum companies. There is no doubt that companies in the same business will show high price correlation to one another; therefore, if this method doesn't work for other petroleum companies, we can say that we overfit the data. We have already applied this method to mining and one agribusiness company with exactly the same rules, so we have hopeful expectations.

Table 6.8 shows the results applied to nine major petroleum companies listed on the NYSE, with ExxonMobil repeated at the top. These companies were chosen simply because of their capitalization and the availability of data. They are:

XOM	ExxonMobil
SUN	Sun
VLO	Valero
EP	El Paso
COP	ConocoPhillips
MRO	Marathon Oil
APA	Apache
APC	Anadarko
CVX	Chevron

On the left are the results from January 2000 through March 2010, and on the right from January 2007 through March 2010. First, we can see that the results are uniformly profitable and consistent with expectations. None of the pairs lost money, and only El Paso had a losing stock market leg. During the most recent three years, there were about 35 trades per pair per year, and the unit returns of $462 per contract and $0.26 per share are well above our threshold for success. We can see from the jump in average values that successful performance was concentrated in the last three years.

Removing the Low-Volatility Trades

Even with good results, we want to look further at what happens if we remove the trades that are taken when price volatility is low. Taking fewer trades means being out of the market more, and that avoids unnecessary risk.

Using the ATR to measure the risk and then converting that to a percentage of price was our way of generalizing a volatility filter. For the mining and agricultural pairs, we found that a filter of 3.0% seemed to yield a consistent improvement; therefore, the same method was applied to the petroleum pairs over both the longer and shorter test periods. The results are shown in Table 6.9.

The averages show that filtering trades improved results in both periods. While the ratios went up about 10%, the unit profits jumped considerably, showing that the trades made during a low-volatility scenario

TABLE 6.8 Performance of petroleum companies, from 2000 through March 2010.

Pair	From 2000 through March 2010						From 2007 through March 2010					
	Corr	Trades	AROR	Unit1	Unit2	Ratio	Corr	Trades	AROR	Unit1	Unit2	Ratio
XOM	0.331	352	14.5	309.46	31.14	1.212	0.441	118	28.0	948.90	53.50	2.337
SUN	0.354	352	4.2	151.94	9.25	0.352	0.353	112	5.4	233.78	19.88	0.453
VLO	0.359	341	2.6	39.29	6.47	0.215	0.376	107	7.3	−116.89	32.73	0.607
EP	0.257	339	5.2	345.22	−0.99	0.432	0.420	108	9.6	802.13	−1.81	0.799
COP	0.402	367	9.4	229.92	14.35	0.783	0.501	117	16.6	421.98	38.49	1.387
MRO	0.404	342	4.5	217.80	2.11	0.378	0.516	101	7.9	336.80	16.57	0.660
APA	0.473	349	9.9	215.90	21.54	0.824	0.564	104	14.7	697.79	29.24	1.229
APC	0.434	339	4.1	67.43	12.54	0.342	0.550	104	4.1	152.50	14.02	0.343
CVX	0.371	361	13.7	292.36	23.05	1.145	0.466	118	20.7	686.44	33.70	1.728
Average	0.376	349	7.6	207.70	13.27	0.631	0.465	110	12.7	462.60	26.26	1.060

TABLE 6.9 Results of oil company pairs using a low-volatility filter.

Pair	From 2000 through March 2010						From 2007 through March 2010					
	Corr	Trades	AROR	Unit1	Unit2	Ratio	Corr	Trades	AROR	Unit1	Unit2	Ratio
XOM	0.331	137	15.0	580.00	74.14	1.251	0.441	63	27.3	1165.56	101.37	2.271
SUN	0.354	253	6.2	271.50	13.67	0.514	0.353	91	9.4	357.91	36.20	0.780
VLO	0.359	264	1.9	-1.89	7.97	0.158	0.376	82	6.6	-284.51	40.98	0.551
EP	0.257	235	8.6	424.04	2.71	0.719	0.420	70	10.0	853.00	0.75	0.833
COP	0.402	213	8.4	247.42	22.09	0.702	0.501	66	14.9	427.43	58.69	1.241
MRO	0.404	254	7.1	139.21	13.56	0.593	0.516	73	13.6	107.81	59.88	1.136
APA	0.473	204	11.4	296.57	47.84	0.949	0.564	75	19.6	809.73	92.56	1.630
APC	0.434	211	7.0	276.16	19.64	0.586	0.550	76	7.1	384.61	22.08	0.594
CVX	0.371	172	10.0	404.77	25.76	0.834	0.466	65	17.3	782.15	49.55	1.443
Average	0.376	216	8.4	293.09	25.26	0.701	0.465	73	14.0	511.52	51.34	1.164

returned smaller profits. The best result would have been that the filtered results of the longer period were as good as the unfiltered results of the shorter time period, but that isn't the case. The period from 2000 to 2010 gave an average ratio of 0.701, still lower than the 2007 to 2010 unfiltered period, which gave 1.060. Because the filtered method does not use hindsight, it is more likely to be realistic.

Comparison of Energy Profits

There are four cases that have been under the microscope with regard to energy pairs:

1. January 2000 through March 2010 with no filters.
2. January 2000 through March 2010 with a low-volatility filter.
3. January 2007 through March 2010 with no filters.
4. January 2007 through March 2010 with a low-volatility filter.

Of these combinations, performance from 2007 was far better because it isolated the biggest moves in the history of the energy markets. Visualizing the results are always useful, and Figures 6.13a, 6.13b, 6.14a, and 6.14b show combinations 1 through 4. Figure 6.13a shows the long period of sideways, slightly positive performance into 2006, followed by more volatile, highly profitable returns through 2008 and mixed results afterward. ExxonMobil is the best performer, followed by Chevron, with the low end held up by Valero and Anadarko. Figure 6.13b used the same test period but applied a low-volatility filter of 3%. Total profits are lower because there are fewer trades, but those trades had higher unit returns and a better average information ratio. Using a filter was better than taking all trades.

The more recent three years are shown in Figures 6.14a and 6.14b. Even though the pairs strategy had an outstanding performance during this period, the filtered results were even better. This is easier to see in the individual profit streams than in the previous tables. While many of the returns start to decline in the last three to six months in the unfiltered performance, many more continue to be profitable when the low-volatility filter is used.

PORTFOLIO OF CROSS-MARKET ENERGY PAIRS

Performance looks different when it's combined into a portfolio. No matter how similar the markets and trades, there are always differences that

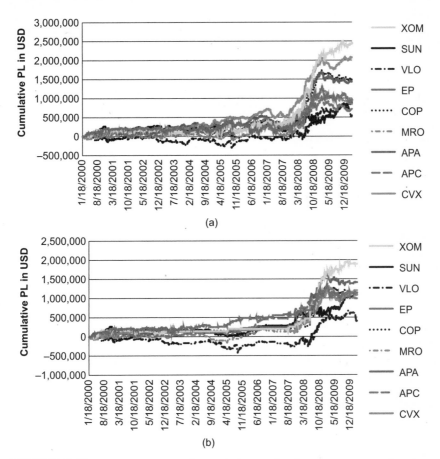

FIGURE 6.13 (a) Comparison of cumulative profits for energy companies, January 2000 through March 2010, no filters, and (b) comparison of cumulative profits for energy companies, January 2000 through March 2010, with a 3% low-volatility filter.

offset risk. When using futures, that risk reduction allows you to leverage up the trading, but with stocks that's not the case. With stocks, you can only bring the leverage down. Still, diversification will lower that risk, which may lower your investment, freeing up capital for other investments.

For pairs trading in energy, we always took a position of 10 contracts in crude oil and then found the number of shares of the stock that would make the risk the same as crude oil. Once we calculate the shares, we know the total exposure, the cost of the position. For this example, we will use the results from February 2010.

To trade one contract of crude oil, we need to deposit a margin amount of $9,788. For those who don't trade futures, margin is a good-faith

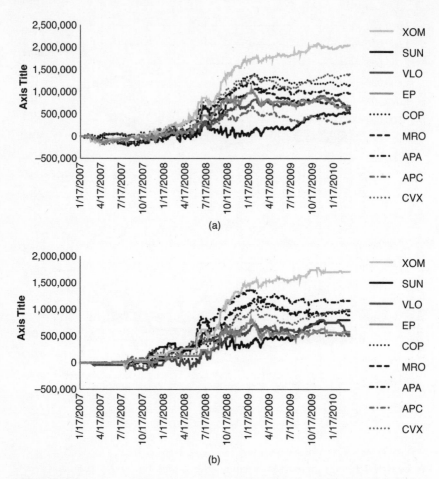

FIGURE 6.14 (a) Comparison of cumulative profits for energy companies, January 2007 through March 2010, no filters, and (b) comparison of cumulative profits for energy companies, January 2007 through March 2010, with a 3% low-volatility filter.

deposit. If the position goes the wrong way, you may owe more. Margin is roughly 10% of the contract value, so with crude at $75 per barrel, a 1,000-barrel contract is worth $75,000. Margin tends to lag prices because it is set by the exchange based on its board's perception of market risk. Even at this level, your leverage is 7.6:1, which is far better than the stock market, which is 1:1.

The daily profits and losses from trading both futures and stocks are shown in Table 6.10. The pattern of positions should be a surprise. Although the momentum for the crude leg is identical for each of these

TABLE 6.10 Daily profits and losses trading energy pairs, February 2010.

Date	XOM	SUN	VLO	EP	COP	MRO	APA	APC	CVX
2/1/2010	0	22058	7147	323	0	0	9726	0	0
2/2/2010	0	0	0	-19090	0	0	-12564	0	0
2/3/2010	0	0	-7755	-1693	0	0	-6568	0	0
2/4/2010	0	20772	11802	4333	0	0	7667	0	0
2/5/2010	0	0	21102	20298	0	0	15928	21131	0
2/8/2010	7575	0	-16934	0	17651	0	0	-13321	23393
2/9/2010	2297	0	-10589	0	-955	0	0	-6264	177
2/10/2010	14163	0	-10904	0	11466	0	0	-2603	16193
2/11/2010	0	0	-7600	0	0	0	2146	7340	0
2/12/2010	0	0	4188	0	0	0	10359	0	0
2/16/2010	0	0	-20547	0	0	0	2014	-5006	0
2/17/2010	0	0	-7907	0	0	0	0	-8610	0
2/18/2010	-12298	0	-21066	0	0	0	0	-4137	0
2/19/2010	-8471	0	9	0	-5771	5718	0	0	0
2/22/2010	-13315	0	-6025	0	-6698	17931	0	0	0
2/23/2010	3915	0	4886	3869	-3343	0	0	0	0
2/24/2010	2637	0	-7804	-10071	-904	0	0	0	0
2/25/2010	8615	0	0	26688	17001	0	0	0	0
2/26/2010	0	0	10750	0	0	0	10191	8817	0

TABLE 6.11 Exposure for each stock based on 10 contracts of crude oil, February 2010.

Stock	Largest Position	Price	Exposure
XOM	230	65.76	$ 15,125
SUN	243	24.94	$ 6,060
VLO	320	19.21	$ 6,147
EP	524	10.61	$ 5,560
COP	210	47.48	$ 9,971
MRO	341	29.95	$ 10,213
APA	94	103.14	$ 9,695
APC	141	69.61	$ 9,815
CVX	156	70.50	10,998
Total			83,584
Futures			
Margin	90	9788	880,920
Total			964,504

stocks, the positions are remarkably different. There are only three days in which five stocks had a position, February 8, 9, and 10, and on those days, the stocks did not have all profits or all losses, as we might expect from a highly correlated group. Fewer signals at the same time might mean that you need less capital than the worst-case scenario, and different profits and losses tell you that there will be a much greater benefit from diversification than originally expected.

To calculate the portfolio investment size, we recorded the largest position size and the corresponding entry price, then calculated the *exposure* for each stock, shown in Table 6.11. The largest position is multiplied by the price at the time of entry, and the total cost is the exposure. Not all positions were taken at the same time, so the table shows the worst-case scenario. It also shows the total margin needed to trade 10 contracts of crude for each of the nine pairs, where the margin for one contract is $9,788. The total investment needed is then $964,504, or $96,450 trading one contract of crude and a tenth the size for stocks.

Using the investment of $964,504, the daily profits and losses can be converted to daily returns, $r(s)_t$, for stock s,

$$r(s)_t = \frac{PL(s)_t}{\text{Investment}}$$

The daily returns for each of the nine pairs are shown in Table 6.12, with the average return (the portfolio return) in the rightmost column.

TABLE 6.12 Daily returns and portfolio returns, with annualized volatility at the bottom.

Date	XOM	SUN	VLO	EP	COP	MRO	APA	APC	CVX	Port Return
2/1/2010	0.0000	0.0229	0.0074	0.0003	0.0000	0.0000	0.0101	0.0000	0.0000	0.0045
2/2/2010	0.0000	0.0000	0.0000	-0.0198	0.0000	0.0000	-0.0130	0.0000	0.0000	-0.0036
2/3/2010	0.0000	0.0000	-0.0080	-0.0018	0.0000	0.0000	-0.0068	0.0000	0.0000	-0.0018
2/4/2010	0.0000	0.0215	0.0122	0.0045	0.0000	0.0000	0.0079	0.0000	0.0000	0.0051
2/5/2010	0.0000	0.0000	0.0219	0.0210	0.0000	0.0000	0.0165	0.0219	0.0000	0.0090
2/8/2010	0.0079	0.0000	-0.0176	0.0000	0.0183	0.0000	0.0000	-0.0138	0.0243	0.0021
2/9/2010	0.0024	0.0000	-0.0110	0.0000	-0.0010	0.0000	0.0000	-0.0065	0.0002	-0.0018
2/10/2010	0.0147	0.0000	-0.0113	0.0000	0.0119	0.0000	0.0000	-0.0027	0.0168	0.0033
2/11/2010	0.0000	0.0000	-0.0079	0.0000	0.0000	0.0000	0.0022	0.0076	0.0000	0.0002
2/12/2010	0.0000	0.0000	0.0043	0.0000	0.0000	0.0000	0.0107	0.0000	0.0000	0.0017
2/16/2010	0.0000	0.0000	-0.0213	0.0000	0.0000	0.0000	0.0021	-0.0052	0.0000	-0.0027
2/17/2010	0.0000	0.0000	-0.0082	0.0000	0.0000	0.0000	0.0000	-0.0089	0.0000	-0.0019
2/18/2010	-0.0128	0.0000	-0.0218	0.0000	0.0000	0.0000	0.0000	-0.0043	0.0000	-0.0043
2/19/2010	-0.0088	0.0000	0.0000	0.0000	-0.0060	0.0059	0.0000	0.0000	0.0000	-0.0010
2/22/2010	-0.0138	0.0000	-0.0062	0.0000	-0.0069	0.0186	0.0000	0.0000	0.0000	-0.0009
2/23/2010	0.0041	0.0000	0.0051	0.0040	-0.0035	0.0000	0.0000	0.0000	0.0000	0.0011
2/24/2010	0.0027	0.0000	-0.0081	-0.0104	-0.0009	0.0000	0.0000	0.0000	0.0000	-0.0019
2/25/2010	0.0089	0.0000	0.0000	0.0277	0.0176	0.0000	0.0000	0.0000	0.0000	0.0060
2/26/2010	0.0000	0.0000	0.0111	0.0000	0.0000	0.0000	0.0106	0.0091	0.0000	0.0034
Volatility	0.1069	0.1112	0.1853	0.1549	0.1084	0.0699	0.1061	0.1175	0.1045	0.0575

The average implies that each pair was equally weighted. The bottom line, marked volatility, is the annualized volatility. Note that the lowest volatility is 6.99% and the highest 18.5%, but the volatility of the portfolio returns is only 5.75%, showing exceptional diversification. It is also important to realize that the standard deviations of the returns of each pair have more days with zero than with actual profits or losses. This reduces the standard deviation so that the volatility of the individual pairs does not reflect the risk on a day when you are trading, but the long-term risk. It may be more accurate, and more descriptive, to include only the days when positions were held (usually nonzero values) in the standard deviation calculation. However, the financial industry doesn't do it that way; therefore, we'll use the traditional method here.

Finally, we can calculate the NAVs for the month of February using the standard formula

$$\text{NAV}_t = \text{NAV}_{t-1} \times (1 + \text{R}_t)$$

where R_t is the average daily return of all pairs. Table 6.13 shows the returns and the final NAVs, and Figure 6.15 shows the corresponding NAVs. Even a successful pattern of performance has both profitable and losing days. The returns for February show a drawdown of 1.18%, even while the month finished up 1.65%. Although this example showed only one month, a volatility of 5.75% is quite conservative, and there is no way to leverage that higher other than to borrow money, a tactic not generally recommended. In Chapter 7, we see that when trading only futures, leveraging up is a simple process. Implementing this strategy using options may also allow more flexibility.

OTHER OPPORTUNITIES

Good traders and good technicians are constantly searching for new opportunities. Many of these come when prices or volatility moves to extremes, attracting participation from the mainstream investor. It is well known that volatility attracts volume. Oil and gold are just the examples used here. It's not possible to say how long these opportunities will last, but there will be others to follow.

During 2007 and 2008, the profits of the airlines seemed to be inversely related to the price of crude oil. Also, the price of gold appeared to be reacting to the drop in the U.S. dollar, in particular the EURUSD. Gold is also attractive when investors feel threatened. The grain markets even began to react to the loss of value of the dollar and were gathered together

TABLE 6.13 Portfolio returns and NAVs for February 2010.

Date	Portfolio Return	NAV
1/31/2010		100
2/1/2010	0.00452	100.452
2/2/2010	−0.00365	100.086
2/3/2010	−0.00185	99.901
2/4/2010	0.00513	100.414
2/5/2010	0.00904	101.322
2/8/2010	0.00212	101.536
2/9/2010	−0.00177	101.357
2/10/2010	0.00326	101.687
2/11/2010	0.00022	101.710
2/12/2010	0.00168	101.880
2/16/2010	−0.00271	101.604
2/17/2010	−0.00190	101.410
2/18/2010	−0.00432	100.972
2/19/2010	−0.00098	100.873
2/22/2010	−0.00093	100.779
2/23/2010	0.00107	100.887
2/24/2010	−0.00186	100.700
2/25/2010	0.00603	101.306
2/26/2010	0.00343	101.654

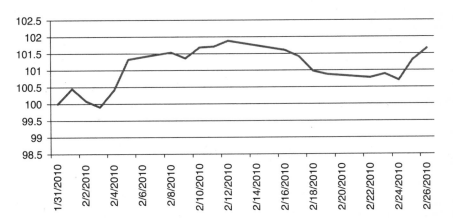

FIGURE 6.15 NAVs for energy pairs, February 2010.

into commodity funds to protect investors against rampant inflation. The most popular of these is the Goldman Sachs Commodity Index (GSCI).

Even if these opportunities last only six months, they are sources of trading profits. The next ones may come when the equity market begins its next rally or the U.S. dollar weakens due to the inflation that will inevitably follow the government bailout and recovery program. We might suddenly realize that the demand on energy far exceeds the supply, or investors again feel that gold is no longer a convenient inflation hedge. And while this program uses only closing prices, there are many more intraday opportunities if this method is applied to 15-minute or hourly data.

SOME FINAL NOTES

All trading methods benefit from diversification, and short-term strategies tend to show differences more often than longer-term approaches because they are more sensitive to smaller changes in price moves, resulting in more frequent entries and exits. The cross-market strategy can produce different signals when crude oil is measured against different petroleum companies, but it is far better to incorporate both oil and metals combinations in the same portfolio. Agribusiness pairs or airlines can also be added. If the commodity markets differ, then the portfolio will gain important diversification.

As with any mean-reverting method, trading at different times of day will increase the opportunities. Markets are more likely to be out of line during the day and come back together on the close. They are also likely to diverge after economic reports or earnings reports. Those are valuable opportunities.

The limiting factor in the cross-market pairs is the inability to increase leverage. This is not the case when using only futures. Other than borrowing funds or using options, selecting more volatile periods to trade seems to be the best alternative.

CHAPTER 7

Revisiting Pairs Using the Stress Indicator

Having introduced the stress indicator in the previous chapter, we would like to look at the most important pairs that were discussed in Chapter 4, "Pairs Trading Using Futures," this time using the stress indicator to generate signals. These are equity index and interest rate futures, both very liquid sectors offering good opportunities for pairs trading. We will find that the results using the stress indicator are very different from the original momentum difference calculations.

FUTURES MARKETS AND THE STRESS INDICATOR

In Chapter 4, we used the difference between two stochastic momentum indicators to generate pairs signals for pairs in equity index and interest rate futures markets. The results were successful but showed that a combination of U.S. and European markets is necessary to produce sufficient profits, rather than just U.S. markets. The correlation between most U.S. markets in either sector is too high, and few trades are generated. Those signals that were produced did not have enough profit to overcome normal commission costs.

In Europe, there is enough difference between the economies, especially if you include Britain, to produce profitable pairs trades in most equity markets, but there is less choice and higher correlations with interest rates. That still leaves a large number of pairs in markets that are highly liquid and have virtually no counterparty risk. Unlike a stock, which can surprise you any day with an announcement of gross mismanagement or fraud, a stock futures index or 10-year government bond doesn't have that problem. The failure of a single stock in the S&P 500 is not a disaster, and the clearing corporation for the Chicago Mercantile Exchange or Eurex has never had a default and has substantial funds and contingency plans to avoid investor losses due to nondelivery or other forms of counterparty risk.

The stress indicator is a simple manipulation of the two momentum values calculated for leg 1 and leg 2 of the pair. By taking the difference in the two values and using those numbers to create a third momentum indicator, we change the dynamics of the trading signals. Essentially, the signals are more uniform and the concept is more generalized, perhaps more robust. However, just like the original momentum values, the stress indicator does not consider volatility. In fact, all sense of volatility is lost during the process. This means that we might need to add a volatility filter in order to take only those trades with the potential for larger returns; otherwise, during a low-volatility period, we could be trapped taking many trades without the possibility of profits exceeding costs.

The following sections compare the original method using the momentum difference with the more generalized stress indicator. A detailed description of the calculations needed to create the stress indicator can be found in Chapter 6.

EQUITY INDEX FUTURES

We had considerable success using the momentum difference for index markets, but a more generalized solution is always best. By converting the final momentum differences using the stochastic formula, we know that any value near 100 is overbought, and values near zero are oversold. The stress indicator will also handle relative changes in volatility differently.

We ran a few simple tests using the stress indicator, shown in Table 7.1. The first test used a calculation period of 4 because that was found to be the most effective for the momentum difference method, and because the shorter calculation periods capitalize on market noise. After $25 costs were applied, the results were quite good, showing small net returns per contract for leg 1 and larger returns for leg 2. An information ratio of 1.521 and annualized returns of 18% were very acceptable.

TABLE 7.1	Stress indicator tests for equity index futures. The top four tests vary the calculation period but leave the entry levels the same. The bottom test uses a volatility filter to find trades with larger per contract returns.

	Trades	TotPL	AROR	Std	Unit1	Unit2	Ratio
4 × 95	347	643,517	18.24	12	68	213	1.521
5 × 95	285	612,443	18.12	12	83	209	1.511
7 × 95	213	587,875	18.33	12	109	202	1.527
10 × 95	154	440,635	13.60	12	147	154	1.134
7 × 95 VF 3	83	464,841	17.34	12	196	221	1.445

However, the average number of trades per pair, 347, was much higher than expected. Over the 4.5-year test period, November 2005 through March 2010, that comes to 77 trades per year, or a new trade every 3.25 days. That seems fast although not necessarily wrong. Still, it would be better if there were fewer trades and larger profits per contract. Note that this is a very different problem than with stocks, when we couldn't get enough trades with sufficient profits.

To accomplish this, tests were run with longer calculation periods: 5, 7, and 10. When selecting these numbers, we keep in mind that the percentage difference in the calculation periods that we test is important, even with a small sample. Moving from 4 to 5 is a 25% increase, 5 to 7 is a 40% increase, and 7 to 10 is a 42% increase. While these are large gaps, going from 9 to 10 is an 11% increase, which is disproportionately small. Given the small numbers and simple test, increasing the space between periods gives the best representation of the method's performance profile.

The next three tests show a steady decline in the number of trades and a comparable increase in the returns per contract. The fourth test, using a period of 10 days, shows a 55% drop in the number of trades but an increase in per contract returns from an average of $140 to $151, a gain of only 7%. While increasing the calculation period showed that the results were stable, or robust, it did not accomplish our goal of significantly increasing the profits per contract.

Volatility Filter

Another way to reduce the number of trades is to apply the volatility filter that was used in Chapter 3. It simply calculated the average true range over the same period as the momentum calculation, divided by the price to get a percent, and then ignored all trades that had volatility below that threshold on the day of entry. Once the trade was filtered out, it could not be entered at another time; the program waited for a new signal to enter.

We previously found that 3% was a good threshold number; therefore, we applied only that one condition to the best of the results, the 7-day stochastic calculation period. As shown in Table 7.1, the filter did much better, drastically reducing the number of trades from the original 213 to 83, a reduction of about 61%, and increasing the profits per contract from an average of $155 to $208. Instead of trading nearly every 5 days, using a filter reduced new signals to once every 13 days.

Comparative Results

It's important to compare results using all pairs, not just the best ones. An improvement in a strategy should improve the losing pairs as well as the profitable ones, even if the losing ones still remain negative. Otherwise, you are focusing on a smaller and smaller set of results, making it far easier to overfit the data.

Table 7.2 compares the results of the momentum difference method from Chapter 4, the basic stress indicator, and the stress indicator filtered with a 3% volatility entry threshold. As seen in the averages on the bottom, the basic stress strategy had the highest ratio and annualized returns, but more trades than we wanted. When we added the filter, the number of trades dropped and the returns per contract increased substantially, while the ratio dropped a relatively small amount, as shown in the panel on the right. In some cases, the filter turned losses into profits, as with the SP-DJIA pair, but it also turned profits into losses, as with the SP-DAX. It may look as though the numbers are jumping around, but Figure 7.1 shows the ratios of each pair grouped together for the three methods. A fast glance shows that the profitable pairs are all similar for the three systems; that is, when one method posted a ratio of about 2, all methods did about the same. The results that changed from plus to minus were all marginal returns in the first place. There are no cases where the stress method shows a ratio of 1.0 and the momentum a ratio of –1.0, a complete reversal. It shows that we are dealing more with subtleties than with structural changes in the strategies. Both are mean reverting, and both are based on similar indicators. Still, we want to trade the strategy that gives us the best chance of success.

Correlations and Returns

In Chapter 4, we showed the relationship between the correlations of index pairs and their return ratios. That relationship is repeated in Figure 7.2. It shows a very clear inverse relationship between correlation and returns; that is, as the correlation declines, the returns increase. Naturally, that is

TABLE 7.2 Comparative results for index pairs using momentum, stress, and filtered stress.

Leg 1	Leg 2	Momentum 4 × 40					Stress 7 × 95					Stress 7 × 95 with 3.0% Filter				
		Trades	AROR	Unit1	Unit2	Ratio	Trades	AROR	Unit1	Unit2	Ratio	Trades	AROR	Unit1	Unit2	Ratio
S&P	NASDAQ	25	−1.6	472	−331	−0.129	199	−5.0	65	−33	−0.420	38	4.5	503	−178	0.378
S&P	Russell	48	−0.4	60	60	−0.037	209	5.8	−144	300	0.483	31	8.0	−606	1099	0.665
S&P	DJIA	5	−5.6	−130	38	−0.469	215	−13.6	−119	107	−1.137	35	9.8	−1051	1065	0.816
S&P	EuroStoxx	26	12.3	218	47	1.027	214	3.8	134	−4	0.320	101	6.6	247	−25	0.547
S&P	DAX	39	5.6	333	−784	0.466	205	1.0	241	−612	0.081	69	−4.0	649	−2421	−0.332
S&P	CAC	73	31.0	96	811	2.581	230	40.0	130	488	3.335	91	28.8	154	778	2.400
S&P	FTSE	85	35.0	153	1175	2.919	232	46.0	157	853	3.831	124	42.6	276	1212	3.553
NASDAQ	Russell	62	6.0	−60	328	0.504	202	4.0	−80	257	0.337	34	3.9	−230	659	0.329
NASDAQ	DJIA	33	−13.8	22	−268	−1.150	209	−8.4	−80	89	−0.701	41	0.3	−258	445	0.024
NASDAQ	EuroStoxx	55	−1.4	34	15	−0.116	209	3.1	40	57	0.262	100	10.0	48	154	0.837
NASDAQ	DAX	52	1.7	−51	668	0.140	204	2.2	88	−139	0.185	75	5.5	178	−345	0.461
NASDAQ	CAC	91	21.3	105	425	1.777	230	34.8	157	342	2.898	95	25.5	157	623	2.123
NASDAQ	FTSE	106	27.2	69	896	2.264	223	29.6	57	685	2.467	116	25.2	89	981	2.097
Russell	DJIA	70	−5.8	128	−165	−0.480	206	−7.5	70	−86	−0.629	27	−0.8	514	−451	−0.067
Russell	EuroStoxx	70	0.0	168	−70	−0.003	211	7.1	207	−5	0.595	93	13.1	492	−57	1.092
Russell	DAX	85	16.3	478	−173	1.362	212	6.0	210	−179	0.500	72	9.3	549	−796	0.773
Russell	CAC	120	30.5	420	420	2.540	224	32.8	281	379	2.731	96	26.5	498	651	2.208
Russell	FTSE	129	30.4	416	611	2.533	225	32.8	195	699	2.736	117	28.7	352	1169	2.392

(Continued)

TABLE 7.2 (Continued)

Leg 1	Leg 2	Momentum 4 × 40					Stress 7 × 95					Stress 7 × 95 with 3.0% Filter				
		Trades	AROR	Unit1	Unit2	Ratio	Trades	AROR	Unit1	Unit2	Ratio	Trades	AROR	Unit1	Unit2	Ratio
DJIA	EuroStoxx	33	0.6	−52	115	0.049	208	0.6	40	47	0.051	92	−1.8	100	−17	−0.149
DJIA	DAX	43	4.2	190	−502	0.351	201	−1.0	173	−629	−0.084	68	−4.1	380	−1717	−0.341
DJIA	CAC	81	31.1	124	752	2.593	226	33.2	84	480	2.768	92	27.3	144	753	2.278
DJIA	FTSE	88	28.3	145	981	2.357	230	39.7	100	834	3.307	113	36.1	242	1157	3.011
EuroStoxx	DAX	3	0.7	−569	2898	0.058	212	−7.8	238	−967	−0.654	85	−3.5	438	−1865	−0.288
EuroStoxx	CAC	28	29.5	−13	1331	2.462	255	61.3	175	377	5.111	105	37.4	240	501	3.113
EuroStoxx	FTSE	45	30.5	36	1502	2.545	236	51.2	148	700	4.269	134	47.8	273	889	3.987
DAX	CAC	35	20.3	−50	1118	1.692	250	46.1	298	474	3.839	108	33.2	414	695	2.768
DAX	FTSE	74	34.7	300	1454	2.888	223	36.3	−1	826	3.022	123	34.7	408	1025	2.892
CAC	FTSE	8	20.1	−395	1904	1.673	63	39.2	193	305	3.263	38	34.9	287	203	2.905
Average		58	13.9	95	545	1.157	213	18.3	109	202	1.527	82.607	17.3	196	221	1.445

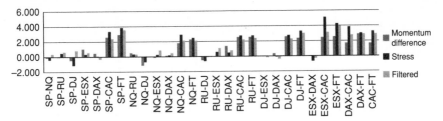

FIGURE 7.1 Comparison of index pairs performance ratios using momentum, stress, and filtered stress.

not a relationship that exists normally, but it does when the pairs are fundamentally linked to each other. The lower correlation shows opportunity, and none of the pairs would have a correlation of zero. The lowest correlation is about .40.

Figure 7.3 shows the same relationship using the stress indicator. While it is similar to the chart produced using the momentum difference (Figure 7.2), the correlations clearly cluster into two groups. We can see why this happens by looking at Table 7.3. All the pairs that have the CAC or FTSE as one leg post the strongest returns and have the lowest correlations. Knowing that, we can reason backward that the French and British economies are very different from the German economy, which dominates Europe and has greater impact on the EuroStoxx. This can be seen because the correlation between the EuroStoxx and DAX is .955, similar to the S&P and DJIA relationship. It is interesting that the top three performers are all European pairs, although in the top two groups, most of the pairs are combinations of U.S. and European markets.

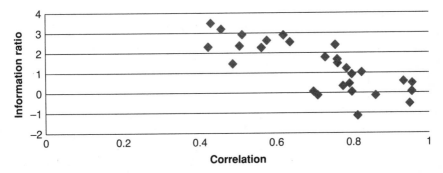

FIGURE 7.2 Relationship between correlation and information ratio for index pairs using the momentum difference method in Chapter 4.

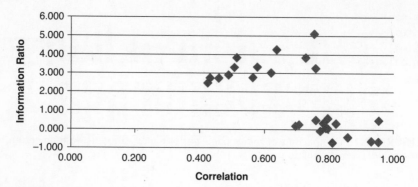

FIGURE 7.3 Correlation versus information ratio for the index pairs using the stress indicator.

TABLE 7.3 Index pairs sorted by correlations, showing the information ratio.

Leg 1	Leg 2	Corr	Ratio
EuroStoxx	CAC	0.754	5.111
EuroStoxx	FTSE	0.637	4.269
DAX	CAC	0.728	3.839
S&P	FTSE	0.513	3.831
S&P	CAC	0.577	3.335
DJIA	FTSE	0.506	3.307
CAC	FTSE	0.759	3.263
DAX	FTSE	0.620	3.022
NASDAQ	CAC	0.488	2.898
DJIA	CAC	0.563	2.768
Russell	FTSE	0.431	2.736
Russell	CAC	0.458	2.731
NASDAQ	FTSE	0.424	2.467
Russell	EuroStoxx	0.797	0.595
Russell	DAX	0.760	0.500
S&P	Russell	0.956	0.483
NASDAQ	Russell	0.783	0.337
S&P	EuroStoxx	0.823	0.320
NASDAQ	EuroStoxx	0.708	0.262
NASDAQ	DAX	0.697	0.185
S&P	DAX	0.791	0.081
DJIA	EuroStoxx	0.797	0.051
DJIA	DAX	0.774	−0.084
S&P	NASDAQ	0.859	−0.420
Russell	DJIA	0.933	−0.629
EuroStoxx	DAX	0.955	−0.654
NASDAQ	DJIA	0.812	−0.701
S&P	DJIA	0.949	−1.137

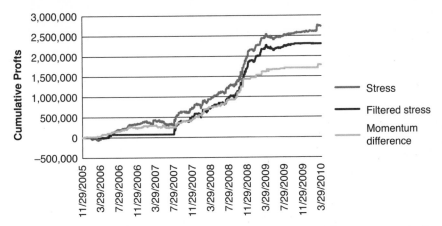

FIGURE 7.4 Comparison of profits using the momentum difference, stress indicator, and the filtered stress indicator for the DAX-FTSE pair.

A visual comparison of the cumulative profits always adds to our information. In Figure 7.4, the results of the DAX-FTSE pair is shown for the original momentum difference method, the stress strategy, and the stress using the standard filter of 3.0. All three profit streams are similar. The filtered stress results, shown as the horizontal line from mid-2006 to mid-2007, also stops trading toward the end of 2009, where it is the middle horizontal line. The momentum difference method does not trade from mid-2009 until recently, when it starts again. These periods of low volatility show the main difference between the three methods. The unfiltered stress method will adjust to all volatility levels and continue to generate trades when it finds relative distortion, even if it cannot produce a profit after costs. By filtering those low-volatility periods, we get a more profitable strategy, but one that was out of the market recently as volatility fell to extreme lows.

The momentum method is fine-tuned but requires that both legs move apart without the benefit of relative volatility. It filters trades much like the filtered stress method.

Of course, we all prefer that a trading system generate trades through all conditions and that those trades are profitable. However, that's unrealistic. Each trading method targets a particular type of trade and market condition. If it can do that consistently, even on a limited basis, it is a success. It is then up to us to find other markets, or other strategies, that work when these methods stand aside.

It is not necessary to go through the exercise of creating a portfolio of pairs from the best of the index group. The DAX-FTSE pair had a ratio of 3.0, about in the middle of the group of 13 best performers. If we created a portfolio from those pairs, it would look excellent, although the reliance on the CAC and FTSE would limit diversification, increase risk, and require that the portfolio is deleveraged to keep risk under control. It's a sacrifice we can all live with.

INTEREST RATE FUTURES

Interest rate futures are among the most liquid markets, so any pairs trading that works will be an important asset in a portfolio. As with the equity index pairs, we will compare the results of the momentum difference method in Chapter 4 with the stress strategy in Chapter 6.

Review of the Momentum Difference Method for Interest Rates

For convenience, Table 7.4 is a recap of the momentum difference results for 14 combinations of the U.S. 30-year bond, 10- and 5-year notes, the Eurobund (maturity of about 10 years), Eurobobl (about 5 years), and the U.K. long gilt (about 8 years). Results are reasonably consistent across the selection of calculation periods and the one entry threshold of ±50. However, for a period of 4.5 years, the number of trades, 22 to 31, is small and causes the annualized returns to be low.

If we look at the results of the momentum difference method in more detail, we see that performance increases as the correlation between the two legs decreases. In Table 7.5, the most correlated markets—the U.S. interest rates—produced only 1 and 2 trades for the 10- and 5-year notes when matched with the 30-year bonds and 10-year notes. The 30 and 5 pair, which has the greatest difference in maturity, posted 10 trades and a good ratio.

As we look down the table at the declining correlations, we see that the biggest gains and the most trades come from pairs using the U.K. long gilt, a longer maturity that allows larger price fluctuations and a market that

TABLE 7.4 Original momentum difference average results for interest rate pairs, Chapter 4.

Test	Trades	TotPL	AROR	Std	Unit1	Unit2	Ratio
4 × 50	31	59,423	4.24	12	335	13	0.353
5 × 50	29	77,229	6.16	12	677	−126	0.513
7 × 50	24	78,720	5.11	12	224	266	0.426
10 × 50	22	86,375	5.51	12	423	142	0.458

TABLE 7.5 Results of the momentum difference for interest rate pairs are dependent on the correlation of the two legs.

	Momentum 5 × 50 Sorted by Correlation			
Leg 1	**Leg 2**	**Corr**	**Trades**	**Ratio**
US 10-Yr	US 5-Yr	0.966	1	−0.361
US 30-Yr	US 10-Yr	0.944	2	0.504
US 30-Yr	US 5-Yr	0.883	10	1.197
US 10-Yr	Bund	0.703	28	0.572
US 5-Yr	Bund	0.697	27	0.936
US 5-Yr	Bobl	0.672	29	−0.093
US 10-Yr	Bobl	0.668	28	−0.180
US 30-Yr	Bund	0.664	23	0.713
Bund	Gilt	0.649	29	0.778
US 30-Yr	Bobl	0.619	39	0.290
Bobl	Gilt	0.607	38	0.450
US 10-Yr	Gilt	0.454	54	0.918
US 5-Yr	Gilt	0.450	55	0.466
US 30-Yr	Gilt	0.425	49	0.992

reflects an economy different from both the U.S. and European countries. The losing combinations all seem to include legs with the shortest maturity, the U.S. 5-year note and the Eurobobl. If we reason backward, one of our better abilities, those markets would have the lowest volatility. If the bobl is paired with the U.S. 30-year bond, the difference in maturity essentially puts them furthest apart on the yield curve and offers the most opportunity for profit, yet the information ratio was still low because the bobl leg would be generating only small returns per contract.

From these observations, we will select a smaller set of pairs for trading. We eliminate all pairs that use only U.S. markets and all pairs that use the Eurobobl—not because the methods pick the wrong entry points, but because, even with the best selection, the volatility of the pairs is not enough to generate profits. The final selection is 7 pairs out of the original 14 pairs. The averages shown in the following examples will include both all markets and the selected pairs. We want both those numbers to show improvement to be comfortable with the results and our conclusions. Table 7.6 shows the results of the selected pairs for the same momentum difference calculation criteria as Table 7.4. All the numbers are far better, although the number of trades is still fairly low, less than 10 per year for any pair. Trading less often should not affect the returns per contract but will lower both the absolute profits and the annualized rate of return. These returns of about 8.5% are not bad, and the few trades mean that the

TABLE 7.6 Results of momentum difference method for seven selected pairs.

		Average of Selected Pairs					
Criteria	Trades	TotPL	AROR	StDev	Unit1	Unit2	Ratio
4 × 50	43	121,045	8.37	12	178	248	0.697
5 × 50	39	127,300	8.39	12	270	203	0.698
7 × 50	31	123,693	7.19	12	96	468	0.600
10 × 50	27	161,979	9.63	12	191	526	0.802

program is mostly out of the market and less exposed to price shocks and unexpected risk.

Results of the Stress Method

Turning to the stress method, results show a very different profile from the momentum difference, even though the test criteria were comparable. Table 7.7 is compared with Table 7.4. The main differences are:

- The stress method had more than seven times the number of trades.
- The total stress profits were large in two of three cases.
- The stress returns were lower.
- The stress ratios were lower.
- The stress returns per contract were too low for comfort.

In previous analysis, selecting trades using a volatility threshold has successfully raised these numbers to good levels. But before that step, Table 7.8 shows the selected set of seven pairs that did not include U.S. combinations and the Eurobobl. Clearly, the three criteria show greatly improved performance. If we compare these results with the same selection using the momentum difference, shown in Table 7.6, we get a very different opinion of the two methods. Now, the stress method still has many

TABLE 7.7 Results of the stress method for all 14 interest rate pairs.

		Average of All Pairs					
Criteria	Trades	TotPL	AROR	StDev	Unit1	Unit2	Ratio
5 × 95	280	42,798	−0.46	12	56	56	−0.039
7 × 95	202	102,077	2.04	12	76	78	0.170
10 × 95	149	104,173	2.65	12	−24	189	0.221

TABLE 7.8 Results of selected pairs for the stress method.

			Average of Selected Pairs				
Criteria	Trades	TotPL	AROR	StDev	Unit1	Unit2	Ratio
5 × 95	288	240,694	10.10	12	56	133	0.842
7 × 95	208	209,389	8.11	12	48	172	0.678
10 × 95	150	186,549	6.60	12	−61	325	0.548

more trades and, at best, twice the profits, a higher annualized return, and a higher information ratio. The profits per contract are still smaller but better than before.

To allow readers to form their own judgment, the detailed summary for each pair, using the stress method with a 5-day calculation period and 95-5 entry thresholds, is shown in Table 7.9. These results include the U.S. interest rate pairs, as well as all the Eurobobl pairs.

Volatility Filter

In the past, we were able to use a volatility threshold filter to select trades that had, potentially, larger profits per contract. The threshold used for all markets was a factor of the average true range of price movement divided by the price, giving us a 3% threshold. The calculation period for the true range was always the same as the momentum calculation period.

When that same approach was applied to the interest rate futures, there were no trades! That is, the volatility of those markets is much less than 3%, so no trades qualified using that threshold. For example, a 3% move in 10-year Treasury notes, now trading at about 116 (this implies a yield of about 3.75%, where 100 is equivalent to 6%), would mean a move to either 119-16 or 112-16, a move so large that it is without precedent.

Instead of 3%, the threshold was lowered to 1%—still a large move, but more realistic. Using 1% generated from 3 to 4 times the number of trades in the momentum difference method and increased the returns per contract by up to 40% while lowering the ratios only slightly. A summary of results is shown in Table 7.10.

Correlation of Momentum Difference and Stress Methods

If we choose the 5-day calculation period for the momentum difference and the 5-day period (filtered) for the stress indicator, we can look at the

TABLE 7.9 Summary of results using the stress method for a 5-day calculation period and entry thresholds of 95 and 5.

Leg 1	Leg 2	Corr	#Trades	TotPL	AROR	Std	Unit1	Unit2	Ratio
US 30-Yr	US 10-Yr	0.944	268	−346,862	−21.6	12	46	−66	−1.801
US 30-Yr	US 5-Yr	0.883	268	−356,551	−16.6	12	−7	−15	−1.385
US 10-Yr	US 5-Yr	0.966	280	−176,850	−22.1	12	67	−46	−1.846
US 30-Yr	Bund	0.664	272	226,761	6.6	12	97	37	0.546
US 30-Yr	Bobl	0.619	275	−33,738	−1.7	12	145	−23	−0.138
US 30-Yr	Gilt	0.425	290	649,691	16.9	12	72	204	1.406
US 10-Yr	Bund	0.703	262	36,559	1.1	12	54	23	0.095
US 10-Yr	Bobl	0.668	275	4,786	−0.5	12	107	−17	−0.040
US 10-Yr	Gilt	0.454	287	256,057	9.1	12	49	135	0.757
US 5-Yr	Bund	0.697	269	−89,830	−7.3	12	−2	26	−0.611
US 5-Yr	Bobl	0.672	265	−86,639	−7.4	12	33	−5	−0.620
US 5-Yr	Gilt	0.450	285	53,984	2.3	12	−25	193	0.195
Bund	Gilt	0.649	312	324,556	21.7	12	105	146	1.810
Bobl	Gilt	0.607	311	137,249	13.0	12	40	194	1.082
Average		0.672	280	42,798	−0.5	12	56	56	−0.039
Selected		0.565	288	240,694	10.1	12	56	133	0.842

TABLE 7.10 Summary of stress method for interest rates using a volatility threshold of 1%.

			Volatility Filtered				
Criteria	**Trades**	**TotPL**	**AROR**	**StDev**	**Unit1**	**Unit2**	**Ratio**
5 × 95 VF1	139	214,652	9.66	12	117	154	0.805
7 × 95 VF1	102	180,288	7.50	12	60	231	0.626
10 × 95 VF1	75	155,512	5.79	12	−103	436	0.483

cumulative profits to see whether the pattern of returns is similar. Figure 7.5 shows that they are quite different, with the momentum difference returning infrequent but steady profits and the stress method showing a strong run of profits from mid-2008 through mid-2009, after a decline at the beginning of 2008. The correlation between the two profit series is .262, indicating that there is at best a weak relationship between the pattern of trading signals. It shows that a small change in technique, calculating the stochastic of the difference, materially changes the strategy. We could take advantage of that by trading signals from both methods. Figure 7.5 also shows the result of equally weighting the two methods. As we would expect, the result is better than either method, with a much smaller drawdown than the stress method and much greater profits than the momentum difference approach.

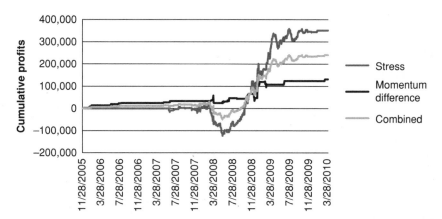

FIGURE 7.5 Cumulative profits for the U.S. 30-year bond–Eurobund pair using both the momentum difference and stress methods, plus the combined results of equal weighting.

A Portfolio of Interest Rate Pairs

Although we created a portfolio of futures in Chapter 4, it seems instructive to go through that same process using the seven interest rate pairs. We first start with the daily profit and loss streams at the inception, November 28, 2005, for each of the seven pairs. We align the data by date because Europe and the U.S. do not always have the same holidays. Remember that the strategy does not trade either an entry or exit if one of the equity index markets is closed and just holds the positions until the next day on which both markets trade; however, there is a change in the returns based on the market that is open. If your data are forward filled, then a simple test of whether the open, high, low, and close today are identical to yesterday would be the same as recognizing a holiday.

Once the data have been prepared, you can accumulate the daily profits and losses into a net profit stream to get a visual understanding of the performance. The cumulative profits, shown in Figure 7.6, will not be used in the calculations, but visual confirmation avoids simple errors. For example, we can see that the filtering of trades resulted in very little trading from the start of the data in 2005 through the middle of 2007. That was a period of very low volatility; therefore, we need to be aware that the 1% filter may keep us out of trading for long periods of time. Reducing the filter size would allow more trades but probably reduce the size of the profits per contract. Traders must decide what low threshold they can tolerate to increase activity.

Note also that the most recent data are also filtered, so that the beginning of 2010 may be inactive. This situation is not likely to continue once

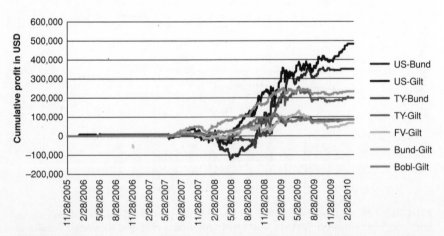

FIGURE 7.6 Cumulative profits for seven interest-rate pairs filtered by 1% volatility.

the central banks start raising rates, but continued concerns about economic recovery and the brewing debt crisis in some European countries might delay an increase in volatility. This is a normal trade-off in the decision process—more activity in exchange for lower unit returns.

It may be tempting to start the portfolio in mid-2007, when volatility and trading activity increased. That way, the annualized returns would be maximized and look better. But that is *ex post* selection, making the decision based on observing past data. In real trading, we will have periods when trades are filtered because of low volatility, and we can't erase those periods from our performance. It's not fair to do that now, so our risk and returns will include all data.

THE PORTFOLIO SPREADSHEET

We began with aligning the daily profit streams, a small part of the data shown in Table 7.11. These values have all been converted to USD at the

TABLE 7.11 Annualized volatility of daily profits and total investment of interest-rate pairs.

A	B	C	D	E	F	G	H
Date	US-Bund	US-Gilt	TY-Bund	TY-Gilt	FV-Gilt	Bund-Gilt	Bobl-Gilt
2/10/2010	0	0	0	0	0	0	0
2/11/2010	0	13304	0	0	0	0	0
2/12/2010	0	6161	0	0	0	0	0
2/15/2010	0	0	0	0	0	792	0
2/16/2010	0	732	0	0	0	0	1197
2/17/2010	0	0	0	6405	4290	2512	1013
2/18/2010	0	0	0	0	0	0	0
2/19/2010	0	0	0	0	0	0	0
2/22/2010	0	0	0	0	0	0	0
2/23/2010	0	0	0	0	0	0	0
2/24/2010	0	0	0	0	0	0	0
2/25/2010	0	1911	0	0	1492	0	625
2/26/2010	0	6260	0	2223	2014	0	−1543
3/1/2010	0	1843	0	3557	1271	0	1980
3/2/2010	0	0	0	−6039	0	0	0
3/3/2010	0	0	0	574	0	0	0
Ann vol	80465	101490	41328	67250	42947	37765	25088
Tot Invest	396,332						

time of the trade so that no currency conversion is needed during the portfolio construction process. At the bottom of each daily profit stream, columns B–H, is the annualized volatility, calculated as

$$\text{Annualized volatility of PL} = \text{Stdev}(\text{B2} : \text{B1121}) \times \sqrt{252}$$

for column B, the 30-year bond and the Eurobund. The result is $80,465. Doing the same for the other pairs and adding all seven gives a total investment of $396,332. This may not be the final investment size because there are other steps that increase or decrease leverage, but it is necessary to have an investment size to calculate percentage returns. Alternatives would be to arbitrarily pick the investment size or to use the investment amount that you have in mind, and then the final numbers will adjust to that investment and show the returns at your target volatility. That will be seen as we move forward.

Using the investment of $396,332, we simply divide the daily profits and losses by the investment size and post them in columns I–O, shown in Table 7.12. Note that each return is divided by the total investment, not by the investment needed for that one pair.

The portfolio returns in column P are now the sum of the seven returns in columns I–O. We again calculate the annualized volatility at the bottom of column P and find that it is 63.9%, far above our target volatility of 12%. To reduce that volatility, we need to deleverage by decreasing the position size while keeping the investment the same, or by increasing the investment size while trading the same number of positions. The factor at the bottom of column P tells us that we would need to reduce our returns, and our position size, to 18.8% of the current size to bring volatility down to 12%. That means, if we were originally trading 10 contracts, we need to trade only 2. That's not good because we won't be able to balance the risk of both legs with only 2 contracts, so the alternative of increasing the investment size is better. Another alternative is to compromise and reduce the position size by half, to 5 contracts, while increasing the investment size by a factor of 2.5 instead of about 5. You must reduce position size, increase the investment, or some combination in order to target the right volatility.

The final step is to create the portfolio NAVs based on the returns in column P and the volatility adjustment factor (VAF) of 0.188. Starting with a NAV of 100 in column Q, the next entry is

$$\text{NAV}_t = \text{NAV}_{t-1} \times (1 + r_t \times \text{VAF})$$

The final NAV is 197.28 (there was a small amount of trading done after March 3, 2010, resulting in a profit). That makes the annualized rate of return 16.6% and, based on a target volatility of 12%, the information ratio

TABLE 7.12 Annualized volatility of daily profits and total investment of interest-rate pairs.

A	I	J	K	L	M	N	O	P	Q
Date	US-Bund	US-Gilt	TY-Bund	TY-Gilt	FV-Gilt	Bund-Gilt	Bobl-Gilt	Returns	NAVs
2/10/2010	0	0	0	0	0	0	0	0	192.35
2/11/2010	0	0.033568	0	0	0	0	0	0.0336	193.57
2/12/2010	0	0.015545	0	0	0	0	0	0.0155	194.13
2/15/2010	0	0	0	0	0	0.001998	0	0.0020	194.20
2/16/2010	0	0.001847	0	0	0	0	0.00302	0.0049	194.38
2/17/2010	0	0	0	0.016161	0.010824	0.006338	0.002556	0.0359	195.69
2/18/2010	0	0	0	0	0	0	0	0	195.69
2/19/2010	0	0	0	0	0	0	0	0	195.69
2/22/2010	0	0	0	0	0	0	0	0	195.69
2/23/2010	0	0	0	0	0	0	0	0	195.69
2/24/2010	0	0	0	0	0	0	0	0	195.69
2/25/2010	0	0.004822	0	0	0.003765	0	0.001577	0.0102	196.06
2/26/2010	0	0.015795	0	0.005609	0.005082	0	-0.00389	0.0226	196.90
3/1/2010	0	0.00465	0	0.008975	0.003207	0	0.004996	0.0218	197.70
3/2/2010	0	0	0	-0.01524	0	0	0	-0.0152	197.14
3/3/2010	0	0	0	0.001448	0	0	0	0.0014	197.19
							Target	Ann Vol	AROR
							0.12	0.639	0.166
								0.188	1.379
								Factor	Ratio

is 1.37, a good number. If you remember, this includes the inactive period from November 2005 through mid-2007. If you lower the target volatility, the ratio remains the same, but the rate of return drops proportionally.

SUMMARY OF PAIRS TRADING

Pairs trading has been covered for stocks, futures, and a combination of both that we called *cross-market trading*. Overall, it has lived up to expectations; that is, it found the right entry and exit points and often returned a profit. It failed only when the volatility of the markets was too low to overcome costs. That could be avoided by waiting patiently for volatility to increase, but traders are not known for their patience. They want to trade all the time.

Futures markets are more interesting than stocks because of both higher volatility and the ability to vary the leverage. Futures trading inherently allows high leverage, and you can tailor it to your personal level of risk. Globalization has been a benefit to the spread trader because U.S. and European markets are now open at the same time, although volume is always highest during the business day in the location of the market being traded, so European volume drops off after 10 A.M. in New York (4 P.M. in Frankfurt). Still, there is enough volume to trade ahead of the U.S. close in both zones. Even now, some Asian markets can be traded 24 hours on an electronic platform, and arbitrage should be expected to increase. Volume is understandably light in Singapore at noon in New York because it is 12 hours earlier. Most people trading in Singapore at that hour are U.S. customers.

Opportunities for trading pairs surface and disappear, but some are always there at any one time. It's not as profitable as it was 10 or 20 years ago, but then we couldn't enter orders electronically, and fills were often disputed. As we've made it easier to trade, the competition has also increased. But that is just a challenge to stay aware and become more technical about how you handle the opportunities and the decisions. Pairs trading is fundamentally sound; it is the basis for the extraordinarily profitable high-frequency trade. Unless all the stocks and futures markets merge into one company, these opportunities are not likely to go away.

CHAPTER 8

Traditional Market-Neutral Trading

A ny strategy that balances longs against shorts can be called *market neutral*. It really means *directional neutral*, where you are not exposed to the risk of outright price direction. You will be able to avoid being long while the stock price is plummeting. It's well known that during uncertain economic times, investors shift to larger, more secure companies, and during boom times, they throw money at small-cap stocks. If that relationship holds true and the economy is robust, you should be able to generate a profit by buying the Russell 2000 and selling the Dow or S&P. That profit would be the result of the relative gain of the Russell over the Dow, regardless of whether the Russell and the Dow went up or down.

One of the greatest advantages of trading a market-neutral strategy is that it is, for the most part, immune to price shocks. If you were long the Russell and short the S&P on September 11, 2001 (volatility adjusted), the losses in the long Russell position would have been offset by the short profits in the S&P. You wouldn't have worried about how much you would lose over the days when the New York Stock Exchange (and most of the other exchanges) was closed. For example, when the markets reopened on September 17, 2001, the S&P had dropped 4.98%, the Nasdaq 5.80%, and the Russell 6.51%. At the lows on September 21, the S&P was off 15.8%, Nasdaq 14.0%, and the Russell 12.3%. Without considering adjustments needed to correct differences in volatility, the exposure would be small. Even leveraged up in futures, typically four times, the exposure would have been smaller than the declines in outright long positions.

In this book, we have focused primarily on pairs trading. The advantages are that you can choose a small set of markets and a modest investment. In addition, the calculations involve only two stocks or futures markets at a time and can be done on a spreadsheet. However, traditional *market-neutral* programs are much broader, serve a somewhat different purpose, and are not correlated to pairs trading, even when both methods are active in the same sector.

This chapter will use similarly related stocks but apply a more general hedging technique. We can then take this method and apply it to stocks that are not closely related, and then to futures markets. The technique used for both stocks and futures will be identical.

HOME BUILDERS

To keep the example of a market-neutral trading program as simple as possible, and still learn as much as we can, the first choice will be the five stocks in the home builders group that were used for the pairs trading example: Hovnanian (HOV), KB Homes (KBH), Lennar (LEN), Pulte (PHM), and Toll Brothers (TOL). The correlations between these stocks can be found in Table 8.1. With pairs trading, we were able to return better than $0.14 per trade; therefore, we have a benchmark to judge the success of the market-neutral approach.

TREND OR MEAN REVERSION?

If you have a set of stocks and plan to go long some of them and short others, it is necessary to decide whether you take a trending position or a mean-reverting one. Do you believe that those stocks that are stronger will stay stronger and those that are weaker will stay weaker than others in the same sector? If we think back at the major trends, it is easy to remember Enron. Once it started down it kept accelerating. More recently, the financial stocks suffered the fastest, steadiest decline on record. We would

TABLE 8.1 Cross-correlations for home builders, 10 years ending March 2009.

	LEN	PHM	KBH	TOL	HOV
LEN	1				
PHM	0.767	1			
KBH	0.787	0.804	1		
TOL	0.472	0.503	0.495	1	
HOV	0.449	0.460	0.495	0.708	1

expect to have produced remarkable profits by selling the financials short and buying everything else (well, maybe not housing) during the second half of 2008.

If you don't believe that trends persist, then you may believe in the *Dogs of the Dow*, a theory advocating that, with qualifications, the weaker companies in the Dow Jones Industrial Average will cycle to become the stronger ones in the near future. After all, they are all solid institutions and just need to get past some short-term issues. At least that was true before the summer of 2008.

How can we decide whether trend or mean reversion is the best approach? For pairs trading, we automatically chose mean reversion, buying when the spread was oversold and selling when it was overbought. But there is always a choice. In Chapter 2, we discussed the level of noise in most markets and how we might use that information. Of all markets studied, the index markets were clustered together and represented the noisiest sector. We also know that applying mean reversion to pairs trading was profitable. The conclusion that was drawn from this was that mean reversion was preferred for stocks and that shorter calculation periods would emphasize the noise. One caveat, however, is that the spread between two noisy stocks might not be as noisy. We'll need to keep that in mind. In Chapter 5, we had a chance to apply a trend to some pairs, but we tilted the game to our advantage by using longer calculation periods, which emphasized the trending nature of some stocks and futures markets.

Another way of deciding whether a trend or mean-reversion method is best would be to find the profitability of a simple trend-following system on these stocks. Although the market-neutral strategy profits from the spread between two stocks, knowing whether the individual stocks trend might make the decision simpler. We'll save that for the next example, applying this method to all Dow components.

BASIC MARKET-NEUTRAL CONCEPT

The first step is to find a measurement that allows us to compare each of the five stocks in the home-building group to decide which are stronger or weaker. There are many ways to do this, and they may all prove to generate similar results. One approach would be to use the same moving average on all stocks, say 20 days, and then compare the 1-day change in the moving average differences. That is done by looking at the change in the moving average from the previous day, $MA_t - MA_{t-1}$, or over n days, $MA_t - MA_{t-n}$. Those stocks with the largest positive change are the strongest; those with the largest negative change are the weakest.

Instead of a moving average, we'll use the slope of a linear regression line. The regression line, the tool of choice for the econometrician, is simply a straight line drawn through the past n daily prices. The slope is the angle of increase or decrease of that line, and it's the same at any point on the line; therefore, if S_t is a point on the line corresponding to day t, and S_{t-1} is the previous point on day $t-1$, then $S_t - S_{t-1}$ is the slope of that line.

Putting All Markets into the Same Units

Comparing the slopes of the lines through price points won't work unless all of the stocks are expressed in the same units, in this case percent. For example, if a stock priced at \$10 went up \$1 each day, the slope would be \$1. If another stock priced at \$5 went up \$0.50 each day, the slope would be \$0.50. If we compared those two stocks without converting to percent, then the higher-priced stock would have the biggest slope and appear to be stronger, when they are actually both rising at the same percentage rate.

Prices are normalized by indexing, which is the same as converting the raw price changes to percentages. Starting each series at 100, the next index value X_t is:

$$X_t = X_{t-1} \times (P_t/P_{t-1})$$

where P_t is the current price and P_{t-1} is the previous price. When the linear regression slope is calculated on each of the five converted home builders, they can be readily compared. Remember that the indexed series are needed only for finding the relative strength of the sector components. When we calculate profits and losses, the original prices are used.

Relative Strength and Weakness

Having chosen to use the linear regression slope to compare the relative strength of all stocks in a sector, we first converted each of the stock series to percentage returns using indexing. The slope is now easily found using the spreadsheet function slope(y, x), where y is the column of dependent variables and the x is the column of independent variables.

Finding the slope of a price series requires only the prices. The independent variable, x, is actually the time. We would use the date for the xs except that stocks don't trade on weekends, and there would be gaps every five days. Instead, we just use the integer sequence $1, 2, 3, \ldots, n$ for as many days as needed in the calculation. For this strategy, we'll use $n = 10$ and apply it to the cash S&P 500 index, or SPX. Table 8.2 shows an example of the slope calculated using Excel. The first valid calculation is in cell D10 and is =slope(B1:B10,C1:C10), giving the result –4.60. That means

TABLE 8.2 Example of a 10-day linear regression slope calculation applied to SPX.

Row	A Date	B SPX	C Seq	D Slope
1	9/2/2008	1287.83	1	
2	9/3/2008	1276.61	2	
3	9/4/2008	1271.80	3	
4	9/5/2008	1233.21	4	
5	9/8/2008	1249.50	5	
6	9/9/2008	1267.98	6	
7	9/10/2008	1227.50	7	
8	9/11/2008	1229.04	8	
9	9/12/2008	1245.88	9	
10	9/15/2008	1250.92	10	−4.60
11	9/16/2008	1188.31	11	−5.94
12	9/17/2008	1210.34	12	−5.61
13	9/18/2008	1157.08	13	−7.70
14	9/19/2008	1213.11	14	−7.92

the SPX is declining at an average rate of 4.60 points per day over the past 10 days. Over the next four days, the index drops even faster, as seen in column D.

The slope can be programmed directly using the formula:

$$\text{Slope}_t = \frac{\sum (x - \bar{x})(y - \bar{y})}{\sum (x - \bar{x})^2}$$

where x is an integer sequence (as in column C) and y is the price (column B). The term x-bar ($\bar{x}$) is the average of the x.

Ranking and Choosing Which Markets to Trade

It's time to do some of the calculations and be more specific about the trading rules. Table 8.3 shows the first day of calculations beginning January 10, 2000. The date and the stock symbols are shown in row 1. The next rows are:

- *Price*, the current price of the stock.
- *Xprice*, the indexed price.
- *Slope*, the value found by using a linear regression.
- *Rank*, the order of stocks when sorted by slope, strongest (1) to weakest (5).

TABLE 8.3 The five home builders showing the calculations needed on day 1 of the first two days.

Day 1

1/13/2000	PHM	KBH	TOL	HOV	LEN
Price	3.87	7.31	4.5	3.09	2.44
Xprice	87.95	108.30	98.25	100.98	113.49
Slope	−1.28	1.11	−0.23	−0.29	1.88
Rank	5	2	3	4	1
Shares	646	−342	0	809	−1025
Chg pos	646	−342	0	809	−1025
Returns	−3	−2	0	−4	−5
Cum ret	−3	−2	0	−4	−5

- *Shares*, the number of shares traded.
- *Chg pos*, the change in the number of shares (used for calculating costs).
- *Returns*, the daily returns in dollars.
- *Cum ret*, the cumulative returns in dollars.

Home builders suffered the brunt of the economic downturn; therefore, it will not be surprising that the period we are using, from 2001 to May 2009, shows wide, volatile price swings. Figure 8.1, repeated from Chapter 3, should be a good reminder.

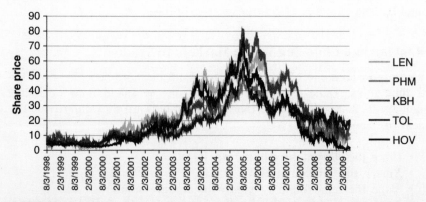

FIGURE 8.1 Prices of five home builder stocks. All five react in a similar manner to the economic changes.

Ranking on Day 1

Table 8.2 shows the prices of the five stocks in row 2 (price) and the corresponding index value in the row 3 (xprice). The index prices started at 100 on January 2, 2000, but Pulte had already dropped more than 12% by January 13 and Lennar had gained more than 13%. Stocks trading at low prices often move in surprisingly large percentages. We'll see the same phenomenon at the end of the test period, when prices drop back to these levels with increased volatility. While volatility is generally good for mean-reverting programs, volatility also means risk and must be treated carefully.

We calculate the slope using an 8-day period in order to have enough data to smooth the direction but not too much as to cause a sluggish reaction to price changes. We also keep in mind that a mean-reverting strategy should only hold a position for a short time, looking for a fast correction in relative price distortions. The longer the holding period, the greater the risk. We have the advantage of knowing that a 7-day period performed well in tests that will be shown later.

Row 4, slope, clearly reflects the direction of the past few days and is consistent with the change in the index value from its start at 100. Pulte, which lost 12%, has the steepest downward slope, while Lennar, which gained 13.5%, is the strongest. Toll Brothers and Hovnanian, with their index value still near 100, fall in the middle.

Selecting the Specific Stocks to Trade

Having ranked the five stocks, the next decision is which to buy and which to sell short. With only five stocks and a mean-reverting strategy we have two choices:

1. Sell the two highest-ranking stocks, and buy the two lowest-ranking stocks.
2. Sell the single highest-ranking stock, and buy the single lowest-ranking stock.

We choose the first option, buying and selling two stocks rather than one stock. Although we have a very small group, four stocks (two pairs) offer some diversification over a single pair.

The two stocks with the most negative slopes, Pulte and Hovnanian, get ranks of 5 and 4, respectively, seen in row 5. The two most positive slopes, although not as positive as the others are negative, are Lennar and KB Homes, with ranks 1 and 2.

Basing the decision entirely on the rank, we buy Pulte and Hovnanian and sell short Lennar and KB Homes. We do not take a position in rank 3, Toll Brothers.

Number of Shares to Trade

Keep in mind that the fundamental purpose of a market-neutral program is to be risk neutral; that is, the risk of the long positions must equal the risk of the short sales. Otherwise, when the market makes a uniform move up or down, you are not protected.

There are two accepted ways to balance the risk:

1. Trading equal dollar amounts for each stock.
2. Volatility adjusting the position size.

We start with the first option because it is commonly accepted on Wall Street—and far easier to calculate. Allocating equal dollar amounts to each stock relies on the loose but generally valid premise that volatility increases as price increases. Although this is generally true, the specific volatilities of two stocks trading at the same price could vary by as much as 50%. If one stock is in the news and the other is under the radar, then the visible stock normally experiences a short-term surge in volatility.

Stocks at very low prices also have erratic volatility, often much larger than those stocks trading at higher prices. It was not surprising to see Bank of America (BAC) or Well Fargo gain 25% near the bottom of the financial crisis in early 2009. A jump from $3.00 to $3.75 is a large percentage for one day, but still a small gain after a drop from above $50. Figure 8.2 shows the path of BAC during the recent financial crisis, and Figure 8.3 shows the corresponding annualized volatility based on a 20-day calculation period. Volatility reaching 250% is unheard of and can be sustained only over short time periods; however, this surge of volatility, in excess of 100%, is now approaching one year. This unusual scenario makes any measurement of volatility subject to problems but is an opportunity to prove that a strategy can survive under stress.

The initial investment for this strategy is $10,000. We will always trade four of the five stocks; therefore, each stock will get an allocation of $2,500. On day 1, we calculate the number of shares to buy for Pulte as $2,500/$3.87 (the closing price) or 646 shares, rounded down. For KB Homes we get $2,500/$7.31 = 342, Hovnanian $2,500/$3.09 = 809, and Lennar $2,500/$2.44 = 1,025.

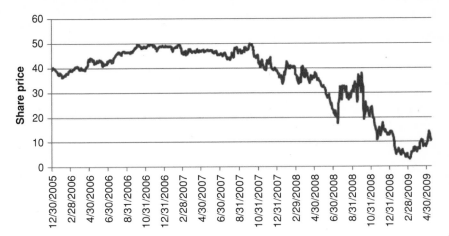

FIGURE 8.2 Bank of America showing increased volatility at lower prices.

We also apply the transaction cost of $0.005 per share. That gives the cost of selling short 1,025 shares of Lennar as $5.12, which is shown only in dollars in Table 8.3; however, the cents are accumulated in the returns. As you will see, transaction costs are very important because the returns per share are typically small for market-neutral strategies in the stock market and the changing of positions may make it difficult to apply costs afterward.

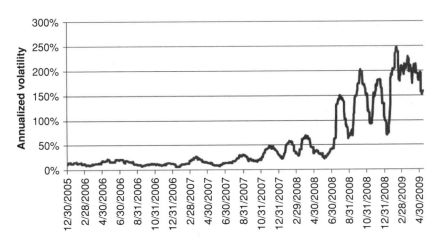

FIGURE 8.3 Bank of America annualized volatility increases as prices drop.

Day 2

At the end of day 1 we have 2 longs and 2 shorts, each committed with $2,500. At the end of day 2 we will do the following:

- Update the prices.
- Calculate the next index value (see Table 8.4).
- Find the 8-day slope of each index series.
- Rank the stocks according to their slope.
- Choose the two strongest markets to sell short and the two weakest to buy.
- Determine the number of shares by dividing $2,500 by the current price.
- Enter orders based on the difference between yesterday's positions and today's.
- Calculate your profit or loss for each stock as the shares held yesterday ("+" for long and "−" for short) times today's close minus yesterday's close.
- Subtract the cost of trading applied to the difference of today's position size and the previous day's size.

On day 2, the stocks kept the same relative strength; that is, Pulte and Hovnanian remained the strongest, Lennar and KB Homes the weakest. Because the prices changed, the size of the positions changed. Lennar's price increased; therefore, the number of shares dropped from 1,025 to 1,011. Because we were short Lennar, 14 shares are bought to reduce the short position. Only three of the four stocks had small adjustments, but the cost of trading is reflected in the PL. The net position lost $24 on day 2, for a cumulative net loss of $38.

TABLE 8.4 Day 2 of calculations.

1/14/2000	PHM	KBH	TOL	HOV	LEN
Price	3.83	7.31	4.63	3.13	2.47
Xprice	87.05	108.30	101.09	102.29	114.88
Slope	−1.13	1.25	0.38	−0.09	2.13
Rank	5	2	3	4	1
Shares	652	−342	0	798	−1011
Chg pos	6	0	0	−11	14
Returns	−26	0	0	32	−31
Cum ret	−29	−2	0	28	−36

TABLE 8.5 Results of the last trading day, May 15, 2009.

5/15/2009	PHM	KBH	TOL	HOV	LEN
Price	9.63	15.56	18.57	2.61	8.81
Xprice	218.86	230.52	405.46	85.29	409.77
Slope	−6.99	−2.76	−6.93	−2.29	−11.33
Rank	4	2	3	1	5
Shares	260	−161	0	−958	284
Chg pos	260	−3	−133	−4	7
Returns	−1	41	−29	10	−61
Cum ret	−7801	1771	−646	7742	9141

The Last Trading Day

Moving forward, the results of the last trading day are shown in Table 8.5. Prices have increased significantly for all but Hovnanian, although the path between the start and end dates of this test was extreme. Hovnanian and KB Homes are the strongest, and therefore they are short, while Pulte and Lennar are the weakest and are long. The cumulative returns on the last line 9 show that three stocks were net profitable and two losing, for a final gain of $10,207. Based on an initial investment of $10,000 that's slightly more than double over a period of about nine years and three months, a simple return of 10.9% per year.

When all the statistics are reviewed, we find that this strategy returned only $0.013 per share, less than 2 cents, certainly not enough to be profitable, even after costs of $0.005 per share. But then, making money isn't easy.

Choosing the Critical Parameter

Up to now, we've referred to the 8-day slope calculation, used to rank the indexed values. But the number of days used to find the slope is the critical parameter for this market-neutral strategy. When the number of days, n, is small, the slope jumps around but is responsive to relative changes in price. As n gets bigger, the linear regression line is smoothed and the slope becomes more stable, changing less often. The size of the returns for each stock is directly related to the calculation period and the holding time.

In Chapter 2, the concept of price noise was discussed. The conclusion was that certain markets were noisier than others, stock markets being the noisiest, and that shorter observation periods emphasized the noise. As the calculation periods get longer, the prices are smoothed, and the trend begins to show. Over the short term, say, 2 to 8 days, there is no trend, only

TABLE 8.6 Market-neutral basic test of the slope calculation period using four stocks.

Period	AROR	p/Share	Ratio
3	10.05	$0.009	0.837
4	9.66	$0.010	0.805
5	8.00	$0.011	0.667
6	6.29	$0.011	0.524
7	6.82	$0.013	0.568
8	5.93	$0.013	0.494
9	4.32	$0.011	0.360
10	2.49	$0.008	0.208

traders reacting to news and investors entering and exiting through large funds not particularly concerned with market timing.

Because we've chosen a mean-reverting strategy, we'll test this strategy for a range of calculation periods, from 3 to 10 days, to be consistent with the concept of noise. The results, shown in Table 8.6, are based on a $10,000 investment, positions in 4 stocks (2 long and 2 short), and an equal dollar allocation to each stock. The four columns show the number of days in the slope calculation, the annualized rate of return (AROR), the profits per share, and the return ratio (AROR divided by annualized risk). This test covered 10 years ending May 15, 2009.

The results of this test have both good news and bad news. The good news is that all tests are profitable, showing that the concept is sound. One of the best measures of robustness is the percentage of profitable tests. In this case, the test spanned the full range of calculation periods that seem reasonable for a mean-reverting strategy; therefore, when all tests show profits, we can conclude that the strategy is sound. As long as the percentage of profitable tests is above about 70%, it would be considered a success.

The bad news is that the profits per share, after taking out costs of $0.005, peak at only $0.013, between 1 and 2 cents per share. That doesn't leave much room for error, and the returns of about 6% don't make this worth the risk. We'll need to explore some alternatives, remembering that we were able to get more than $0.13 per share using pairs trading.

Filtering Low Volatility

The most obvious way to boost profits per share is to remove trades taken when a stock is doing nothing. "Doing nothing" usually means that prices are exhibiting very low volatility. We found this method successful for

TABLE 8.7 Using a volatility filter on the 8-day slope strategy.

Low Filt	AROR	p/Share	Ratio
1.0	7.43	$0.015	0.619
2.0	12.11	$0.024	1.009
3.0	11.59	$0.025	0.964
4.0	12.07	$0.029	1.006
5.0	12.52	$0.031	1.043
6.0	14.59	$0.038	1.215
7.0	13.11	$0.036	1.092
8.0	12.85	$0.039	1.071
9.0	12.78	$0.044	1.065
10.0	13.70	$0.049	1.142
11.0	14.31	$0.053	1.193
12.0	14.88	$0.059	1.240
13.0	15.57	$0.062	1.298
14.0	15.39	$0.063	1.282
15.0	13.21	$0.057	1.101

various other pairs trading. The filter is based on a 10-day standard deviation of the returns, expressed as a percent. The 10-day standard deviation is annualized by multiplying by $\sqrt{252}$, which we've done before. Unless the current volatility is above our threshold, no trades are entered. Without a filter, the strategy returned 6.82% annualized and $0.013 per share. The results of using the volatility filter are shown in Table 8.7.

The low-volatility filter is shown in whole percent in column 1. To keep it simple, these tests all use the 8-day slope. When the 10-day annualized volatility is below 1%, performance increases slightly to a return of 7.43% and $0.015 per share. Notice that the volatility filter works as expected: The AROR generally increases as the filter increases, and the profits per share move from our no-filter case of $0.013 to a maximum of $0.063 when the filter is at 14%. The ratio also increases, showing that the low-volatility filter is a legitimate way to approach the problem. To confirm our belief that the filter is working correctly, we plot the resulting NAV with and without a 6% filter, shown in Figure 8.4. Having not seen the original NAVs, we find it surprising that the strategy had a long declining period; however, the volatility filter shows that the decline was the result of low volatility—exactly the result we are looking for. The filtered results show a much stronger performance at the end because both NAV series are adjusted to 12% volatility. If we leave them unchanged, then the original NAV series would simply have no trades in the middle years.

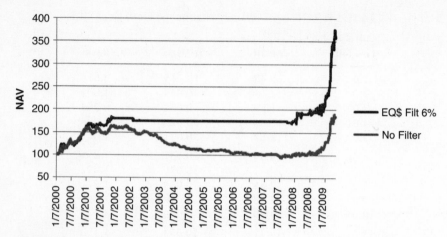

FIGURE 8.4 Home builders original NAV and results using a low-volatility filter of 6%, both adjusted to a target volatility of 12%.

Applying a volatility filter turned out to be very useful, but a profit per share of slightly over $0.06 is still marginal. The $0.13 using pairs remains more attractive. However, the filter has all the right characteristics and will be used for other strategies to boost results. A filter has the added advantage of reducing costs.

Quantizing to Reduce Costs

Another technique for reducing costs is to hold the same position size unless that size changes by more than a threshold percentage. In engineering, this method is call *quantizing*. For example, without the filter, if we are long 1,000 shares of Lennar and the next day the volatility declines by 5%, we would add 50 shares and be long 1,050. With a 10% filter threshold, we would not add the 50 shares but wait until volatility had dropped by 10%. There is a good chance that volatility will increase tomorrow and we would just be resetting all or part of today's trade. Instead, the volatility must change by at least 10% to trigger an additional purchase or sale of 100 shares or more. This method won't be tested here, but it is a common and successful way of minimizing trading costs.

Price Filters

Another filter that might increase returns per share is a simple price threshold. A stock that falls under $2, perhaps even $3 or $4, might be considered unstable. At low levels, prices make much larger percentage moves than stocks trading at, say, $30 per share. This is particularly true if it was once trading at a much higher price, such as Bank of America. Removing the low-priced stocks from the mix might save both aggravation and risk, along with some costs.

Trading Only the Extremes

In an effort to increase the profits per share, we must return to an earlier decision to trade the two strongest and two weakest of a total of five stocks. Instead, we'll trade only the extremes, the two stocks that show the steepest positive and negative slopes. Naturally, trading a set of only five stocks has its limitations. One of those limitations can be that none of the stocks show enough volatility to generate sufficient profits per share. With a larger set of stocks, we might get both diversification and volatility.

The first step is to repeat the basic test of various linear regression calculation periods, this time only going long the one weakest stock and short the one strongest stock. We are sure that the profit potential is greatest for this pair, but we don't know by how much. By limiting the number of stocks trading, we also expect the risk to increase. In this case, we have removed all chance of diversification. The results are shown in Table 8.8.

Compared with the results of using two longs and two shorts, these are clearly better. The average AROR, profits per share, and ratio for the earlier test, using four stocks (Table 8.6) were 6.70, $0.0107, and 0.558. The averages for these tests are 7.99, $0.0152, and 0.666. The ratios are much higher and very stable, showing that we have improved the risk profile. Unfortunately, the best per share return is only $0.022, a 69% increase, but still too low.

	Home builders mean-reversion strategy
TABLE 8.8	using only the two stocks with the strongest and weakest slopes.

Period	AROR	p/Share	Ratio
3	8.56	$0.009	0.713
4	8.40	$0.011	0.700
5	8.34	$0.013	0.695
6	9.55	$0.017	0.796
7	6.83	$0.014	0.569
8	7.31	$0.017	0.609
9	8.74	$0.022	0.729
10	6.23	$0.018	0.519

TABLE 8.9 Applying the low volatility filter to the 2-stock case.

Low Filt	AROR	p/Share	Ratio
1.0	5.95	$0.013	0.496
2.0	11.16	$0.024	0.930
3.0	11.44	$0.025	0.954
4.0	10.90	$0.026	0.910
5.0	11.59	$0.029	0.966
6.0	12.72	$0.034	1.060
7.0	16.47	$0.043	1.372
8.0	15.49	$0.043	1.291
9.0	14.60	$0.046	1.216
10.0	13.05	$0.045	1.087
11.0	14.58	$0.052	1.215
12.0	14.11	$0.056	1.176
13.0	13.11	$0.052	1.093
14.0	12.90	$0.055	1.075
15.0	10.45	$0.048	0.870

When applying the low-volatility filter to the 2-stock case, we again see that the numbers are better, but not as much of an increase as we saw when we used two longs and two shorts, a total of four stocks. The results are shown in Table 8.9. The best returns per share are not as large as when we used two longs and two shorts, and the averages are all marginally lower.

VOLATILITY-ADJUSTING THE POSITION SIZE

At the beginning of this chapter, we discussed two ways of calculating position size. The first was allocating equal dollar amounts to each stock and then dividing by the current price to get the number of shares. This relied on a general relationship that volatility increases as price increases.

This general risk relationship is not very accurate because some stocks trading at about the same price can be much more volatile than others. In this section, we'll find the volatility of each stock and adjust them so they have the same risk. In addition, we'll be sure that the net long positions have the same risk as the net short positions, in the event there are an uneven number of longs and shorts.

We feel strongly that this is the correct way to size positions. At the same time, we hope that this increases the profits per trade. Even if it does

TABLE 8.10 Calculating the number of shares from the volatility.

Day 1

1/13/2000	PHM	KBH	TOL	HOV	LEN
Price	3.87	7.31	4.5	3.09	2.44
Xprice	87.95	108.30	98.25	100.98	113.49
Slope	−1.28	1.11	−0.23	−0.29	1.88
AVOL	0.624	0.711	0.540	0.243	0.784
Rank	5	2	3	4	1
Size	0.28	−0.524	0	0.72	−0.476
Shares	361	−358	0	1164	−974
Chg pos	361	−358	0	1164	−974
Returns	−2	−2	0	−6	−5
Cum ret	−2	−2	0	−6	−5

not improve returns, there is a clear element of chance introduced when you trade equal dollar amounts of each stock. If you can fix the problem, you are obligated to do so.

Beginning again on day 1, this time the annualized volatility is calculated over the same 8-day period that is being used for the slope. The annualized volatility is the standard deviation of price changes over the calculation period multiplied by the square root of 252 for annualization. Row 5 of Table 8.10 shows PHM at 0.624, an annualized volatility (AVOL) of 62.4%. When we use a very short calculation period, the annualized volatility can exceed 100%, but over a long period, even these numbers will average out to the same value as those using a longer-term calculation period.

The steps for finding the number of volatility-adjusted shares follow, and the values associated with each step are shown in Table 8.10.

- Calculate the 8-day standard deviation of price changes for each stock, i.
- Calculate the annualized volatility for each stock as

$$\text{AVOL}_i = \sigma_i \times \sqrt{252}$$

- Create a volatility adjustment factor, VAF, for each stock equal to your target volatility divided by the annualized volatility:

$$\text{VAF}_i = \frac{\text{TV}}{\text{AVOL}_i}$$

TABLE 8.11 Step-by-step process for finding volatility-adjusted share size.

	PHM	KBH	TOL	HOV	LEN
Stdev	0.039	0.045	0.034	0.015	0.049
AVOL	0.624	0.711	0.540	0.243	0.784
VAF	0.192	0.169	0.222	0.494	0.153
Signed VAF	0.192	−0.169		0.494	−0.153
Normalized	0.280	−0.524		0.720	−0.476
Shares	362	−359		1165	−976

where the default target volatility is 12%. Note that this inverts the volatility so that markets with higher volatility will get smaller allocations. Actually, the target volatility can be any number such as 1, which will invert the annualized volatility. Later, we will scale this to the investment size.

- Set VAF_i to negative if the position is to be short (highest ranks).
- Normalize the volatility factors by finding the sum of the long factors, *LFV*, and the sum of the short factors, *SVF*. Then divide each of the long factors in (4) by LFV and the short factors by SFV.
- 6. Calculate the number of shares for each stock as

$$\text{Shares} = \frac{\dfrac{\text{Investment}}{2} \times \text{Volatility adjustment factor}}{\text{Stock price}}$$

In row 6 of Table 8.11, the investment of $10,000 is divided by 2 in order to get the amount allocated to only longs or shorts; then the number of shares for PHM is

$$\text{Shares} = \frac{\$5,000 \times .28}{\$3.87} = 361.7$$

In Table 8.11 we show the number of shares rounded up, but in the actual trading strategy, we truncate the number of shares to avoid exceeding the investment size.

If we compare the number of shares from this volatility-adjusted method with the equal dollar allocations (from Tables 8.3 and 8.10), the numbers are sufficiently different. PHM is only half the equal dollar

TABLE 8.12 Day 2 calculation and performance detail for home builders.

Day 2

1/14/2000	PHM	KBH	TOL	HOV	LEN
Price	3.83	7.31	4.63	3.13	2.47
Xprice	87.05	108.30	101.09	102.29	114.88
Slope	−1.13	1.25	0.38	−0.09	2.13
AVOL	0.564	0.597	0.510	0.251	0.731
Rank	5	2	3	4	1
Size	0.308	−0.551	0	0.692	−0.449
Shares	401	−375	0	1103	−908
Chg pos	40	−17	0	−61	66
Returns	−15	0	0	46	−30
Cum ret	−16	−2	0	40	−34

method, and HOV is more than 20% different. This difference should be enough to change the final outcome.

	PHM	KBH	TOL	HOV	LEN
Vol	361	−358	0	1164	−974
Equal	646	−342	0	809	−1025

On the second day, the stocks that are long and short remain the same, but the position size changes slightly. This can be compared to day 2 using the equal dollar method, shown in Table 8.12.

In the end, using the volatility-adjusted position sizes seems to be the right method, but the annualized returns were 4.45%, and the per share profit was only $0.008, less than the approach using equal dollar allocations. We'll need to look further.

ARBING THE DOW: A LARGE-SCALE PROGRAM

A large-scale market-neutral program trades a basket of long positions against a basket of short sales. Our example of only five stocks in one group is not a fair indication of its success. When you have many markets, there should be bigger divergences and more volatility among the stocks. This will lead to larger profits. The previous small example was just an exercise to show how a market-neutral program is constructed and traded.

One important point to remember is that pairs trading uses a timing device, some form of momentum indicator to find relative differences. We've used both a simple stochastic difference and the stress indicator. Trades are not entered until that indicator reaches an extreme, which provides entry timing. Of course, that extreme could occur under conditions of high or low volatility. If it's low volatility, then the per trade returns would be small, but over the entire period, entry prices will be at relative extremes and average higher returns than methods that choose entry points more arbitrarily. Pairs trading will also be improved by filtering out low-volatility situations.

Market neutral has no timing. Each day, the slopes are calculated, and the steepest slope is sold. If you use some other form of ranking, then the highest-ranking stocks are sold. Although a mean-reversion entry benefits from timing, at no point did the market-neutral method try to decide if this was a good place to sell or if the relative price of one stock was at an extreme compared with its own history or the price of another stock. As soon as one stock moved into the top zone, it was sold. If it continued to strengthen relative to the other stocks, it would produce a loss rather than a better opportunity for entry.

Success in market-neutral trading requires two key attributes: high volatility if the method is mean reversion and a reversal in the strength or weakness of one stock compared to the others. If trend following, then we would want continued strength or weakness of each stock, keeping them in the buy or sell zones.

Are the Dow Components Trending or Mean Reverting?

We need to decide if the large-cap stocks in the Dow tend to move away from each other, exhibiting trending, or whether they keep switching from being in the strongest zones to being in the weakest, a mean-reverting trait. We have two pieces of information to help us. If the Dogs of the Dow work, then we should expect any large company that has underperformed its peers to rotate back up to the top. To have stayed on the top, companies such as Microsoft and General Electric seem to figure out how to evolve.

More important, our study of price noise in Chapter 2 showed that the stock markets in all developed countries exhibit a large degree of erratic price movement. The equity index markets were the noisiest of all markets and resisted profits based on trending methods. Most individual stocks also show the same characteristics. Then mean reversion is the likely scenario, and we'll take that approach.

Specifying the Rules of the Market-Neutral Method

To make this as transparent as possible, we will begin with the following rules:

- An investment of $100,000.
- Equal investment in each of the 29 stocks, $3,448 (we found a data error in one of the Dow components and removed it).
- Buy and sell zones each with 13 stocks, a neutral zone with 3 stocks.
- Cost per transaction of $0.005 per share.

We know that if we use a very short calculation period, then the trades will all be held for a shorter time, and the returns per share will be small; therefore, we tested periods of 5, 10, 15, and 20 days. Trading began on January 11, 2000, and ended on June 18, 2010. Table 8.13 shows the detail of calculations and positions on the second day of trading.

Table 8.13 is simply a bigger version of Table 8.12, which showed the home builders. The symbols are along the top and the rows are:

- Stock price.
- Stock index value (converted from price).
- Linear regression slope using the index price.
- Annualized volatility of price using the index.
- Sorted rank based on the linear regression slope, where 1 is the strongest stock.
- If long, the size is the volfactor divided by the sum of the volfactors of all long positions; if short, it is the volfactor divided by the sum of the volfactors of all short positions.
- Number of shares entered based on equal investment sizes.
- Number of shares that changed from the previous day.
- Returns, in USD, based on yesterday's position sizes and today's price moves.

On the far right of part C are the total changes in shares and the total profits or losses for the day.

Performance

When we test this method using the four calculation periods, we get the results shown in Table 8.14. As with our other tests, these results would be excellent if only the returns per share were higher. Considering that costs

TABLE 8.13 Second day of trading the DJIA.

(a) The first 10 stocks.

1/12/2000	AA	AIG	AXP	BA	C	CAT	DD	DIS	GE	GM
Price	35.73	1382.88	39.49	31.97	27.31	14.86	53.5	30.98	41.98	61.88
Xprice	103.15	105.13	98.48	109.86	105.81	111.23	108.21	114.02	101.62	102.91
Slope	-0.61	1.07	1.12	-0.49	0.19	-0.96	-1.57	3.40	1.04	1.29
AVOL	0.49	0.59	0.36	0.65	0.67	0.87	0.65	1.36	0.30	0.61
Rank	22	14	13	21	16	24	28	3	15	11
Size	0.09	0	-0.129	0.068	0	0.051	0.068	-0.034	0	-0.075
Shares	108	0	-97	120	0	259	72	-124	0	-62
Chg pos	1	3	0	-1	-149	-8	0	-9	92	-128
Returns	-41	-128	26	22	209	117	22	294	-16	226

(b) Stocks 11–20.

1/12/2000	HD	HON	HPQ	IBM	INTC	JNJ	JPM	KO	MCD	MMM
Price	55.69	50.03	37.24	107.89	42.56	33.51	34.14	49.84	33.18	33.49
Xprice	93.10	105.82	93.64	103.35	105.27	102.01	95.85	111.45	110.38	110.53
Slope	0.03	1.43	3.45	1.58	4.04	-0.04	-0.99	2.03	2.95	-0.37
AVOL	0.64	0.46	1.17	0.39	0.69	0.56	0.37	0.65	0.41	0.86
Rank	18	10	2	9	1	19	26	8	4	20
Size	0.069	-0.101	-0.04	-0.117	-0.067	0.079	0.12	-0.071	-0.113	0.052
Shares	69	-77	-103	-36	-90	115	113	-77	-116	115
Chg pos	1	1	-103	-72	2	115	-1	1	-116	230
Returns	-34	-44	-1	18	-72	-1	33	-54	-1	-16

TABLE 8.13 *(Continued)*

(c) Stocks 21–29 plus totals.

1/12/2000	MRK	MSFT	PFE	PG	T	UTX	VZ	WMT	XOM	Today
Price	56.18	47.17	27.21	46.27	28.22	22.86	37.74	58.56	29.14	
Xprice	113.79	89.78	113.56	111.87	85.10	104.72	91.40	97.10	109.76	
Slope	2.06	−0.99	2.15	2.36	−1.17	1.17	−1.78	0.08	−0.81	
AVOL	0.91	0.40	0.61	0.78	0.61	0.69	0.50	0.66	0.71	
Rank	7	25	6	5	27	12	29	17	23	
Size	−0.051	0.111	−0.076	−0.059	0.073	−0.067	0.088	0.067	0.063	
Shares	−68	82	−141	−83	136	−168	102	66	132	
Chg pos	2	3	6	−1	10	6	5	130	1	1197
Returns	−101	−141	−166	31	−291	−125	−189	76	−33	−377

TABLE 8.14 Results of market-neutral trading using the DJIA for varying calculation periods.

Slope Period	AROR	Per Share	Ratio
5	15.19%	0.0251	1.266
10	13.13%	0.0423	1.094
15	12.50%	0.0558	1.042
20	11.66%	0.0646	0.972

TABLE 8.15 Results using a 2 percent low-volatility filter.

Slope Period	Low Filter	AROR	Per Share	Ratio
5	2.00	13.43%	0.0491	1.119
10	2.00	10.61%	0.0650	0.884
15	2.00	11.79%	0.0990	0.983
20	2.00	8.59%	0.0909	0.716

have already been taken out, information ratios above 1.0 are very good, and annualized returns are also attractive.

We again fall back on the need for a volatility filter to increase the profits per share. In this case, we found that a 2% filter was best. Smaller filters improved the per share returns, but not by enough. Results of using the 2% filter are shown in Table 8.15. The slope period of 15 shows the highest per share returns of nearly $0.10, with only a small decline in annualized returns and information ratio. Figures 8.5 and 8.6 show the cumulative profits

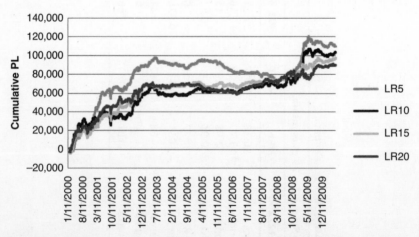

FIGURE 8.5 Unfiltered results for market-neutral program.

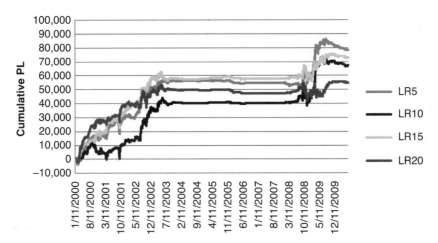

FIGURE 8.6 Results of the market-neutral program using a low-volatility filter.

of both the unfiltered and filtered tests for the four slope periods. Performance is not very different for any of the calculation periods, and using the filter eliminates trading for the four-year period in the middle of the test. Again we see that mean-reverting strategies should not be traded during periods of low volatility.

There is still one last option to test, changing the number of stocks in the buy and sell zones. By including 13 in the current test, we are not selecting those stocks that might have moved further apart from the other stocks. By reducing the number of stocks in each zone, we might add some element of timing plus a higher average volatility. Instead of 13, we'll use 8. With 8 in each zone, we have 13 in the neutral area that are not traded. We won't go to 4, 2, or 1 because we lose diversification and increase switching costs, as the few stocks move in and out of the buy and sell zones. Results are shown in Table 8.16. Although using 8 stocks has a slightly lower return per share, it has an impressive improvement in both the annualized

TABLE 8.16 Using only 8 stocks in the buy and sell zone, with and without a low volatility filter.

Slope Period	Number of Stocks	AROR	Per Share	Ratio
15	13	12.50%	0.0558	1.042
15 LF 2	13	11.79%	0.0990	0.983
15	8	16.13%	0.0697	1.344
15 LF 2	8	13.67%	0.0956	1.139

returns and the information ratio. If we can produce the better returns trading fewer stocks, then that's a better choice. The trade-off is that fewer stocks present greater risk, regardless of what the numbers show.

THOUGHTS ABOUT MARKET-NEUTRAL TREND FOLLOWING

The statistics show that mean reverting is a better strategy for stocks in the long term. However, we must all feel that there are times when that's not true and those times could present higher risk. Ideally, if we could identify when these markets are trending, then we might switch to a different trading mode. This concept has been called *regime switching*.

Most regime switching has been unsuccessful, mainly because of the lag needed to identify one regime from another. In addition, each time we switch from trending to mean reverting, we would need to change all the long positions to short and all the shorts to long. That can be a very large cost unless you hold the positions long enough to make up the cost.

One criterion for making the switching decision would be the slope of the equally weighted average of those stocks in the portfolio. If the slope is nearly flat, then there is no dominant trend in the market, and mean reversion would be the best choice. However, when the entire stock market trends, and even the laggards in the Dow show a rising slope, then a trending regime may be the way to make the most profits. At the same time, to emphasize the trend, you would want to increase the calculation period for the slope to 60 or 80 days. The longer the calculation period, the more likely we'll see a sustainable trend.

Unfortunately, research is a never-ending process, and regime switching won't be covered here. It is, however, an intriguing approach to improving many trading programs.

MARKET NEUTRAL USING FUTURES

Futures markets would be an ideal venue for a market-neutral program. There is high leverage and the ability to go long or short with no restrictions. We discussed pairs trading for both equity index and interest rate futures in Chapters 4 and 7; now we'll look at using a traditional market-neutral method applied to interest rate futures.

The fixed-income futures markets are among the most liquid trading vehicles in the world. Eurodollar futures alone trade an average of 2 million contracts per day, each contract having a face value of $1 million, for a total notional value of $2 trillion. The 10-year Treasury notes, considered the benchmark interest rate, trade more than 300,000 contracts each day for a notional value of $30 billion. Entering and exiting do not pose a problem, and there is even a modestly active after-hours market.

Unlike stocks, trading futures provides exceptional leverage. To buy one contract of 10-year Treasury notes with a face value of $100,000, an investor needs only $2,700 in margin. Note that margin for futures is not the same as stocks. It is a good faith deposit and is based on the volatility of the market, not the face value. At this time, the 30-year bond margin is $4,860, the 10-year note margin is $2,700, and the 5-year note margin is $1,755. A study of the volatility of these three markets will show that the margin requirements closely parallel relative volatility.

It is important to understand margin because it provides extremely high leverage, but few traders take advantage of the maximum levels. For example, if June 2009 Eurodollars rates (to distinguish it from EURUSD FX) are trading at 99.025, and the face value is $1 million, then every 1.0 move is worth $2,500 (only 25% of the value because it is a 3-month delivery). The margin requirement is only $500. If you were long and the price dropped 20 basis points, all your margin would be gone—a 100% loss. And because margin is a good faith deposit, you are responsible for any additional losses.

Most traders deposit 3 to 4 times the amount of margin, reducing the amount of leverage normally to about 4:1. For our market-neutral program, we will calculate how much money needs to be invested to target returns reflecting 12% volatility. Unlike stocks, we will not find out that our investment wasn't enough to buy all of the contracts that we need.

The contract size of each futures market presents problems for traders with a small amount of capital on hand. In our example, we will track 9 markets and trade 4 long and 4 short. If each market requires a margin of $1,000 per contract, then we need at least $8,000. If we want to deleverage, and have reserves for losses, we should invest about 4 times that amount, or $32,000.

But the strategy also requires that we volatility-adjust each position so that they all have the same risk. From the margins for the 30-year, 10-year, and 5-year rates given earlier, we can see that we would need to trade approximately 3 of the 5-year notes, 2 of the 10-year, and 1 of the 30-year to have any similarity in volatility across markets. That means a lot more margin. And unless we trade a large number of contracts and invest millions of dollars, it will be difficult to fine-tune the size of the positions, unlike the stock market, where you can add one share at a time.

With that in mind, let's look at the market-neutral strategy for fixed-income markets. The process will be similar to arbing the Dow, but perhaps simpler. We'll calculate position sizes differently.

The Rules for Mean-Reversion Trading with Futures

When we applied pairs trading to both equity index and interest rate markets, we found that all the profits were made when the pairs consisted of one market from the U.S. and one from Europe. Keeping that in mind, we chose those nine most active interest rates to include Eurodollars, U.S. 30-year bonds, U.S. 10-year notes, U.S. 5-year notes, Euribor, short sterling, Eurobunds, Eurobobls, and the long gilt. Since 2005, these markets close each day at the same time.

The other rules are:

- An investment of $100,000.
- 2, 3, or 4 markets in the buy and sell zones.
- A $50 cost per round turn for each trade in one futures market.

The gilt presents a problem because it closes one hour earlier than the U.S. markets, but that could be resolved by posting prices for all markets just before the gilt close or eliminating the gilt from the strategy. For now, we'll leave it as part of the mix. Markets are usually very quiet in Europe toward the end of the day. Although there still may be active U.S. markets, the reality is that not as many European traders are interested in staying in front of their screens until 10 P.M. That may change.

The contract size will play an important role in our ability to balance the number of contracts to create equal volatility. It will also be used to calculate the correct daily PL:

$$\text{Today's PL} = \text{Signal} \times \text{Position size} \times \text{Conversion factor} \\ \times (\text{Today's price} - \text{Yesterday's price})$$

where *signal* is +1 for long and −1 for short, and the *conversion factor* is the value of a 1 big point move in the futures market. For 30-year bonds, the conversion factor is $1,000, representing the value of a move from, for example, 115.00 to 114.00. Conversion factors are

Market	Conversion Factor
Eurodollar rates	$2,500
U.S. 30-year bonds	$1,000
U.S. 10-year notes	$1,000
U.S. 5-year notes	$1,000
Euribor	€2,500
Eurobund	€1,000
Eurobobl	€1,000
Long gilt	£1,000

Many of these markets now have mini versions. These minicontracts would have more flexibility for balancing the portfolio; however, commission costs are not reduced in proportion to the contract size, so trading the larger, original contracts whenever possible is more cost effective.

At some point, we will need to deal with the currency conversion. Ideally, we should know the currency rates on each day throughout our test history and repatriate both euros and sterling back to U.S. dollars after the close. We won't do that for these tests, but we can treat all non-U.S. trades as though prices were always at the current rates of EURUSD 1.30 and USDGBP 1.45. That is easily done by changing the Eurobund and Eurobobl conversion factors to $1,300 and the gilt conversion factor to $1,450.

As we did with the Dow, the second day of trading is shown in Table 8.17. All of the rows are the same as in the previous example except that, instead of *shares*, there are *contracts*. The number of contracts may seem large, but the correlations between these interest rates are very high, and the risk of being long one and short another is surprisingly small. Because of that, the profits are also small.

Results of Interest Rate Trading

Interest rate differences correct very quickly, so the calculation periods need to be short. We found that this was true when we first looked at pairs trading in stocks. We also tried buy and sell zones with 2, 3, and 4 markets. Table 8.18 shows the information ratio (a), profits per contract (b), and annualized rate of return (c) for these combinations. The lower right corner of the table, the 4-day calculation period and only two markets in each zone, is the best combination; however, most combinations were good.

The returns per contract, which are net of $50 round-term commissions ($25 for each leg although trading them as spreads will reduce that amount), show a very safe margin of error for trading and make this an attractive method. Given the results we had applying pairs trading to equity index markets in both the U.S. and Europe, we would expect similarly good results with those futures markets.

MARKET-NEUTRAL COMMENTS

Traditional market-neutral programs applied to stock sectors or industries were the first of the major algorithmic trading methods. They profited mostly during the 1990s, when competition was not as keen and markets were less noisy. They took advantage of a new level of computing power that had become more broadly available.

TABLE 8.17 Detail of the second trading day for interest rate futures using two markets in each of the buy and sell zones.

1/11/2005	Eurodollars	U.S. 30-Yr	U.S. 10-Yr	U.S. 5-Yr	Euribor	Short Sterling	Eurobund	Eurobobl	Long Gilt	Today
Price	96.4500	101.3594	94.4531	97.0234	96.5600	95.4250	110.7700	107.6300	105.0900	
Xprice	99.907	100.340	99.687	99.567	100.052	100.021	100.353	100.186	100.114	
Slope	-0.017	0.257	0.031	-0.032	0.001	0.008	0.094	0.045	0.014	
AVOL	10.648	33.928	18.356	13.473	7.410	3.778	9.774	6.048	23.654	
Rank	8	1	4	9	7	6	2	3	5	
Size	0.559	-0.224	0	0.441	0	0	-0.776	0	0	
Contracts	259	-247	0	258	0	0	-226	0	0	
Chg pos	0	0	0	0	0	0	0	0	0	0
Returns	0	0	81	35	0	0	0	0	32	149

TABLE 8.18 Market-neutral results for interest rate futures showing the (a) information ratio, (b) profits per contract, and (c) annualized rate of return.

(a) Information ratio

	Number of Stocks in Zone		
Calc period	4	3	2
7	0.024	0.311	0.640
5	−0.001	0.643	0.552
4	0.687	0.931	1.030

(b) Profits per contract

	Number of Stocks in Zone		
Calc period	4	3	2
7	26	251	1196
5	11	237	355
4	105	219	301

(c) Annualized rate of return

	Number of Stocks in Zone		
Calc period	4	3	2
7	0.29	3.74	7.69
5	−0.01	7.72	6.62
4	10.58	11.17	12.36

The principles of market-neutral trading, separating the strongest and weakest stocks within a fundamentally related set and then either buying the strongest and selling the weakest or, less often, selling the strongest and buying the weakest, are still sound. Only now, we need to be more selective.

Success in trading a market-neutral program can be in two areas: an above-average interval of volatility in stocks or the cross-regional use of futures. By far the best payout is in using futures. Both equity index and interest rate futures offer profitable opportunities because globalization has caused all of these markets to be linked, even if it might be seen as a *dirty* link. They don't follow exactly, but they don't drift too far apart without reacting back. That makes mean reversion the strategy of choice. With U.S. and European markets now open at the same time, every investor has an equal chance of profiting.

CHAPTER 9

Other Stat-Arb Methods

*S*tat-arb is short *for statistical arbitrage*, a traditional way of identifying and profiting from price distortions in related stocks. We've used the term *pairs trading* instead. For years, this was a bread-and-butter trade for the institutions. They simply watched for companies within a sector to perform differently from one another and then placed a trade that profited from the two stock prices coming back together. It was just short of printing money. Unfortunately for us, competition has become keen in every area of trading, with stat-arb being a primary target. Any system that removes directional risk and avoids the brunt of price shocks is in high demand. The big investment houses have migrated their approach to high-frequency trading, where even the proximity to the source of data gives one company milliseconds of an edge against another. Some exchanges have just recently required that users have their computers no closer than 500 feet to the exchange transmission source. It's their attempt to even the playing field. We can't compete in that venue, but there still are selected areas where we can be profitable and have no directional risk. Some of the primary opportunities have been covered in the previous chapters.

This chapter will look at a few different approaches to trades that don't have directional risk. First we'll see what happens when we create our own index and use that for one leg of the pair, or use one of the mutual funds available from a number of different companies. Then we'll see if it makes sense to create pairs from the components of the Dow or the S&P. We'll also look at creating a market-neutral strategy from stock rankings provided by companies that specialize in that service.

TRADE-OFFS

We can't know which combination of trading frequency, size of returns, and risk that any one trader will choose. Some traders prefer risk avoidance; others are risk seekers. That's a characteristic called *investor risk preference*. In most of the approaches discussed in this book, we've taken a centrist approach, trying to find the greatest common denominator.

Pairs trading is best when it's short term and mean reverting. All mean-reverting strategies have the same risk and reward trade-offs. If the entry point is set closer, there are more trades with smaller profits. If the entry is further away, there are fewer trades but larger profits per trade. As far as risk is concerned, entering a trade sooner means you must hold the trade with a larger open loss if it moves against you, but you will take smaller profits more often. By entering at a point of greater distortion, you will not suffer an unrealized loss that is as large, but you will need to wait longer for each new trading opportunity. For our purposes we are interested in which trade-off has the best return to risk ratio, which is our ultimate measure of preference. A fast trading method may have smaller losses, but a series of losses can be equally as large as a single, poor trade using a slower system. The final performance for a mean-reverting method has the shape of a short-options profile—many small profits and a few large losses. You can't change this shape, although you can scale the leverage up or down.

SYSTEM BRIEFS

There are trading methods that are difficult to backtest, although they may be perfectly thought out and fully systematic. For the first method discussed in this section, taking advantage of upgrades, downgrades, and promotion on the television or radio, the computer has not yet reached the level where it can be substituted for the human brain. In the second method, the availability of historic data is scarce and sometimes requires a hefty fee to participate. Both are classic stat-arb trading methods, both are systematic, and both can be very profitable.

Taking Advantage of Upgrades and Downgrades

We are all familiar with the daily market alerts on the financial news networks that say "Microsoft has been upgraded from neutral to buy" or from "buy to hold" (whatever that means) or occasionally from "neutral to underweight" (rarely do they give an outright "sell," even for Enron). Other shows, such as *Mad Money* with Jim Cramer, cover a number of companies with less tactful recommendations to buy or sell those shares.

Recommendations by large financial institutions, such as Bank of America, influence many investors. Clients of Bank of America, J. P. Morgan, or any other big investment house will have already received those recommendations and acted on them. After all, it doesn't seem right to offer the benefit of their research to the general public, without payment, before or at the same time as their own clients. And Cramer fully discloses that his recommendations may have been disseminated beforehand. None of that is a problem. One web site where you can find upgrades and downgrades posted each day is www.TheStreet.com.

Stat-arb trading triggers an action after the market has moved; therefore, we want the recommendations to cause investors to stampede, buying or liquidating en masse. While that's unlikely to happen, we would be satisfied with a move in the target company that differed from the market as a whole. It would be difficult to identify whether the buy recommendation had investors rushing to acquire the stock if both the target and the entire S&P index moved up by the same amount. Without the recommendation, perhaps the company would have declined in price while the rest of the market rallied; however, that's more difficult to measure than if the company being recommended rose more than the overall market.

Our stat-arb trade looks for moves in individual stocks that are clearly stronger or weaker than the overall market, but only under three certain conditions:

1. The move must be preceded by a visible recommendation by a service, financial institution, or television show with a large following.
2. It cannot be caused by a quarterly earnings report.
3. It cannot be caused by an announcement of a merger, scandal, or major event internal to the company.

Note that we are looking for buying and selling recommendations, not structural changes in the company or in the price of its stock. The impact on the company share value must be temporary and inconsistent with the movement of the market as a whole. A quarterly earnings report is a structural change. If earnings are below expectations, then you can expect that company to underperform the S&P index, but it does not provide an opportunity to buy.

The premise of this traditional arbitrage is that analyst recommendations are badly timed and have no lasting significance on price movement. A buy recommendation pushes prices up as investors buy *at the market*, without regard to getting a good price. And it always happens after the fact. For example, Merck will announce that a new drug has passed the next step in the FDA approval process. Prices rise. A few days later, because prices have risen, an investment house recommends that its clients buy. Of course, the recommendation is intended to take advantage of the longer-term effect of the announcement, not a 2- or 3-day price move. But the market has already moved up to discount the longer-term move as best it can. Our best trade is to sell the rally for a very short-term profit.

But what if we sell and the overall market is rallying due to generally good economic news? That would mean we were right about Merck but lost money anyway.

We can protect against that contingency by selling the S&P when we buy Merck, volatility-adjusting the position sizes to be the same. That effectively hedges the position and isolates the *alpha*. We make money only if we were correct about the distortion of the Merck price and cannot have either a windfall profit or loss because of moves in the overall market. Alpha means that we make money if we're smarter.

These trades will be more obvious for smaller companies than for members of the Dow. Even if Cramer recommends buying General Electric, it is unlikely that a surge of buying will be seen in the price move. The company is just too big. However, if he recommends a small-cap company making hydrogen batteries, then it is very likely that we would see a market impact. So the size of the company will make a big difference. For larger investors, these smaller companies will have limited liquidity and limited returns; however, results should be better.

The steps to follow for this classic stat-arb trade are:

- Watch for all upgrades, downgrades, and other recommendations to buy or sell given by investment houses, research firms, or television reports.
- Wait for the market to open stronger or weaker than the S&P, confirming the direction of the buy or sell recommendation. Normally, these recommendations are disseminated after the close on the previous day.
- Be careful to check that there is no news just released by the target company that would cause a structural change in the share price. This could be an earnings release, merger, change of management, or other major announcement.
- If the price is up, then sell the individual stock and buy the S&P, being sure that you have correctly volatility-adjusted the position sizes so that they have the same risk.
- Take off the position when the stock gives back its gain or loss relative to the S&P, but no longer than three days, perhaps less.

Do not substitute a sector ETF for the S&P. When one company in a sector is upgraded, it is often the case that other companies benefit. For example, when the first of the microchip manufacturers or computer companies reports its quarterly earnings, the market takes that as an indication of how the rest of that sector will perform. If Dell has an unexpected rise in sales and its price jumps by 3%, it is very likely that Hewlett-Packard will also rise.

Based on this sympathetic movement, it is possible to sell the sector ETF and buy the S&P to capture the temporary move across a broader range of companies. Of course, the move when averaged out will be smaller for the sector than for the target company, but it still may be an attractive trade. And arbing an ETF and S&P futures means that the position can be leveraged and there are no awkward short sales.

Creating a Stat-Arb Trade Using a Rating Service

There are quite a few firms offering services that rank stocks in order of expected performance. By searching the Internet, you can find "stock rankings systems" or "stock ranking services" that are computer programs you can buy or services to which you can subscribe. The best ranking systems seem to have proprietary black box algorithms. They won't tell you how they do it, but they will sell the rankings each day. Many other services are free but require much more effort to rank stocks if you have more than one criterion. This discussion is not intended to recommend any of these services or assess which one is better than another. Part of the process of generating a successful strategy will be to determine that yourself.

The intriguing part of a ranking service, or any ranking method, is that you can find forecasts for both the best and the worst expected performance. The stat-arb trade is created using the most actively traded stocks and then buying the highest ranking stocks and selling short the lowest ranking. This gives you a classic market-neutral portfolio. The only calculation you must make yourself is to size the positions according to volatility, so that the risk of all the long positions equals the risk of all the shorts.

The hard part of this process is determining if the forecasts are credible. That is, the minimum requirement is that those stocks that ranked in the upper 10% should perform above average and those in the lower 10% should perform below average. That doesn't seem to be a particularly demanding requirement, but you cannot assume that it will happen. It may be more reasonable to look at those stocks ranked in the top 80–90% range, or even 70–80%, under the theory that the highest-ranking stocks are experiencing an abnormal, short-lived period in the spotlight, while the ones in a more modest position are the slow but steady performers. Whatever you decide, you must prove that the rankings have forecasting power before they can be used.

The problem of forecasting ability is particularly true if you are creating your own ranking. Do you rank by the P/E ratio? By the size of the dividends? By the recent or long-term performance? It may be interesting to know that the U.S. government's *Leading Economic Index* (LEI) includes many components, but the most important and most reliable is the previous move of the stock market, for example, the S&P. If the S&P has risen recently, then the LEI is likely to be positive. It may seem as though it's a dog chasing its tail, but the point is that a rising stock price can be a strong indicator of continued success.

Ranking for Hire   Value Line Publishing, Inc. has the oldest continuous ranking service, initiated in 1965. They rank stocks by three qualities: timeliness, safety, and technicals. They boast that the returns on their timeliness ranking are in excess of 26,000% since 1965, compared with the return on the DJIA of 826%. Their web site posts a list of charges for their services.

Starmine (a Thomson Reuters company) is considered one of the high-end providers of analytic tools, as well as stock ranking. They offer newsletters with "earning surprise forecasts" and those companies expected to have material or structural changes in earnings. They target a mostly professional clientele at a fee.

Other services, such as www.TheStreet.com, Cramer's *Mad Money*, Reuters, and *The Motley Fool* (www.fool.com) provide both premium and free stock ratings. Examples of the free services are shown in the next section. It is worth repeating that claims of success are a normal part of marketing a product, but whether you are buying a service or doing your own ranking, you must prove that it works.

Not Quite a Rating Service   If you can't afford to pay for a proprietary rating service, there are other options. Many web sites allow you to sort stocks by one characteristic, such as price/earnings ratio (P/E), but *MSN Money* offers a summary of analyst recommendations. Table 9.1 shows 27 recommendations for Microsoft on May 25, 2010, grouped from strongest to weakest, plus the 3-month history of recommendations. The bottom line gives the mean recommendation, which is interpreted as 1.0 = *strong buy*, >1.0 to 2.0 = *moderate buy*, >2.0 to 3.0 = *hold*, >3.0 to 4.0 = *moderate sell*, and >4.0 = *strong sell*.

TABLE 9.1   Analyst recommendations provided on the *MSN Money* web site.

Recommendations	Current	1 Month Ago	2 Months Ago	3 Months Ago
Strong buy	14	13	14	15
Moderate buy	5	5	5	5
Hold	8	9	8	9
Moderate sell	0	0	0	0
Strong sell	0	0	0	0
Mean rec.	1.76	1.83	1.76	1.78

This seems to be exactly what we would want. The only inconveniences are that:

- You must enter each stock individually and record its recommendation in a spreadsheet.
- You will need to develop a history of performance relative to the recommendations to be sure that the best recommendations bear some relationship to successful performance, or at least fall in the upper 50% of performance of the candidates.

On the other hand, the price is right. *MSN Money* also has its StockScouter Ratings, which have features similar to other services we are discussing.

In addition to access to the Jim Cramer *Mad Money* daily recommendations, www.TheStreet.com provides both premium and free ranking services. It provides individual stock rankings by sector, shown for airlines in Table 9.2, and Cramer's stock calls are shown in Table 9.3. As with many other services, how the rankings are arrived at is not disclosed.

TheStreet.com Ratings stock model compiles and examines all available financial data on a daily basis to gauge stocks' probabilities of moving up or down. The model scores stocks on various factors—including growth, financial solvency, stock price performance and volatility—which, when taken together, have shown strong correlation with future stock performance. The aim is to deliver investors with stock ideas that we feel have the best chance at delivering top risk-adjusted returns.

TABLE 9.2 From www.TheStreet.com rankings for airlines.

Symbol	Equity	Rating
ALGT	ALLEGIANT TRAVEL CO	B+
CPA	COPA HOLDINGS SA	B
HA	HAWAIIAN HOLDINGS INC	B
LFL	LAN AIRLINES SA	C+
LUV	SOUTHWEST AIRLINES	C+
TAM	TAM SA	C
GOL	GOL LINHAS AEREAS INTELIGENT	C
RJET	REPUBLIC AIRWAYS HLDGS INC	C
PNCL	PINNACLE AIRLINES CORP	C
JBLU	JETBLUE AIRWAYS CORP	C

Source: www.TheStreet.com.

TABLE 9.3   Jim Cramer's *Mad Money* daily stock calls (May 24, 2010).

Company	Date	Segment	Call	Price
Citigroup (C)	24-May	F	▲	$3.78
Caterpillar (CAT)	24-May	L	▼	$59.22
Hitachi (HIT)	24-May	L	▼▼	$39.53
Macy's (M)	24-May	L	▼	$21.15
MGM Mirage (MGM)	24-May	L	▼▼	$11.79
Perrigo (PRGO)	24-May	F	▲	$57.04
Sprint Nextel (S)	24-May	F	▲	$4.79
SandRidge Energy (SD)	24-May	I	▲	$5.40

The Segment column tells which part of the show produced the recommendation—
F for feature, L for lightning round, I for interview—and the Call column gives the
strength or weakness of the recommendation.
Source: www.TheStreet.com.

Investor's Business Daily also ranks stocks. In an academic paper, "A
Test of the Investor's Daily Stock Ranking System" (*Financial Review* 33,
no. 22, March 9, 2005), Olsen, Nelson, Witt, and Mossman conclude that
"the best system provides market adjusted abnormal returns of 1.8% per
month." While not free, the cost is not excessive.

Do-It-Yourself Ranking   The Morningstar Stock Quickrank offers a
fully technical ranking approach applied to the major equity sectors, stock
funds, ETFs, and some other investment vehicles. You can choose to rank
by market cap, sales, year-to-date total return, dividend yield, return on
equity, earnings growth, price/earnings ratio, relative strength, and other
features. Once selected, you get a list of stocks as shown in Table 9.4.

The Morningstar ranking is similar to many others available on the Internet. You can rank only one feature at a time, so you'll need to copy the
table and move it to a spreadsheet, which is allowed. Then you can give
each stock a ranking value, probably just a sequence number where 1 is the
best, 2 is next, and so on, and combine the rankings from various attributes
to get a composite score. Once that is done, you need to keep a record of
whether your ranking reflects the relative success of performance.

MSN Money offers a similar service called StockScouter Ratings on
its web site. Enter a stock symbol, and you get a ranking from 1 to 10,
with 10 being the best. You can rank sectors, but there are only a few factors to choose from: fundamental, ownership, technical, and valuation. You
can also qualify the choices by various levels of capitalization. The actual
method of ranking is not disclosed, but then analyst rankings are also not
explained.

TABLE 9.4 Sample of Morningstar's Stock Quickrank for all stocks, return on equity.

Ticker Symbol	Name	Return on Equity %
NEGI	National Energy Group, Inc.	244.19
FXEN	FX Energy, Inc.	240.06
MRIB	Marani Brands, Inc.	231.92
MARPS	Marine Petroleum Trust	231.11
SPNG	Spongetech Delivery Systems Inc.	230.45
TIRTZ	Tidelands Royalty Trust	227.77
PAY	VeriFone Systems Inc.	223.74
ARB	Arbitron Corporation	216.63
IHG	Intercontinental Hotels Group PLC	212.39
AH	Accretive Health, Inc.	199.92
BJGL	Beijing Logistic Inc.	198.76
AJGH	American Jianye Greentech Holdings Inc.	196.74
LGBS	Legends Business Group, Incorporated	196.36
SNSTA	Sonesta International Hotels Corporation	195.48
SWKH	SWK Holdings Corporation	194.00
PNGXQ	PNG Ventures, Inc.	192.56
ESI	ITT Educational Services, Inc.	184.17
IMMU	Immunomedics, Inc.	183.92
WLSA	Wireless Age Communications, Inc.	183.35
MILL	Miller Petroleum, Inc.	181.59

Return on equity (ROE) measures a firm's return on shareholder investment (the shareholders' equity or the net worth of the company). ROE is a useful gauge in determining how efficiently a company is using shareholders' investment. Unlike return on assets, it considers the amount and cost of the firm's debt.
Source: Morningstar.

Rules for Using Ranking Systems
To summarize the use of ranking services:

- Research the services that are available. Those that provide a record of the success of past recommendations may be the best place to start, but you will need to confirm those results yourself or find a review from some other source with no conflict of interest.
- If you prefer to try to rank stocks yourself, then choose any of the free services available on the Internet. Decide the sector(s) and the criteria, and then rank the stocks daily. Transfer the rankings to a spreadsheet for tracking.
- Record the performance of those stocks in the ranking zone that you've decided to track. That could be the top and bottom 10%, or those in the 70–80 percentile range versus the 20–30 percentile range. The goal is

that those stocks in the upper range remain in the upper range and those in the lower range remain lower.

- Choose the stocks to be bought and sold. Calculate how many shares of each stock are needed to have the same risk. This is done by measuring the annualized volatility and then finding the multiplication factor for each stock that brings the position size to a common target volatility or risk.
- Enter your positions.
- Monitor the ranking and either hold the stocks for a predetermined period based on your ranking success or remove those stocks that fall out of your ranking zone, replacing them with the new stocks that are now in that zone. Positions must be volatility adjusted. To avoid switching too often, if you are using a zone of 70–80, then switch when the stock falls below 65 or 60. If it moves above 80, then all the better. Similarly, stocks in the 20–30 zone are held below 20 but are switched if they move above 35 or 40.

NEW HIGHS AND NEW LOWS

An interesting variation on a ranking arbitrage is to trade all stock prices making new highs and new lows, buying the new highs and selling the new lows short. At the extreme, this could be limited to historic (life of the stock) highs and lows or modified to recognize 5-year or 2-year extremes. The longer, the better. The idea is that stocks making all-time highs or lows have something structurally good or bad happening, and this method would profit from that trend continuing.

Once a position is set, you'll need an exit criteria. A reversal from the high or low by 20% could work well. Each time you add or remove a stock, you'll need to rebalance both sides of the trade. It may be important to monitor the stocks making new lows to be sure they are moving; otherwise, you will be leveraging them up in large numbers to offset the obvious price movement in those stocks at the top. That presents two risks: The first is event risk, where a low-priced stock reverses on high volatility. The second is that you effectively trade only the longs, and the shorts offer no risk protection.

MERGER ARB

Merger arb is an interesting area of trading that some traders consider to be an arbitrage, but it's really not. We'll describe it here to remove any confusion.

Merger arb is an arbitrage between the purchasing company (the *acquirer*) and a to-be-acquired company (the *target*). This can be traded a number of different ways.

The most successful arbitrageurs try to anticipate the acquisition. On the one side, they know a company is not profitable because of debt, overhead, some crisis (such as loss of crops or a tainted product), or a temporary drop in demand that puts pressure on their cash flow. On the other side, there might be companies such as IBM, Intel, or Berkshire Hathaway that are looking to either complement their portfolios or add a missing piece of technology to their services. The traders may buy an option on what they perceive as the target candidate that pays off with either higher prices or higher volatility, both of which happen when a buyout or acquisition is announced. The trader who is correct about the acquired company even one in five times gets a very big payout because the price of that stock jumps to near the level of the acquisition price. At that point, they may take their profits or join the second group of arbitrageurs.

The second group is more conservative. They wait until the acquisition is announced and the board of directors has approved the deal. If the acquirer is paying a 100% premium for the stock, say, $30 for a company currently trading at $15, then the price jumps immediately to $28. The $2 difference is the uncertainty factor. If the market thinks the deal has a high probability of closing, then the difference between the stock price shortly after announcement and the target price is very small. If the market doesn't like the deal, then the difference is large.

Some traders buy the target company and sell the acquiring company, under the theory that the purchase adds to debt and uncertainty, thereby lowering the price of the acquiring company. Although that may appear to be a market-neutral trade, the movements of the two stocks are not very predictable; therefore, there is no assurance that one move will offset the other and reduce risk.

The greatest risk in a merger arb trade is that the deal falls through. This most often happens when an audit of the company books produces unacceptable surprises. More recently, it happened because tight money made it impossible for some acquiring firms to borrow enough to close the deal. At that point, the stock of the nearly acquired company collapses, normally back to the preoffer price but many times much lower. The company no longer has its anticipated support and, if it was losing money, it might spiral into bankruptcy. A trader who has sold the acquiring company may or may not benefit, but in the best of cases, the benefit would never offset the loss of buying the target company near the target price and then seeing the share price decline by half.

Although a merger arb program can have large risk, it is considered to have a short options profile. That means there are many small profits from successful deals closing and a few large losses. A merger arb program typically generates a return of about 8% annually for investment houses and offers a special type of diversification. Most deals close, so that the large losses are rare and can be absorbed by the higher frequency of small gains.

CREATING YOUR OWN INDEX ARBITRAGE

If you can create your own stock ranking, can you also create your own index and use it for an arbitrage? In the previous chapters, we've used individual stocks and individual futures markets to create pairs. We've looked at using ETFs as well with some success. An ETF is convenient because there are no restrictions on short selling and it allows leverage. If you substitute an ETF for the short sales in stocks, you reduce the returns because the distortion in one stock is not reflected in the average of all stocks. Instead of capturing the entry points where two stocks or futures markets diverge, you are only capturing the point where one stock moves away from the index. That may be only half the potential profit. During a high-volatility period, that can still generate profits.

Selecting the two markets to use in the arbitrage can be done in a number of different ways. Many traders test their strategy on a wide choice of stocks and then pick the best performers. That's generally not a good method because you may have overfit the data and squeezed profits out of a few stocks by fine-tuning the parameter choices, which in turn identifies entry and exit points. As we saw in the previous chapters, parameters that are fine-tuned may work beautifully on one period of data but have too many or too few trades during other time intervals, usually because of changing volatility. If we are going to have confidence in a method, then it should produce profits using an arbitrary set of related markets and a wide range of parameters.

Another entirely statistical way of selecting the pairs is to find the correlation in price movement of the two legs. Correlations that are over 0.90 reflect markets that are too similar and have little chance of a profit that exceeds the cost of trading. Correlations below about 0.35 diverge for extended time periods, thereby introducing a very large risk each time you trade. Those markets with correlations of about 0.60 would be ideal, provided it's not just a short-term effect. We've looked at cases where the EURUSD and gold would be highly correlated for short periods due to immediate concerns about inflation. Those are excellent trading opportunities, but they can disappear quickly.

In the next section, we'll look at what happens if we create our own index and use it as one leg of a pair. It's similar to trading one stock against an ETF of that sector, when there is no ETF.

Mining Shares and the PMI Index

We were very successful trading pairs of gold, platinum, and copper against the physical commodity in Chapter 6, but not everyone wants to trade futures.

Gold is already familiar to us, and the precious metals sector has a relatively small number of active stocks; therefore, it will be our starting point. By looking at the Yahoo! web site, we can find the precious metals (mining) stocks that are most active. They are shown in Table 9.5, in order of volume.

All other stocks traded fewer than 2 million shares per day. The individual stocks' price histories are shown in Figure 9.1. We create an index that we call the PMI (Precious Metals Index) by equally weighting the prices of the six stocks. That index is shown in Figure 9.2. It is easy to see that the index tracks the rise and fall of precious metals prices in a way that is even more exaggerated than the pattern of gold prices themselves. Besides supply and demand, profitability of mining companies is sensitive to operating margins, labor issues, and corporate management. At the time this index was created, gold was above $900/ounce after touching $1,000 (and on its way higher), and the PMI index is about 17 after topping 35, a drop of 50%.

None of the six companies in the index was chosen based on suitability. You might observe that Coeur d'Alene, CDE, shown as the bottom price line in Figure 9.1, is far different from the other five stocks. It is also trading at the lowest price and might be delisted from the NYSE. It has a large business in silver, which might be reflected in the somewhat different price pattern. Perhaps a better index could be created by paying more attention

TABLE 9.5 Six most active precious metals mining stocks.

Symbol	Name	Current Price
CDE	Coeur d'Alene Mines Corp	$0.63
ABX	Barrick Gold Corp	$28.76
NEM	Newmont Mining Corp	$38.90
AUY	Yamana Gold Inc	$8.70
GG	Gold Corp	$29.70
NG	NovaGold Resources, Ltd	$2.70

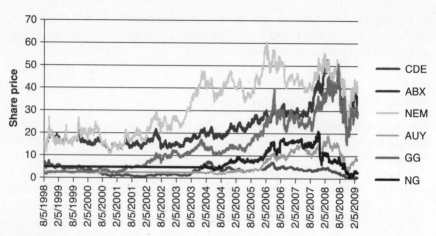

FIGURE 9.1 Six precious metals mining stocks with the highest daily volume.

to fundamentals, but our intention is to show that an arbitrage strategy works on an arbitrary set of stocks and a simple index.

One way to see if the components are reasonable choices is to calculate the cross-correlations, as shown in Table 9.6. Low correlations give us an idea that some of these companies are not affected by the same factors. For example, CDE has a low correlation against all other companies and only 0.163 against the index, while ABX, NEM, and GG are all very highly correlated. Correlations that are this low can occur randomly, but we expect that, being in the same sector, there is some fundamental relationship between CDE and the other stocks. For that reason, we'll leave it in this study because it may offer valuable diversification.

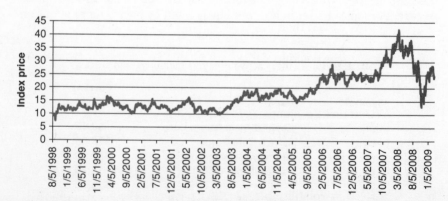

FIGURE 9.2 Precious Metals Index (PMI), an equal weighting of six mining stocks.

TABLE 9.6 Cross-correlations of six mining stocks and the Precious Metals Index, July 19, 2002, through March 6, 2009.

	CDE	ABX	NEM	AUY	GG	NG	PMI
CDE	1						
ABX	0.108	1					
NEM	0.089	0.823	1				
AUY	0.177	0.675	0.646	1			
GG	0.131	0.842	0.803	0.678	1		
NG	0.110	0.400	0.321	0.384	0.378	1	
PMI	0.163	0.935	0.932	0.750	0.922	0.442	1

The Rules

As with the other steps that we've followed in previous chapters to identify a trade, we'll follow a standard set of calculations and rules:

- Standardizing the data so both the stock prices and the index are in the same terms. That should be done by indexing.
- Identifying the size of the entry distortion needed to capture sufficient profits to overcome costs.
- Trading different quantities of each in order to equalize the risk.
- Deciding at what point to exit the trade.

Because the PMI is an average price, it can be treated in the same way as each of the stocks in the index. We'll need to get the daily returns, based on the prices, using

$$r_t = \frac{P_t}{P_{t-1}} - 1$$

The return, r_t, can then be used to calculate the annualized volatility (AVOL) of the two series over the past 10 days, and the ratio of the two volatilities gives the volatility factor, VAF, used to equalize the two series.

$$\text{AVOL(index)} = \text{standard deviation (index returns)} \times \sqrt{252}$$

$$\text{AVOL(stock)} = \text{standard deviation (stock returns)} \times \sqrt{252}$$

$$\text{VAF} = \frac{\text{AVOL (index)}}{\text{AVOL (stock)}}$$

The 10-day calculation period is chosen because it is short enough to reflect changes in volatility but long enough to have enough data to be stable. Reducing the period to five days is tempting but would cause the volatility to jump around. Many traders might find that using a 20-day period is more in line with standards such as implied volatility or value at risk. With a much longer period, such as 250 days, the volatility will change very slowly and won't be responsive to some of the exceptionally volatile periods we've seen during 2008 and 2009.

The volatility adjustment factor, VAF, will be used for determining the number of shares to trade for every 100 units of the index. The position size for one side of the arbitrage must be fixed, and the other is then determined from the ratio.

Entry Points

Finding good entry points will be the most important step. For this, we again use VAF to equalize the relationship between the index and stock price. The basic way of finding distortions is by using the standard deviation of the differences or, in our case, the returns. These will be called the volatility-adjusted differences (VAD). We will also need the average of the VAD values. This is different from previous methods that used a momentum oscillator to identify extremes.

$$\text{Volatility-adjusted differences (VAD)} = \frac{\text{Returns (index)}}{\text{Returns (stock)} \times \text{VAF}}$$

Both of these calculations, the standard deviation of VAD and the average VAD, are based on only the past 10 days in order to be responsive to changes in volatility. It is now time to choose a key parameter, the standard deviation factor that determines how close or how far away the entry points will be placed. We know from statistics that using 1 standard deviation will capture 16% of these distortions (the part remaining on the outside of the distribution curve to the right). If we choose 2 standard deviations, we will only capture 2.5%, although those distortions will be much larger. We're going to choose a value that is smaller, 0.5 standard deviations, with the intention of having many more trades but enough profit to cover costs. Traders may decide to make this number bigger or smaller depending on their own preference for trading frequency and cost. If the standard deviation factor, F, is 0.5, the entry points are then calculated as follows.

Buy the index and sell the stock if VAD falls below the previous value of the average VAD minus the factor F times the previous value of the standard deviation of VAD.

If

$$\text{VAD}_t < \text{Average (VAD}_{t-1}) - F \times \text{Standard deviation (VAD}_{t-1})$$

then buy the index and sell the stock.

If

$$\text{VAD}_t > \text{Average}\,(\text{VAD}_{t-1}) + F \times \text{Standard deviation}\,(\text{VAD}_{t-1})$$

then sell the index and buy the stock.

In both cases, buying and selling, the exit occurs when the current VAD returns to the average VAD over the past 10 days. If the VAD values drift during the time a position is held, results may be better or worse than expected. There are no stop-losses and no maximum holding period. Risk is reduced primarily by diversification and is naturally minimized because there is no directional exposure.

Implementation and Liquidity

The size of the positions is determined by the volatility adjustment factor, VAF. If we always trade 100 units of the index, then the number of shares of the stock is $100 \times \text{VAF}$. Because we are using the PMI index that we created ourselves, we would buy or sell 1/6 of 100 (16.67) shares in each of the six companies in the index.

Selling short is always an issue, and not all stocks are available, so we need to know in advance which companies can be readily sold. If they cannot, they should not be part of the index. In this stat-arb example, we haven't checked on the status of any of the companies. It is best that we create the index, or trade the strategy, using the most liquid stocks, and those stocks are most likely to allow short selling. They will also have smaller execution slippage because they have a narrower bid-asked spread.

Precious Metals Results

When we test the strategy on the six stocks for the 10 years ending March 2009, we get the results shown in Table 9.7. All results are adjusted to 12% annualized volatility, meaning that one standard deviation of the stock returns calculated over the entire 10-year period, times the square root of 252, will be 12%.

Of the six stocks, four were profitable, with the average result showing a return ratio of 0.284. There were nearly 100 trades per stock per year. The two companies that posted losses, AUY and NG, did not trade during the first half of the test period. The three stocks with the highest volume all posted profitable returns. Remember that there are no costs taken out of the results, and the stock trades posted a net loss of $0.0278 offset by the index gains of $0.027 on higher volume. These are marginal returns even for professional traders. Electronic trading can be done at very low cost, but profits this small are a concern. The performance pattern of each company can be seen in Figure 9.3. However, there is better news.

298

TABLE 9.7	Results of stat-arb using PMI and six mining companies, about seven years.

				Arb with PMI, June 19, 2002, through March 6, 2009					
Arb	**Trades**	**%ProfTR**	**CumPL**	**NAV**	**AROR**	**Risk**	**UnitX**	**UnitS**	**Ratio**
CDE	748	52	3570	196.0	6.58	12	0.081	−0.0183	0.548
ABX	833	51	3132	250.9	9.10	12	0.063	−0.0712	0.758
NEM	822	48	1176	134.7	2.86	12	0.039	−0.1107	0.238
AUY	392	51	−640	76.6	−2.49	12	−0.053	0.0298	−0.208
GG	670	51	4848	250.6	9.08	12	0.039	0.0441	0.757
NG	399	47	−2190	60.3	−4.68	12	−0.008	−0.0406	−0.390
Average	644	50	1649	161.5	3.41	12	0.027	−0.0278	0.284

First, there is the advantage of diversification. In Figure 9.3, two of the stocks, ABX and NEM, continue higher during the last year while the other four swing lower before beginning a recovery. If we combine the six NAV streams into an equally weighted portfolio, the individual NAV volatility of 12% is reduced to 5.8%, less than half. This shows a significant amount of diversification, considering these stocks all belong to the same narrow industrial group. The final portfolio can then be leveraged back up to 12% using a factor of 2.05, yielding an annualized return of 8.18% from July 2002, shown in Figure 9.4.

Volatility is an important factor in arbitrage. It makes the distortions larger and reduces the impact of costs. It should be no surprise that the

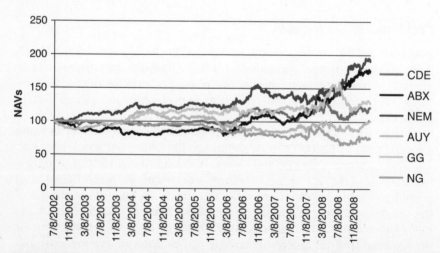

FIGURE 9.3 Performance of components and portfolio for the PMI arbitrage.

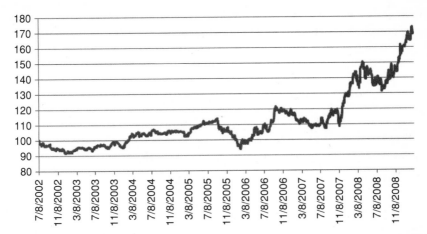

FIGURE 9.4 Combined performance NAVs of six mining companies traded against the PMI.

volatility of nearly all markets increased dramatically during the past two years, and this is reflected in the performance. During that period, the annualized return of the portfolio of six markets was 22.4%. The trading profiles from January 1, 2006, are shown in Table 9.8. We again see that volatility is an ally of the trader.

Even during this ideal time, NovaGold (NG) posted a loss. Remember that it is currently trading at a very low price, which may make the absolute size of the price moves small. We should understand that, given enough time and hindsight, we can explain why one market lost and another gained and convince ourselves that we should remove the worst performers and keep the best ones. But we really don't know what will happen in the future.

TABLE 9.8 Performance of each mining company traded against PMI for the period from January 1, 2006, through March 2009.

	Arb with PMI from January 1, 2006, through March 6, 2009								
Arb	Trades	%ProfTR	CumPL	NAV	AROR	Risk	UnitX	UnitS	Ratio
CDE	217	49	2896	118.4	8.47	12	0.371	−0.0358	0.456
ABX	250	58	5766	177.6	19.86	12	0.442	−0.2287	1.655
NEM	245	48	4085	144.2	12.23	12	0.286	−0.1638	1.019
AUY	243	53	1018	107.0	2.16	12	−0.003	0.0224	0.180
GG	242	48	1340	111.4	3.47	12	0.149	−0.1023	0.289
NG	232	48	−786	93.7	−2.03	12	0.088	−0.0523	−0.169
Average	238.2	51	2387	128-4	6.86	12	0.222	−0.0934	0.572

As long as these companies qualify according to their fundamentals or by their correlations, they should be included.

One caveat discussed in an earlier chapter concerned distortions in positions. When one market trades at a high price with normal volatility and another at a very low price with corresponding low volatility, the size of the position taken in the low-priced stock would need to be much larger to equalize the risk. This presents a real leverage risk, the possibility that any surprising news involving the low-price stock could cause a very large loss in those pairs using that stock. Our earlier conclusion (see the *distortion ratio*) was that no pair should be traded if one stock has more than twice the shares of the other stock.

Substituting a Mutual Fund for the PMI

There are some practical issues concerning the construction of our own index. The strategy has been set up to trade 100 shares of the index and the volatility-adjusted equivalent of each stock. If we are buying the index and there are six companies, we then buy 16.6 shares of each. We need to be able to sell short the other side of the trade. Because we chose companies with the highest volume, we should have less trouble. If volatility is high, as it's been during the past two years, there may be a choice of using options; otherwise, the overhead might be too high.

One way to simplify the problem is to find an ETF or mutual fund for precious metals. Either will track the cash price of the stocks. They have the advantage of allowing long and short positions without penalty and without size limitation. In the case of ProFunds, which offers a broad selection of tradable mutual funds, the precious metals fund PMPIX is twice leveraged and has competitive costs built into the transaction. PMPIX is only a bull fund—that is, you can only go long—but there is a large number of listings by SPDR, ProShares, Rydex, PowerShares, and iShares that offer various combinations of long, short, and long-short funds. We'll use PMPIX because ProFunds allows downloading historical data easily; therefore, anyone can test strategies.

First we need to see how PMPIX correlates to our six mining stocks. Table 9.9 shows that our six stocks are nearly identical, giving an overall

TABLE 9.9 Correlations of PMI and PMPIX with each of the six mining stocks and with each other.

	CDE	ABX	NEM	AUY	GG	NG	PMPIX	PMI
PMPIX	0.126	0.911	0.905	0.722	0.900	0.394	1	
PMI	0.163	0.935	0.932	0.750	0.922	0.442	0.981	1

TABLE 9.10 Results of six mining pairs using PMPIX, June 19, 2002, through March 5, 2009.

							Arb with PMPIX, June 19, 2002, through March 6, 2009		
Arb	Trades	%ProfTR	CumPL	NAV	AROR	Risk	UnitX	UnitS	Ratio
CDE	480	52	2737	121.5	2.95	12	0.137	−0.0170	0.246
ABX	522	53	4728	176.8	8.86	12	0.175	−0.0902	0.738
NEM	533	52	5568	190.7	10.10	12	0.170	−0.1104	0.841
AUY	395	51	494	100.9	0.13	12	−0.029	0.0165	0.011
GG	505	48	2360	128.0	3.74	12	0.123	−0.0729	0.312
NG	397	47	−3120	78.5	−4.10	12	0.015	−0.0417	−0.342
Average	472	51	2128	132.2	3.61	12	0.099	−0.0526	0.301

correlation of 0.981 with the mutual fund and showing only small variations in the individual stocks. We can then test the six pairs of mining stocks with PMPIX and get the results shown in Table 9.10.

Compared with Table 9.7, these results are all better, and they should also improve during the past three years. The net return was a positive $0.03 per share, and the ratio improved from 0.284 to 0.301, which includes the administration mutual fund fees, which are reflected in the daily price. Overall, using a mutual fund, when it is available, is a better choice and simplifies trading.

ARBING THE DOW

A natural next step might be to try this stat-arb process on the components of the Dow Jones Industrial Average (DJIA) against that average. Those companies are certainly more liquid and are all available for short selling. In addition, the Dow trades as a number of ETFs, including the Diamonds (DIA) on NASDAQ.

Without going through the tedious process of showing results, the conclusion is that stat-arb does not work for the Dow and its components. Consider that we need to find distortions in one stock with respect to the index, and those distortions must correct quickly back to the average value of the index. If all the stocks are part of the same industrial group, as we tried to construct with precious metals, then the same fundamental factors affect all of them. We have reason to believe that any news affecting one company within the group will often have a corresponding, but not equal, effect on the other stocks in the same group. In addition, when one company has good news, it leads the index; then others follow as investors buy the laggards in the belief that they will benefit from the same news.

The result of arbing all 30 Dow components against the index was slightly worse than zero, a small net loss, even before costs were subtracted. With the aid of hindsight, we can say that the Dow components are a diverse group, and one component can keep going up, such as Wal-Mart, while another is going down, as with Bank of America, particularly during the financial crisis of 2008–2009. Buying Bank of America and selling the DJIA would have resulted in a huge loss, only to be repeated by other huge losses. In reality, half of the stocks generated a profit, and half a loss, which indicates diverse fundamentals.

While arbing one stock against the index doesn't work, a very large business exists in program trading, the process of keeping the cash stock index in line with the futures market or other index markets that track, primarily the S&P, and producing some trading profits along the way.

ARBING THE S&P 500— INDEX ARBITRAGE

Index arbitrage is a subset of program trading and is an essential part of market pricing. Professional traders track the cash S&P 500 index (SPX) and the nearby S&P futures contract and wait for these two markets to diverge. That often happens when a large pension fund or hedge fund sets an outright position in S&P futures, driving the price up or down without regard to the cash price. This may be an outright trade intended to be profitable or insurance against existing positions. In addition, recommendations by brokers or investment houses can cause the general public to move back into the stock market, pushing up the actual stock prices but not directly affecting futures.

Program trading is a pure arbitrage—a market-neutral program. If the futures markets move up faster than the cash market, then traders will sell futures and (theoretically) buy all of the stocks in the S&P in proportion to the cap-weighted holdings in the S&P cash index. This brings the two markets into equilibrium. If the cash market moves first, then they buy the S&P futures and sell the stocks. Selling short all the stocks in the S&P requires planning and adds considerable risk, so it is not nearly as desirable as trading in the other direction. When a trigger point is hit, program traders use computers to automatically generate and execute orders to buy or sell all stocks in the S&P. Some traders try to use a smaller set of stocks to represent the whole index, which, on one hand, can save money and speed up execution but also introduces tracking risk.

It is estimated that all program trading, which includes index arbitrage and algorithmic trading, accounts for nearly 50% of all volume trading on the New York Stock Exchange. The exchange defines *program trading* as a trade involving 15 or more stocks with an aggregate value in excess of $1 million.

Trigger Points

The key to index arbitrage is finding the trigger point at which to activate the trades and generate a profit. This is where the fair value of forward price of the S&P component stocks differs from the futures price, or ETF, or options price, by some minimum threshold. The fair value at time t is calculated as

$$FV_t = SPX_0 \times [1 + (RF_t - D_t)]$$

where FV_t is the fair value at some future date, t days ahead, SPX_0 is the current value of the cash S&P index, RF_t is the risk-free rate of return for the calculation period, and D_t is the accumulated dividends of the S&P components between now and t days ahead. Normally, t is chosen to correspond to the delivery date of the futures markets, around mid-month in March, June, September, and December. As the date gets closer, the accumulated dividends get smaller, and the fair value approaches the cash value of SPX. It is essential that futures and cash prices converge on the delivery date because the futures delivery is in cash, and hedgers must be sure that any shorts taken in futures to insure against cash stock market losses do indeed perform as expected.

Traders typically look for the difference in the futures price and fair value to exceed $5 or fall below –$5 to trigger a trade, but competition may cause some traders to jump ahead of that threshold. Once a program trade has been set, stocks and futures should converge within a short time, but the worst-case scenario is that they converge at delivery. The sooner they converge, the sooner traders have their investment back and can use those funds for another trade. If stocks and futures take a long time to converge back to equilibrium, the traders are effectively losing money.

Volatility plays an important role in triggering index arbitrage opportunities. Volatility causes all markets to move quickly, often independent of one another. At the same time, volatility attracts volume. The combination assures that index arbitrage will come into play.

The S&P is traded in many ways, and all of them are subject to a similar arbitrage to keep prices in equilibrium. There is also a large selection of ETFs that mimic the S&P cash price. The best known of these is SPY ("Spyders"), traded on NASDAQ, but a wide range of leveraged funds are offered by ProShares, ProFunds, Rydex, iShares, and other financial companies.

There are many variations on index arbitrage. It might be possible to sell S&P futures and buy the SPY ETF, or buy S&P futures and sell SPY, avoiding all the short-sale issues. Program trading is a big business, and professionals hold a so-called book of positions in such a way that short-selling can be done instantly. The elimination of the uptick rule and the move to trading pennies instead of eighths have facilitated program trading. The negatives are that, if the S&P drops more than a fixed percentage in one day, all program trading is halted, an awkward situation if you're in the middle of a trade. Also, competition has caused some traders to select a smaller set of stocks to represent the S&P futures in order to reduce costs and expedite the process. They might set the arbitrage with marginal profit expectations just to enter sooner than other traders waiting for bigger opportunities. It is a clear case of competition improving the spread and liquidity of the market.

How Can We Participate?

If we're going to participate in this arbitrage, then the practical answer is to choose a smaller set of markets that has an index that can be traded. Of the futures markets, that would be the DJIA, which has 30 components. Tracking the fair value of the Dow futures would be a straightforward process on a spreadsheet. Each day you would change the number of days to delivery and get a number that can be used all day to monitor differences in the cash and futures prices.

On even a smaller level, you can calculate the fair value of single stock futures and find a trigger point that makes that a profitable trade. While others are out there looking at the same opportunities, taking a slightly smaller profit and a slightly bigger risk may give you an edge.

About the Companion Web Site

T his book includes a companion web site, which can be found at www.wiley.com/go/alphatrading (password: alpha). There you will find a series of six Excel spreadsheets:

1. An Excel spreadsheet showing the calculations needed for creating a pairs trade made with two stocks plus trading signals. You can enter your own signal threshold levels and costs to test the results.

2. An Excel spreadsheet showing the calculations needed for creating a pairs trade using two futures markets plus the trading signals. You can enter your own signal threshold levels and costs to test the results.

3. An Excel spreadsheet showing the calculation of the stress indicator.

4. Two more Excel spreadsheets similar to (1) and (2) showing pairs calculations using the stress indicator.

5. An Excel spreadsheet showing the calculations needed for a crossover pairs trade, one stock and one futures market.

6. An Excel spreadsheet showing a simple portfolio of pairs (or any assets), including volatility-adjusting.

About the Author

Perry Kaufman has 40 years of experience in financial engineering and hedge funds, and is well known for his role in algorithmic trading. Beginning as a rocket scientist in the aerospace industry, he worked on the navigation and control systems for the Gemini project. Since 1971, Mr. Kaufman has specialized in the development of fully systematic trading programs in derivatives and equities, as well as risk management and leverage overlays. During his career, Mr. Kaufman headed trading operations for large firms and has partnered three successful hedge funds. He is the author of *New Trading Systems and Methods, Fourth Edition* (John Wiley & Sons, 2005), *A Short Course in Technical Trading* (John Wiley & Sons, 2003), and other books and articles that have gained worldwide acclaim.

Index